APPALACHIAN MOUNTAIN CLUB

Quiet Water

Canoe Guide

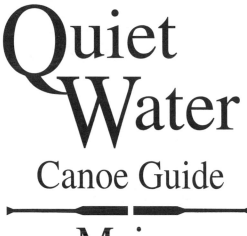

Maine

BEST PADDLING LAKES AND PONDS FOR ALL AGES

Alex Wilson and John Hayes

D0324798

APPALACHIAN MOUNTAIN CLUB BOOKS
BOSTON, MASSACHUSETTS

Cover photograph: Jerry and Marcy Monkman
Drawings: Marrin Robinson
Book design: Carol Bast Tyler
All photographs by the authors unless otherwise noted.

Distributed by The Globe Pequot Press, GPP, Inc. Old Saybrook, CT.

Library of Congress Cataloging-in-Publication Data
Wilson, Alex, 1955—
    Quiet water canoe guide, Maine: best paddling lakes and ponds for all ages / Alex Wilson and John Hayes.
        p. cm.
    At head of title: Appalachian Mountain Club.
    Includes index.
    ISBN 1-878239-36-8 (alk. paper) : $14.95
    1. Canoes and canoeing—Maine—Guidebooks. 2. Lakes—Maine—Guidebooks. 3. Ponds—Maine—Guidebooks. 4. Maine—Guidebooks. I. Hayes, John. II. Appalachian Mountain Club. III. Title. IV. Title: Appalachian Mountain Club quiet water canoe guide, Maine.
GV776.M2W55 1995
797.1'22'09741—dc20   94–47665
                                                                                        CIP

The paper used in this publication meets the minimum requirements of the American National Standard for Information Sciences—Permanence of Paper for Printed Library Materials, ANSI Z39.48–1984.∞

**Due to changes in conditions,
use of the information in this book
is at the sole risk of the user.**

Printed on recycled paper.
Printed in the United States of America.
10 9 8 7 6 5 4 3 2 1   95 96 97 98 99 00

Contents

Northern Region *242*

Nature Essays

"I want to go soon and live away by the pond, where I shall hear only the wind whispering among the reeds. It will be success if I shall have left myself behind. But my friends ask what I shall do when I get there. Will it not be employment enough to watch the progress of the seasons?

Henry David Thoreau

Acknowledgments

COMPILING this guide to Maine's lakes and ponds provided us with many, many days of wonderful paddling in gorgeous spots. For the opportunity to carry out this research, we are grateful to the Appalachian Mountain Club and especially Editor Gordon Hardy. While the authors alone accept blame for any missing or incorrect information, we did receive help and suggestions from many people in bringing this book from concept to reality. We offer our sincerest thanks to all those who assisted us:

First, we thank our families, both for joining us on our more extended trips and for putting up with our many weekends away from home, late night meetings, and deadlines: Jerelyn, Lillian, and Frances Wilson; Joanne, Andrew, and Stefanie Hayes. Thanks to our close friends who joined us on our research expeditions, put us up far away from home, or offered tips on great paddling spots: Malcolm, Karen, Randy, and Kirsten George; Sally Andrews; Jet Thomas; Wyatt Wade; Joseph Kahn; John Nevins and Cherrie Corey; Bob Engel; Randy Knaggs; Malcolm Moore; Caleb Wilson; Nadav Malin; Allyn and Mary Copp; Russell Heath; and Philip Demay. Plus, a special thanks to Ted and Andy Crowley, who kept the Wilson research team warm and dry and entertained two young daughters on a cold, windy, rainy day on Sysladobsis Lake, and to the Hatt family on Round Pond who did the same for the Hayes research team.

Thanks to the professional Maine Guides and recreation professionals who offered advice during the project: Don Kleiner of Maine Outdoors and the Maine Professional Guides Association, Martin Brown of Sunrise Country Canoe Expeditions, Garrett and Alexandra Conover of North Woods Ways, Eddie Raymond of Katahdin Outfitters, Darrell Whittaker of Whittaker Camps, Rick LeVasseur of Katahdin Shadows Campground and Penobscot River Outfitters, Kevin Harding of the Downeast Outdoor Recreation School, Larry

McIntosh of Wildwater Outfitters, Craig Ten Broeck of the Maine Bureau of Public Lands, Howard Weymouth of Bowater–Great Northern Paper, and Al Cowperthwaite of North Maine Woods.

For information on Maine's wildlife, we thank Sally Stockwell of the Maine Audubon Society, Maurry Mills of the Moosehorn National Wildlife Refuge, Molly Docherty of the State of Maine Natural Areas Program, and Karen Morris of the Maine Department of Inland Fisheries and Wildlife.

For assistance with our map research we thank Floyd Merritt of the Robert Frost Library at Amherst College and Dr. Klaus Bayer of Keene State College. For the meticulous work of drawing maps we thank Nadav Malin, John Sawers, and John Catlin. For skillful photographic printing in the face of looming deadlines we thank Sheila Roth. For the wildlife illustrations in the book we are deeply indebted to Marrin Robinson.

Introduction

MAINE'S quiet waters—its hidden treasures—receive much less attention than its famous rivers. Indeed, Maine offers some of the finest river canoeing in the eastern United States: places such as the Allagash, the St. John, the West Branch of the Penobscot, the Kennebec, the Androscoggin, the Machias, and the Saco. With all the attention on these wonderful rivers, many overlook the superb paddling opportunities in the state's many hundreds of quiet lakes and ponds. That's what this book is about.

What lures us to quiet-water canoeing is the peaceful solitude one encounters on out-of-the-way lakes and ponds; the playful antics of a river otter in crystal-clear, pine-tree-bounded lakes; the beautiful plumage of wood ducks and hooded mergansers in shallow, marshy coves; the thrill of spotting a moose—its mouth full of pond weeds— as you round the next bend in a winding inlet channel; the fascinating morphology of pitcher plants and the diminutive sundew; the haunting cry of the loon on a summer evening.

With quiet-water canoeing, you can focus on *being* there instead of *getting* there. You don't need to portage around rapids or arrange complex drop-off and pickup logistics. You don't need a lot of fancy equipment and high-tech gear—though a nice light canoe is great if you have to portage into the more out-of-the-way places. Other than a paddle and life vest, your most important gear is a pair of binoculars and field guides to the fauna and flora you're likely to encounter on your explorations. This is not to say that quiet-water canoeing is without risks—you certainly can get yourself into lots of trouble and even life-threatening situations on the larger lakes in bad weather (see below)—but for the most part the risks are low: low enough that one of our daughters donned a life vest for her first canoe trip on her one-month birthday.

Being avid paddlers, we have logged many miles, searching for the best lakes and ponds to paddle in Maine. Sometimes our trips have proved fruitless, as the pond we sought turned out to be off-limits to boating, ringed with cabins, or chock-full of speedboats. Finding out where you can canoe—and where you might *want* to canoe—has not always been easy. In bookstores and outdoors stores that had whole shelves of whitewater boating guides, we had long been frustrated by the lack of books on lake and pond canoeing—the sorts of places we could enjoy with young children and without complicated logistics. This book and the series of AMC Quiet Water Canoe Guides that preceded it fill a void in the literature on paddling.

How We Selected These Lakes and Ponds

Because this guide includes only a small percentage of the lakes and ponds in Maine, it is obviously a *selective* listing. We began the selection process with some definite prejudices when it comes to paddling: pretty scenery; limited development; few motorboats; a varied shoreline with lots of coves and inlets to explore; and interesting plants, animals, and geological formations.

We sought to include a variety of types of bodies of water in the book as well: some big lakes for when you really want to exercise your muscles over miles of paddling and some small protected ponds that are just right when your time is limited, your children lack the patience for extended outings, or conditions preclude venturing out on the big lakes. To make the book useful to as many people as possible, we paid particular attention to lakes and ponds in the more populated regions of the state, even though many bodies of water in remote parts of eastern and northern Maine better fit our standards for what is an ideal paddling spot. This focus makes the book useful not only to vacationers looking for paddling destinations but also to a Bangor business executive wanting to do some paddling on her afternoon off or a family with a free Saturday morning and a sense of adventure.

We had a few favorite canoeing spots in Maine when we took on this project, but we knew we'd be exploring mostly new places. Finding the nicest would take some work. We contacted friends and friends-of-friends—anyone we could find who shared our interest in quiet-water canoeing—asking for suggestions. We studied DeLorme's excellent *Maine Atlas and Gazetteer* and maps from North Maine Woods and Bowater–Great Northern Paper. We filled our files with information from the state's Bureau of Land Management, and we spent many days poring over the U.S. Geological Survey (USGS) 7.5-minute topographic maps of the state—all 600-plus. From the USGS topos, you can get a good sense of the development on a lake or pond, although some of these maps are quite dated.

We compiled an initial list of more than 200 lakes, ponds, and tidal estuaries that we visited, and we paddled on more than 150 of them. We found nearly 120 of these suitable for inclusion; they are described in the book's 78 sections.

We have by no means found all the very best places. As our research proceeded, we constantly discovered new places— either through someone's tip, a reexamination of the maps, or just coincidence as we came across a great spot during our travels. We are sure there are still many dozens of other lakes and ponds around the state that really *should* be in a guide like this. That's what future editions are for. If anyone has suggestions of other lakes and ponds that belong in this book, please pass them along to us (Alex Wilson or John Hayes, c/o AMC Books, 5 Joy Street, Boston, MA 02108). Also, please bring to our attention any inaccuracies you find and suggestions for improvements and clarifications to make future editions better.

Do We Really Want to Tell People about the Best Places?

Throughout this project, many people have asked us how we could, in good conscience, tell others about our favorite hidden lakes and ponds—the more remote, more pristine places, still unspoiled by too many people. After all, increased visitation would make these places less idyllic. That has indeed been a difficult issue for us—one we've spent many an hour grappling with as we paddled along.

We believe that by getting more people out enjoying these places—people who value wild remote areas for what they are—we will be able to build support for greater protection of these bodies of water. For many lakes and ponds, protection will mean the purchase of fragile surrounding areas by such groups as the Nature Conservancy or the state to prevent further development. On other bodies of water, the best form of protection is restriction of high-speed boating, which generally is handled by state government.

We hope you will become involved in helping to protect some of our most treasured water resources. For many of the lakes and ponds in Maine, the most vocal users right now are fishermen in motorboats and water-skiers, people who have the greatest impact on these delicate environments. The policy makers need to hear from the low-impact users as well. We hope that by the time this book is updated in a few years, we'll be able to report that some of the lakes and ponds included here are better protected than they are today, and thus likely to remain enjoyable to quiet-water paddlers for years and years to come.

Safety First

You might be attracted to quiet water because you have small children and don't want to risk capsizing in a swift-flowing river. Or maybe you just don't like dangerous places—like raging whitewater on rivers in the spring—or places where you have to concentrate too much on your paddling skills. So you turn to the lakes and ponds, envisioning tranquil paddling on mirror-smooth water reflecting the surrounding hills.

You certainly will find these places, including the idyllic mirror-smooth surfaces of quiet ponds at daybreak. But if you spend any time at all paddling on Maine's lakes and ponds, you will also encounter quite dangerous conditions. Strong winds can come up very quickly, turning tranquil lakes into not-so-quiet, whitecap-filled inland seas. On big lakes, strong winds can whip up two- to four-foot waves in almost no time—waves big enough to swamp a canoe. Unlike on rivers, you are often far from shore on larger lakes, and capsizing in cold water can bring on hypothermia very quickly. Along Maine's coast, tidal rivers and estuaries can have very swift currents—in some places faster than you can paddle against. If not approached with proper caution, these places can be very dangerous.

The U.S. Coast Guard and state law in Maine require that personal flotation devices, or PFDs, be carried in all canoes and kayaks for every person in the boat (see further discussion of PFDs in the equipment section on page xv). We recommend that everyone in your canoe wear PFDs at all times. *Certainly* all children should wear them, and with children in the boat, you too should wear a PFD so that if the boat capsizes you can be of more help to the children.

If you don't normally paddle with your PFD on, at least put it on when wind comes up, or when you're crossing large lakes or are likely to encounter substantial motorboat wakes. It may be an inconvenience, it may make you a little hotter in the summer, it may interfere a bit with your paddling. But it could save your life.

Also, in the name of safety, be ready to change your plans. If you've just driven eight hours to reach your destination and it's blowing a gale, be ready to find a more protected pond or go hiking instead. We've made it a point to include in this guide small ponds

Children should always wear life jackets on the water. This well-prepared fellow also has on a cap for the sun, a warm pile top, plenty of water, and a whistle in case of emergency.

near some of the larger, better-known lakes for just this reason. Even if the forecaster promises a beautiful sunny day with no wind, by afternoon it could be blowing a gale and pouring. So be flexible in your plans.

On some lakes, ponds, and marshes described in this guide, particularly the shallow, marshy ones, waterfowl-hunting season can bring a big influx of activity. Avoid these areas during waterfowl-hunting season, especially if you see hunting blinds and decoys in the water. To find out the hunting-season dates, contact the Maine Department of Inland Fisheries and Wildlife, 284 State Street, Augusta, ME 04333; 207-287-3371.

Starting out Right: Equipment Selection

To get started with quiet-water canoeing, you don't really need a whole lot of fancy, high-tech gear. Most any canoe will do, as long as it isn't a high-performance racing model or a tippy boat designed just for whitewater. If you're new to canoeing, try to borrow a canoe for your first few trips. Once you've had a little experience, you'll be in a much better position to select the right one to buy.

If you're ready to buy a canoe, look for one that's stable. Canoe manufacturers often refer to both the *initial stability* and the *secondary stability* of their boats. A canoe with good initial stability and poor secondary stability will be unlikely to begin tipping, but once it tips up a bit it may keep going (this is the case with some older aluminum canoes). Look for a model that does pretty well with both initial and secondary stability. The best canoe for lake and pond canoeing has a keel or shallow-V hull and flat keel line to keep it tracking pretty well across the water, even in a breeze. Whitewater canoes, on the other hand, have rounded bottoms and what's called *rocker* (a curve to the bottom from front to back).

If you like out-of-the-way lakes and ponds, especially those that require portaging, you should try to stretch your budget to afford a Kevlar® canoe. Kevlar is a very strong fiber somewhat like fiberglass but much lighter. The rugged, high-capacity, 18' 4" Mad River Lamoille canoe we paddle on many trips weighs just sixty pounds, and our solo 15' 9" Mad River Independence (also Kevlar) weighs less than forty pounds. If you plan to do a lot of canoeing by yourself, you should consider a solo canoe, in which you sit (or kneel) close to the center of the boat. You will be amazed at the difference a well-designed solo canoe makes compared to a standard two-seater used for solo canoeing.

Another option for the solo paddler is to purchase a sea kayak. Lightweight ones can be quite expensive, but they move along quickly and track extremely well if equipped with a foot-operated rudder. To keep from swamping in rough water, a spray skirt is mandatory.

Look for a good canoe rack. We prefer a simple two-bar system that clips onto the car's rain gutters. With newer cars that do not have gutters, you need to buy specialized mounting hardware suited to the specific car model. You can often save money by purchasing just the mounting brackets and cutting sections of 2x4 for the racks. If your bumpers permit it, tie down the front and back of the canoe as well as securing the canoe to both racks. The sales personnel in any good outdoor-equipment store should be able to help you get set up with an easy-to-use system suitable for your vehicle.

A portage yoke in place of the center thwart on the canoe is essential if you plan on much portaging. A padded yoke makes for a much more comfortable carry. If your yoke isn't padded, a life vest with padded shoulders accomplishes pretty much the same thing. Attach a rope—called a *painter*—to the front of the canoe so you can secure the canoe when you stop for lunch, line it up or down a section of stream, and—if the need ever arises—grab onto it in an emergency.

Paddles should be light and comfortable. Our favorite paddle is relatively short (fifty-six inches), with a blade made of laminated basswood and other hardwoods. It also has a special synthetic tip to protect the blade from damage if you hit rocks or push off from shore. You might want to try out one of the new bent-shaft paddles, which we have come to prefer.

As mentioned above, PFDs are a must—both by common sense and by law. The best type of life preserver is a Coast Guard–approved Type I, II, or III PFD. A Type IV PFD (floating cushion) is acceptable by law, but it is far less effective than a life vest you wear. A good life vest is designed to keep a person's face above water, even if he or she loses consciousness. There must be one PFD in the boat for each occupant, according to Maine laws. With children, it is extremely important that the PFD be the right size so that it won't slip off. Adult PFDs for children are not acceptable. Although Maine law does not require that PFDs be worn at all times, we strongly recommend that you do so, especially when paddling with children.

Adults should wear life jackets for their own safety and to encourage children to do likewise.

As for clothing, plan for the unexpected—especially on longer trips. Even with a bright sunny day forecast, we have frequently had a shower come up by afternoon. So we make it a habit to bring along a small stuff sack with rain gear. On longer trips, we also carry a dry change of clothes. Along with rain coming up unexpectedly, temperatures can drop very quickly, especially if you like paddling in the spring or fall—when you can avoid the crowds. Bring along plenty of warm clothes if you will be out for a few hours with children. Be aware that they are probably just sitting while you are doing the work. Even though you may be plenty warm from paddling, they may be getting cold. Watch for signs of their discomfort.

Canoeing Technique

As with equipment selection, canoeing technique is a lot more critical with whitewater canoeing—where it can mean literally the difference between life and death—than it is with quiet-water paddling. On a quiet lake or pond it doesn't really matter whether you're using the proper J-stroke, or if you know the sweep stroke, the draw, or the reverse J. Learning some of these strokes, however, can make a day of paddling more relaxing and enjoyable. We watch lots of novices zigzagging along as they frantically switch sides while shouting orders back and forth. It doesn't have to be so difficult. If you are not familiar with paddling strokes, buy a book on canoeing or participate in a canoeing workshop, such as those offered by the Appalachian Mountain Club, equipment retailers, a few canoe manufacturers, and L.L. Bean. Among the books we recommend on canoeing are *Beyond the Paddle* by Garret Conover (Tilbury House, 1991); *The Complete Wilderness Paddler* by Davidson and Gugge (Vintage, 1983); *The New Wilderness Canoeing and Camping* by Cliff Jacobson (ICS Books, 1986); and *Pole, Paddle & Portage* by Bill Riviere (Little, Brown & Co., 1969).

If you're a novice canoeist, we suggest starting out on the smaller lakes and ponds. Practice paddling into the wind, with the wind, and across it. Becoming comfortable with paddling isn't hard, it just takes some practice. On a warm day close to shore, you might even want to practice capsizing. That sounds odd, but intentionally tipping your canoe over will give you an idea of its limits and how easy or difficult it is to capsize (refer to the previous discussion of initial and secondary stability). If you go that far with practicing, you might also try to get back into the canoe when you're away from shore. With two people, you should be able to right the boat, getting most of the water out (you'll need a bailer to get it all out). Getting back in is a bit of a trick. Try it sometime—preferably *intentionally,* and with an empty canoe, near shore.

Recreation on Private Land in Maine

Most of the wild lakes in eastern and northern Maine are surrounded by private land—mostly that of large paper companies. Nearly all of these companies keep their land open to recreational use, for which we should be very thankful. In eastern and central Maine, access is generally uncontrolled and camping permitted anywhere at no cost. In some areas, it is necessary to obtain landowner permission to camp; never camp on land that is posted No Trespassing. In roughly five million acres in northern Maine, access is controlled by gates and usage fees must be paid. Understanding the access to this land can be difficult.

The controlled land in northern Maine is divided into two large tracts that are managed separately. Bowater–Great Northern Paper owns and manages 2.1 million acres in the region around the West Branch of the Penobscot River north and west of Millinocket (see map). A larger tract of about 2.8 million acres to the north is owned by approximately 20 different companies or families but managed cooperatively as North Maine Woods. Access to this land is controlled by staffed gates or checkpoints.

Bowater–Great Northern Paper operates three checkpoints: the Debsconeag checkpoint near Millinocket (open twenty-four hours a day in 1994); the Sias Hill checkpoint north of Greenville (open 4:00 A.M. to 11:00 P.M. in 1994); and the Twenty Mile Checkpoint northwest of Moosehead Lake (open 4:00 A.M. to 11:00 P.M. in 1994). North Maine Woods maintains fourteen checkpoints, including five on the U.S.–Canada border. The Six Mile Checkpoint in Ashland is open twenty-four hours a day (1994); others have various hours of operation, usually from 5:00 A.M. or 6:00 A.M. to 8:00 P.M. or 9:00 P.M. We advise that you contact North Maine Woods to check on the hours of operation for any checkpoint you plan to cross.

When you cross a checkpoint, you pay a usage fee. (Here's where it really gets confusing, because Bowater–Great Northern and North Maine Woods maintain different fee schedules for day use and camping.)

1994 BOWATER–GREAT NORTHERN PAPER FEE STRUCTURE
(fees collected *per vehicle*)

	Maine Vehicle Registration	Non-Maine Vehicle Registration
Vehicle use	$4/day	$8/day
	$24/season	$48/season
Camping	$3/site/night	$6/site/night

1994 NORTH MAINE WOODS FEE STRUCTURE
(fees collected *per person*)

	Maine Resident	Nonresident
Day use	$3.50/person/day	$7/person/day
	$20/person/season	$40/person/season
Camping (in addition to day-use fee)	$4/person/night	$4/person/night
Day use plus camping	$55/person/season	$90/person/season

To complicate matters further, there are some state camping areas that you enter and pay for (at different rates) through either the Bowater–Great Northern or North Maine Woods checkpoints. These areas include Lobster Lake, sections of the West Branch of the Penobscot, Allagash Lake, and the Allagash Wilderness Waterway. You pay these state camping-registration fees at the checkpoints, which pass them on to the state.

1994 MAINE DEPARTMENT OF CONSERVATION CAMPING FEES

	Maine Resident	Nonresident
Lobster Lake and West Branch (children under ten free)	$3/person/night	$4/person/night
Allagash Wilderness Waterway and Allagash Lake (children under ten free)	$4/person/night	$5/person/night

If you are passing through Bowater–Great Northern Paper land to reach North Maine Woods land there is no charge by Bowater. If you are going the other way—through North Maine Woods land to Bowater–Great Northern land—you will be charged a day-use fee by North Maine Woods. Finally, if you are staying in a commercial establishment within these lands (such as a sporting camp) there is a flat fee (round-trip), as follows:

	Maine Resident	Nonresident
Bowater–Great Northern	$4/vehicle	$8/vehicle
North Maine Woods	$12/person	$18/person

These logging roads are private, built by the corporate owners to move timber to paper and lumber mills. Logging trucks have the right of way. Because trucks are not regulated here as they are on public roads, you may see some mammoth loads of logs. We've seen tandem trucks barreling along these gravel roads, carrying at least double the legal load permissible on public roads. If you see one of these coming, pull over and let it pass. We owe the industrial landowners this courtesy in return for making their land available for our recreational use.

For North Maine Woods access, we recommend calling first, because there are quotas at several of the checkpoints on the number of recreational vehicles that can enter. North Maine Woods can be reached at 207-435-6213 from 8:00 A.M. to 11:30 A.M. and 1:00 P.M. to 4:30 P.M. Registering to camp on Bowater–Great Northern or North Maine Woods land does not provide you with a fire permit. For most, but not all, camping sites on these lands you need to obtain a fire permit if you want to build an open fire (see below).

Fire Permits

Because Maine depends highly on forest products, the state takes great care to reduce the risk of fire. Although one can kindle a fire without a permit in state-park campgrounds and in private campgrounds, most other sites require fire permits. There are two types of designated campsites: *authorized* campsites where you may carefully build a fire without obtaining a fire permit; and *fire-permit* campsites where you may build a fire only after obtaining a permit. On sites requiring fire permits and nondesignated campsites, no permit is required if you use only a camp stove.

To obtain a fire permit, contact the Maine Forest Service at one of the numbers listed in the write-up. The *Maine Atlas and Gazetteer* identifies authorized and permit campsites by a closed tent symbol and an open tent symbol, respectively. Based on inspections, the

Maine Forest Service changes these designations from time to time; we recommend buying the most up-to-date *Maine Atlas* available. We do not distinguish between these two types of campsites on the maps in this book.

Other Lodging Options

Along with camping on or near most of the bodies of water covered in this book, there are often options for other nearby lodging. For information on other options, check your local bookstore or library for guides to bed-and-breakfasts or country inns, many of which can be found near the lakes and ponds in this guide. Information on inns around the state is available from the Maine Innkeepers Association, 305 Commercial St., Portland, ME 04101; 207-773-7670. You might also want to contact local Chambers of Commerce for listings not included in the Maine Innkeepers directory, as well as for names of restaurants and area attractions.

In remote northern and eastern parts of the state, scattered sporting camps, that harken back to a bygone era of life without a lot of conveniences, offer comfort and protection from biting insects. Most sporting camps have five to twenty cabins and a central lodge for meals; some are set up for housekeeping (you cook your own meals). For information on sporting camps, refer to the new book *In the Maine Woods: The Insiders' Guide to Traditional Maine Sporting Camps* by Alice Arlen, published in 1994 by AJ & Co., 25 Warren St., Hallowell, ME 04347. A more complete listing of sporting camps is available from the Maine Sporting Camp Association, P.O. Box 89, Jay, ME 04239.

Bringing the Kids Along

Quiet-water canoeing is a *great* activity to do with kids—but pay attention to weather forecasts and take adequate safety precautions. Maintain flexibility in your plans in case of adverse weather, and always make it a rule to wear life preservers in the canoe. Perhaps the most important suggestion when canoeing with kids is to make it fun. If the parents argue about who should paddle on which side of the boat, or yell about rocks ahead, that will affect the kids. Try to keep calm. Your kids will do better, and you'll have a better time. On long paddling excursions, set up a cozy place where young children can sleep. After the initial excitement of paddling fades, the gently rolling canoe often puts young kids right to sleep, especially near the end of a long day. If you haven't taken your kids canoeing before, they might be anxious on the first trip or two, but after they are used to it, they will be much more relaxed.

Respect for the Outdoors

Lakes and ponds show the effects of recreational use. Keeping them in good shape requires special attention. Even a low-impact pastime such as canoeing can have a substantial effect on fragile marsh habitat. Our wetlands are extremely important ecosystems for wildlife and are home to many rare and endangered species. An unaware paddler can disturb rare turtles, nesting loons and eagles, and even fragile bog plants. Please use care as you enjoy these waters.

You can go even further than the old adage, "Take only photographs, leave only footprints." On the most pristine of our lakes and ponds, we make it a habit to carry along a trash bag and pick up the leavings of less thoughtful individuals. If each of us does the same, we will enjoy more attractive places to paddle. While motorboaters tend to have a bad reputation when it comes to leaving trash, we want canoeists to have the opposite reputation—which could come in handy when some of us seek greater paddling access on some of Maine's more remote lakes. Remember, most of the lakes and ponds in the northern part of Maine are surrounded by private land; use it with respect. To learn more about how to enjoy a wild area without damaging it, see the excellent book *Soft Paths* by Hampton and Cole (Stackpole Books, 1988).

What You'll See

Wetland ecosystems are diverse and exciting—by far the richest ecosystems accessible to us. In Maine, you can visit everything from salt-water estuarine marshes to deep, crystal-clear mountain ponds and unique bog environments. You'll have the opportunity to observe hundreds of species of birds; dozens of species of mammals, turtles, and snakes; and literally thousands of plants. Some of these species are quite rare and exciting to discover—such as a delicate bog orchid, or a family of otters. But even the ordinary plants and animals contain a storehouse of information, leading to exciting discoveries and providing hours of enjoyable observation.

We've picked out a few of the more interesting animal species you might encounter on the lakes and ponds of Maine and written up some notes on them. You will find these write-ups—and accompanying pen-and-ink illustrations by Marrin Robinson—interspersed in the lake and pond descriptions. By learning a little more about these species, you'll find them all the more fun to watch.

Have a Great Time

The purpose of this guide is to help you enjoy and appreciate our outdoors. We hope you will enjoy using this book as much as we enjoyed researching and writing it. Let us know what you like or dislike about the places we've described, and tell us about any others you think should be included.

Finally, don't consider this guide as a limit to the areas you can visit. There are other lakes and ponds—literally thousands more in Maine, many of which offer excellent quiet-water canoeing. Buy some topographic and other maps and explore. You'll find, as we did, that many of the ponds shown on maps have no public access. Others are too built-up with summer homes. But there are many gems out there that are not included in this guide—hidden beaver ponds, quiet meandering channels of slow-moving streams and rivers, old mill ponds with ruins of long-abandoned mills, bird-filled estuaries. These are places whose secrets you can either reveal to others or keep to yourself. And that's as it should be.

Alex Wilson
John Hayes
October 1994

How to Use This Book

FOR each lake or pond included in this book, we provide a short descriptive write-up and map. Most maps show the roads or highways that provide access to the body of water, as well as boat-launch sites. Some launch sites have boat ramps suitable for trailered motorboats as well as canoes, but many require a carry to the water—we do not distinguish between these types of launch sites on the maps.

The maps and write-ups included in this guide are designed to accompany road maps. If you are not familiar with your destination, do not try to rely on just these write-ups and maps to get there. Obtain a copy of the DeLorme Mapping Company's *Maine Atlas and Gazetteer.* Each lake in this book is keyed to this atlas, which divides the state into twenty 10" x 14-1/2" maps. These detailed maps include most boat-access locations and lakeside campsites. For more detail, refer to the USGS topographic maps. The 7.5-minute USGS maps for the lakes described are listed at the end of each section.

For many of the lakes and ponds, we describe or show campsites or nearby campground locations. Refer to the introduction for information on camping and fire permits on private land in Maine, as well as for ideas on other lodging options.

Finally, while the book is about quiet-water *canoeing,* the information applies equally well to kayaking. In fact, tidal areas and big lakes are actually better for sea kayaking because of wakes and choppy water that can splash into an open boat. We hope that whatever boat you choose, you will be careful and enjoy many hours of quiet-water paddling on the lakes and ponds of Maine. Happy paddling!

Locator Map

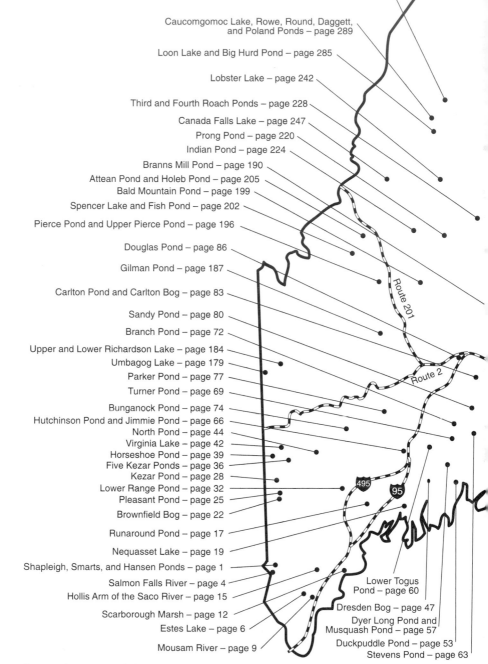

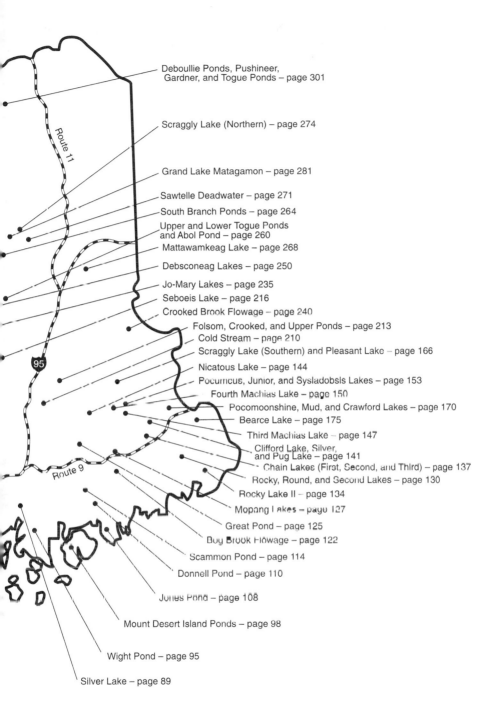

Route 11

Route 9

95

Deboullie Ponds, Pushineer, Gardner, and Togue Ponds – page 301

Scraggly Lake (Northern) – page 274

Grand Lake Matagamon – page 281

Sawtelle Deadwater – page 271

South Branch Ponds – page 264

Upper and Lower Togue Ponds and Abol Pond – page 260

Mattawamkeag Lake – page 268

Debsconeag Lakes – page 250

Jo-Mary Lakes – page 235

Seboeis Lake – page 216

Crooked Brook Flowage – page 240

Folsom, Crooked, and Upper Ponds – page 213

Cold Stream – page 210

Scraggly Lake (Southern) and Pleasant Lake – page 166

Nicatous Lake – page 144

Pocumcus, Junior, and Sysladobsis Lakes – page 153

Fourth Machias Lake – page 150

Pocomoonshine, Mud, and Crawford Lakes – page 170

Bearce Lake – page 175

Third Machias Lake – page 147

Clifford Lake, Silver, and Pug Lake – page 141

Chain Lakes (First, Second, and Third) – page 137

Rocky, Round, and Second Lakes – page 130

Rocky Lake II – page 134

Mopang Lakes – page 127

Great Pond – page 125

Bog Brook Flowage – page 122

Scammon Pond – page 114

Donnell Pond – page 110

Jones Pond – page 108

Mount Desert Island Ponds – page 98

Wight Pond – page 95

Silver Lake – page 89

Map Legend

⌢	Tent site
◢	Lean-to
⌐	Picnic area
⋏	State or federal campground
⌂	Private campground
⌣	Boat access
P	Parking area
⋅⋅⋅	Marsh
☼	Peak

Interstate highway	══════
State highway	──────
Paved road	─·─·─·─·
Graded dirt road	════→═══
Rough dirt road	= = = = = = =
Foot path	··············
River	══→══
Stream	──→──

arrow indicates direction of flow

# Southwest Region

Shapleigh, Smarts, and Hansen Ponds
Shapleigh

MAPS
> **Maine Atlas:** Map 2
> **USGS Quadrangle:** Great East Lake

INFORMATION
> **Hansen Pond area:** 30 acres; maximum depth: 8 feet
> **Smarts Pond area:** 20 acres; maximum depth: 5 feet
> **Shapleigh Pond:** no data
> **Prominent fish species:** largemouth bass and chain pickerel in
> Hansen and Shapleigh ponds; smallmouth bass in the stream;
> chain pickerel in Smarts Pond

Small, shallow, and with a tiny, rustic boat access, Shapleigh Pond sees few visitors. Several houses cluster near the boat access, but the rest of the area is fairly free of development. If you paddle up the Little Ossipee River into Hansen and Smarts ponds, you undoubtedly will be alone in this little patch of wilderness.

Paddling up the right-hand side of Shapleigh Pond, we encountered fresh beaver cuttings. As we rounded a bend, sure enough, there was a beaver swimming in front of the boat. It let us get quite close before slapping the water with its broad tail in typical beaver fashion and diving into the underwater entrance to its lodge. A little farther along, up in the northwest arm, we surprised a white-tailed buck who, after flagging us with the underside of its very white tail, stood a few feet back in the alders and snorted with indignation for several minutes at being interrupted while taking his evening drink. Hermit

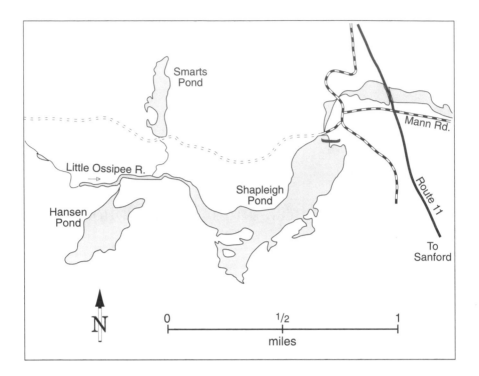

thrushes, with their beautiful flutelike notes, serenaded us from the dense understory. Here was a habitat not overrun by humans.

Continue paddling up the right side into the Little Ossipee River with its barely perceptible current. Stick to the main channel, especially during drier times of the year, as it gets quite shallow. You will have to wend your way through acres of aquatic vegetation, which was loaded with feeding black ducks when we visited. The river channel narrows, then opens up a bit with a lot of aquatic vegetation on the right side. At this point, if you search carefully on the right, you will find the outlet from Smarts Pond. The outlet stream is narrow, shallow, and dammed by beavers. Although we did not travel past the first beaver dam, we suspect that you would have to get wet several times before making it to Smarts Pond, which is a few hundred yards through the brush.

The real reason we did not check out Smarts Pond, we have to confess, is because it was one of those warm, humid evenings in June, when you would be drenched if you wore a long-sleeved shirt. With no wind to keep the bugs down, the mosquitoes were out in droves, and the thought of dragging a boat through a brush-filled passageway for a couple hundred yards . . . well, sometimes the mosquitoes win.

Travel up the river a little farther, keeping your eye out for the channel choked with pickerelweed leading to Hansen Pond on the left. In contrast with the outlet from Smarts Pond, this entryway is easily navigable. Because of its small size and the encroaching tree canopy, Hansen Pond has a real wilderness feel to it, though it does have one cabin on it. Large white pines line the eastern shore of this shallow, plant-choked pond, while short red maples, alders, and other scrub vegetation dominate the marshy western shore.

Except during high water in the spring, you won't be able to travel upriver more than about a quarter-mile past the outlet from Hansen Pond. The river here actually has a little current to it; more importantly, it gets narrow and quite shallow. The rocks, however, are not coated with boat paint, indicating that, indeed, this is not a heavily traveled waterway.

Getting There

From Sanford, travel north on Routes 11 and 109 until they split. Turn right, following Route 11 north. At the Shapleigh Corner Store, there is a flashing yellow light as the road takes a hard left. Start marking mileage here. Go 4.8 miles to a crossroads. Mann Road goes off to the right; instead, turn left here onto an unmarked blacktop road. Go a quarter of a mile, and turn left at the Village Thrift Shop and Post Office. In half a block, take a right, and go about one more block to the access, right next to the iron bridge. There is very little parking; you can get two wheels off the pavement on the left-hand side. If it's hot, cool off by swinging out and dropping into the water from a rope that dangles from a tree on the far side of the iron bridge.

Salmon Falls River
Acton

MAPS
Maine Atlas: Map 2
USGS Quadrangle: Great East Lake

This river forms the boundary between lower Maine and New Hampshire. For most of its considerable length, it is but a small stream. However, in Milton Mills there is a dam that causes the river to widen to canoeable proportions.

Although this section of the river is only about two miles long, if you paddle here it will seem much longer. The channel meanders through endless acres of aquatic vegetation. Given the vast amount of underwater structure, there are healthy fish populations, including, we are told, some huge smallmouth bass lurking under the lily pads.

There are two put-in access points, one at the dam site and the other 0.5 mile upstream. The dam site has more parking, but if you put in at the upper site, you will avoid paddling literally through the back yards of two houses. Once past these, the evidence of human civilization is slight. A second reason for putting in up above is that the lower section is choked with barely submerged rocks. Go slowly here.

This is a great place to paddle if you enjoy exploring the pond life among the lily pads, pickerelweed, and rushes. In places, the main channel is masked by vegetation. What looks like a widened channel turns out to be a dead end, while the real channel snakes through a dense stand of pickerelweed. There are many hours to be spent exploring here without motorboats, although you may see an occasional fisherman in a canoe, especially on weekends.

Getting There

From Milton Mills, with the U.S. Post Office on your right and the Milton Mills Village Store on your left, drive straight uphill. Do not turn right here. Go 0.3 mile and turn off to the right onto Hopper Road (unmarked). Drive 0.55 mile up Hopper Road. The boat access is just over the bridge, up on the left.

Alternatively, from Sanford, take Routes 109 and 4A to neighboring Springvale. Continue on Routes 109 and 11 west. Start measuring mileage with your trip odometer when Routes 109 and 11 split. Take

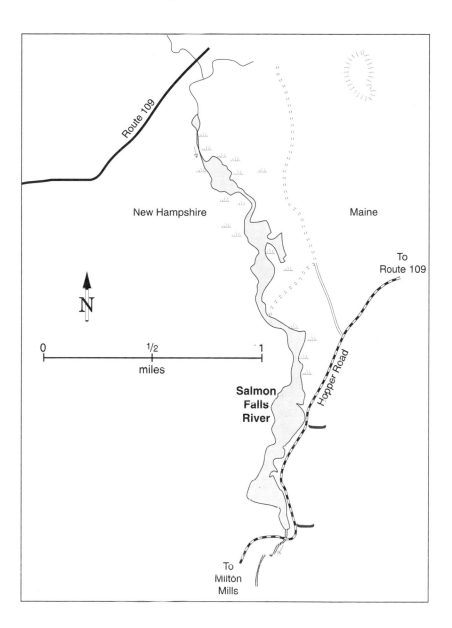

Route 109, the left fork, drive for 3.6 miles, and turn left onto Old Route 9, which cuts diagonally across Route 109. At this junction there is a small U.S. Post Office sign, followed immediately by the genuine article on the right. At 3.8 miles, take the left fork onto Hopper Road (unmarked). The boat access is on the right at 6.9 miles.

The alternate put-in is back toward Sanford about 0.5 mile; this access avoids the first two back yards and the submerged boulders.

Estes Lake

Sanford

MAPS
  Maine Atlas: Map 2
  USGS Quadrangle: Alfred

INFORMATION
  Area: 387 acres; maximum depth: 30 feet
  Camping: Apache Campground, Bernier Road, Sanford, ME
    04073; 207-324-5652 or 5563. Open May 15 to October 15.
  Prominent fish species: smallmouth bass, largemouth bass, and
    chain pickerel

Estes Lake is a long, widened section of river, backed up behind a small hydroelectric dam on the Mousam River. The northern three-quarters of Estes Lake is actually part of the Middle Branch of the Mousam River, as the main river comes into the lake near the south end. As of this writing, there is no official public boat access on Estes Lake. As a result of the recent Federal Energy Regulatory Commission relicensing procedure, however, the dam operator must provide public access. Because of pressure from the Estes Lake Association, the dam operator will provide only carry-in access, probably at Goodwins Bridge, halfway down the lake, and at the dam. According to the

pine

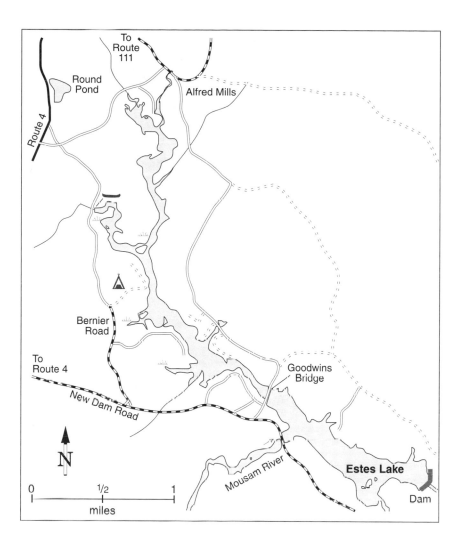

staff at Berniers Apache Campground, who own quite a bit of land along the lake, reasonable boat access exists on Hay Brook, a tributary on the northwest end. Even after the provision of public access, we would still prefer the Hay Brook access, given its location on the unpopulated northern end. You can also put in at Apache Campground if you are camping there.

Paddling from the access on Hay Brook, you pass through cattails, horsetails, and many other marsh plants. Wood duck nesting boxes dot the shoreline, most of them put up recently. The only occupant we saw was a tree swallow peering out of one of the holes. Eastern kingbirds darted out from exposed perches to snatch insects from the air, and hermit thrushes sang from the understory, along with rufous-sided towhees and common yellowthroats. The water everywhere here is quite shallow and choked with aquatic vegetation. There is supposed to be good bass fishing in the weed beds.

As you enter the main lake, off to the right you will see Apache Campground and a few houses on the opposite shore. Paddle around to the left, heading north. Besides the many marshy coves to explore, you can paddle up each of the two main tributaries for a couple of miles before they become impassable. The varied vegetation here, ranging from scrubby marsh plants to tall deciduous trees and pine plantations, enhances the scenic character of upper Estes Lake.

You should not see many power boats here. No access exists for large boats, the Estes Lake Association tries to limit motors to 10 hp, and the large number of barely submerged rocks and stumps make speedboating dangerous. We paddled here on a warm Saturday in late June and saw no other boat—human- or motor-powered.

Getting There

From Sanford, take Route 202 toward Alfred. Turn right onto Grammar Road just outside of town. Cross Route 4, after which Grammar Road becomes New Dam Road, and turn left onto Bernier Road, following the signs for Apache Campground. Upon reaching the campground in about 0.8 mile, the paved road turns to gravel. Go about half a mile to the short iron bridge that spans Hay Brook. There is parking along the road for a couple of small cars.

Mousam River

MAPS
    Maine Atlas: Maps 2 and 3
    USGS Quadrangles: Alfred and Kennebunk

The Mousam River provides an outstanding paddling resource for much of its length, from Mousam Lake down to Kennebunk Beach. The section included here runs upstream from a dam just west of I-95, Exit 3. The river meanders so much that you rarely see much of it at once. Side passages abound, and the main channel has no perceptible current, at least late in the summer and at other times of low water.

    Throughout this section of the river, standing dead trees seem to sprout from the water, and the many marshy areas are adorned with the typical assortment of aquatic plants and shoreline shrubs. In bloom in June are rhodora (early), sheep laurel, and a viburnum, probably arrowwood. Extensive patches of iris bloom in marshy areas, wherev-

great blue heron

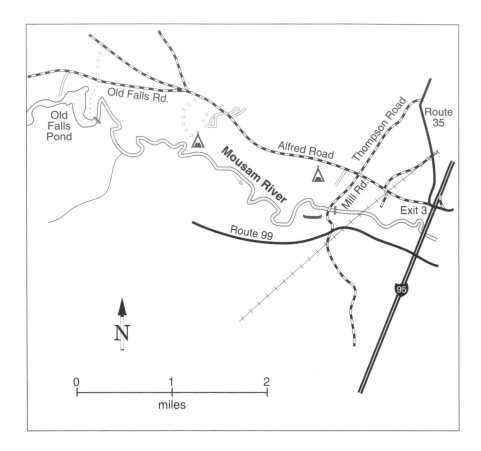

er the canopy is open. If you get as far as the high-tension wires crossing overhead, look for the black locusts hanging out over the water.
These trees belong to the pea family and are loaded with clusters of
white flowers in June.

Great blue herons stalk fish and amphibians along the shoreline,
double-crested cormorants dive for fish, and herring gulls patrol the
air, hunting for dead things floating in the water, always ready to
snatch food away from other birds that venture near. Beaver cuttings
and lodges occur all along the shore, and this should be a good place
to look for river otters.

The privately owned shoreline has very few No Trespassing
signs. In the more secluded reaches, you probably could picnic on the
flat grassy spots, but if you do so, please treat the land with respect so
that it is not posted off-limits to others who follow. An occasional

Irises growing along the bank of the Mousam River.

house or camp punctuates the shoreline, but in places you can paddle for a mile without seeing any evidence of civilization. The presence of this wild river, given its location within a few miles of Kennebunk, I-95, and thousands of summer vacationers, is remarkable. Boating here on a warm Saturday in June, we saw nary another human being.

Getting There

From I-95, Exit 3, drive northwest on Alfred Road toward West Kennebunk and Alfred. Go 0.8 mile, getting to a crossroads where Thompson Road goes to the right and Mill Road goes to the left. Turn left onto Mill Road and drive a half-mile to the bridge at the dam. Access is from either end of the bridge on the upstream side. It is easier to get in the boat on the eastern (approach) side.

Scarborough Marsh

Scarborough

MAPS
   Maine Atlas: Map 3
   USGS Quadrangles: Prouts Neck and Old Orchard Beach

INFORMATION
   Scarborough Marsh Nature Center, Maine Audubon Society, 118
      U.S. Route 1, Falmouth, ME 04105; 207-883-5100. The nature
      center is open from 9:30 A.M. to 5:30 P.M.

Preserved by the Wetlands Protection Act of 1972, Scarborough
Marsh is a 3,100-acre estuary of fresh, brackish, and salt water filled
with birds, mammals, insects, and crustaceans. Native Americans of
the area called marshes *owascoag,* which means "land of many grasses," and indeed there are endless acres of cordgrass, cattails, rushes,
and sedges—and many other aquatic plants.

   There is much to learn about the ecology of estuaries and their
value as producers of huge quantities of biomass, about tenfold more
than equivalent acreage in farm fields, pine plantations, or even tropi-

*Acres of cordgrass, cattails, rushes, and sedges greet paddlers as they ven-
ture out onto the serpentine rivers of the Scarborough Marsh.*

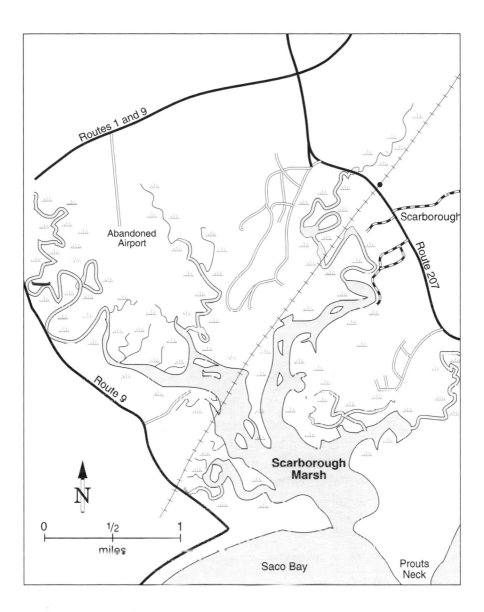

Routes 1 and 9

Abandoned
Airport

Scarborough

Route 207

Route 9

N

Scarborough
Marsh

0   1/2   1
miles

Saco Bay

Prouts
Neck

cal rain forests. The Maine Department of Inland Fisheries and
Wildlife is in charge of the preservation of Scarborough Marsh, and
through a cooperative agreement allows the Maine Audubon Society
to operate a nature center here, which is open from late April to September. Not only are there nature trails, canoe rentals, and a boat-
launch site at the nature center, but the staff is more than willing to
provide helpful information about the life of the marsh and about how
best to canoe it.

The marsh area is a birdwatcher's paradise. The nature center has a list of birds seen recently. One bird of interest found here in relatively large numbers is the glossy ibis, which looks black at a distance, but at close range is an iridescent purple. The bird is about two feet long with a three-foot wingspan. It is an odd-looking bird with a long, decurved bill specialized for poking around in marshy areas and hunting up crustaceans or whatever else can be found. Formerly, it ranged only as far north as the mid-Atlantic states, but it has recently expanded its range all the way into Canada; nobody seems to know why.

We have included Scarborough Marsh with some reservations, not because it isn't a worthy place to paddle but because of the ten-foot tides. When we paddled here, the tide was rising and reached full high tide. The current was not particularly swift, but the wind blows almost constantly, with no trees to block it. Paddling against both the tide and the wind can be quite tiring, and it is almost inevitable that this combination will confront you on windy days, because the serpentine rivers double back on themselves every few hundred feet. This will not be a problem for strong paddlers, but families with children should be aware. We strongly recommend that all paddlers wear PFDs at all times in Scarborough Marsh.

The Audubon Society recommends that you paddle out against the tide while you are fresh and then allow the tide to help carry you back in. This is very wise advice, and indeed, with a little planning, you could ride both out and back in on the tide as it turns. Contact the nature center just before your trip to find out the local tide times. The staff also told us horror stories of people who paddle up narrow creeks and get stranded as the tide runs out, leaving them in hip-deep mud. It is safest to stick to the many miles of main river channels, which do not go dry at low tide.

Getting There

From Portland, take Route 1 south. Turn left onto Route 9 toward Pine Point, and drive 0.8 mile to the nature center on the left. You will see a raft of bright red Old Town rental canoes out front.

Hollis Center Arm of the Saco River

Hollis and Dayton

MAPS
    Maine Atlas: Map 3
    USGS Quadrangle: Bar Mills

INFORMATION
    Information of area, depth, and prominent fish species not available.

The Saco River drains the White Mountains of Maine and New Hampshire, meandering southeast until it dumps into the Gulf of Maine at Saco. Whitewater dominates the upper reaches, but once it crosses from New Hampshire into Maine the Saco becomes a quiet-water paddler's dream. From Swans Falls in Fryeburg it meanders slowly for

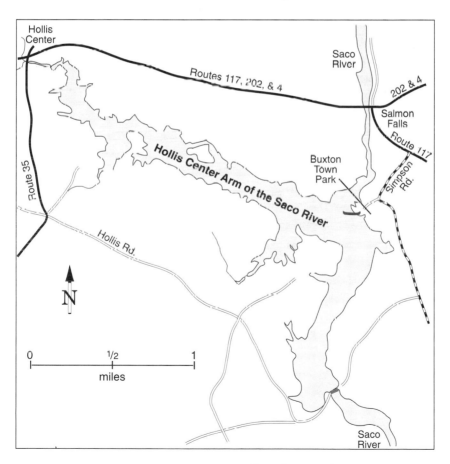

miles down to Hiram and seems to be bank-to-bank with canoeists for most of the summer, inducing anyone who wants a modicum of solitude to seek less traveled ways. The Hollis Center Arm, just south of Salmon Falls and southeast of Hollis Center, backed up behind a dam, sees far fewer paddlers and is the section described here.

The access is from the Buxton Town Park, which has a gate that is open from sunrise to sunset. In practice, because this is a popular fishing and recreation area, the gate closes nearer to 8:30 or 8:45 P.M. If you wish to paddle in the cooler evening hours, check on the gate-closing hour with the caretaker, who often sits in his truck near the park entrance.

Large deciduous trees line the shore and the hillsides around this wide lake, with a smattering of lofty conifers, mainly white pine, interspersed. Huge granite boulders poke up here and there along the shoreline. Numerous coves, some of them quite deep and with jagged shorelines, beg to be explored. With all of the maples, oaks, and other deciduous trees lining the banks and covering the hillsides, this should be a beautiful spot to paddle in the fall when the leaves are turning. Avoid midsummer weekends if possible, because this is a popular recreation spot. When we paddled here, there were canoes out on the water, but we saw only one small motorboat.

Getting There

From Hollis Center, drive east on Routes 202, 4, and 117 to Salmon Falls. Cross the bridge over the Saco River and turn right immediately, following Route 117 (Routes 202 and 4 continue straight). Continue on Route 117 for 0.4 mile, and turn right onto Simpson Road. Go 0.3 mile, and turn right onto a gravel road leading to the boat access in another 0.2 mile. Do not drive down to the water unless your vehicle has four-wheel drive; park on the flat areas up above, keeping as far off the road as possible.

Runaround Pond

Durham

MAPS
  Maine Atlas: Map 5
  USGS Quadrangle: North Pownal
INFORMATION
  Area: 91 acres; maximum depth: 18 feet
  Prominent fish species: largemouth bass and chain pickerel

Runaround Pond is really two shallow weedy streams, teeming with wildlife and aquatic vegetation. It takes several hours to paddle back to the farthest navigable reaches of each stream, but the effort will be well worth it. You will see wood ducks, black ducks, great blue heron, muskrat, turtles, fish, and myriad other wildlife. When we paddled

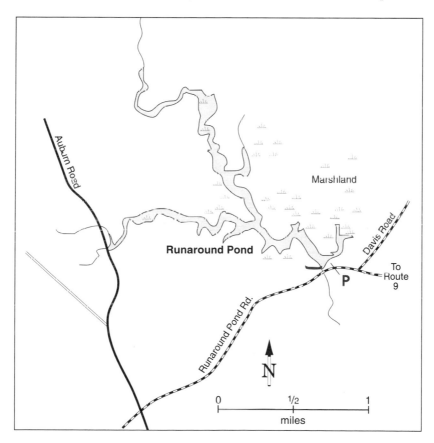

here on a beautiful Sunday morning in July, we met only one other canoe. Aquatic vegetation severely limits access for motorboats.

There are several large, flat boulders at the boat access, overhung by red pines: perfect for a picnic. From the access, you can paddle into a beautiful little cove by going through one of the two large culverts under the road. The creek emerges in a walled canyon with large white pines above.

As you return to the boat access and head upstream, huge rafts of beautiful bright blue-flowered pickerelweed greet you, abuzz with the constant drone of thousands of bumblebee pollinators. Water shield, fragrant water lily, bullhead lily, and yellow bladderwort are your constant companions. The water is tea colored from the tannic acids released during plant degradation.

When the stream channel forks, go left, weaving your way back up the meandering channel. The wide valley here is choked with shrubs and aquatic vegetation, leaving open only a narrow channel. Back on higher ground, maples dominate the shoreline, along with scattered pines, pointed balsam fir, and red oak. You can paddle all the way to Auburn Road—more than two miles—where the stream becomes impassable.

A great horned owl took off from one of the many side coves as we approached. Kingfishers scolded us all the way up the stream. Several great blue herons took off as we approached, and wood ducks and black ducks exploded from the surface as we rounded several of the numerous stream bends. We did not expect to see a cormorant on this shallow, weedy stream, but there it was as we rounded a bend. You should see muskrats and turtles, and if you paddle here in the evening, you should see one or more of the numerous beavers whose presence is evident everywhere.

The right-hand fork is not quite as long, has thicker aquatic vegetation, a less open channel, and lots of duckweed obscuring visibility into the water. Nonetheless, it offers much of the same beauty as the left fork and is well worth paddling.

Getting There

Take Route 136 south out of Auburn. Start measuring mileage when Route 9 splits off to the right in Durham. Drive south on Route 9 for 2.2 miles. Look for a crossroads sign, with Rabbit Road taking off to the left and Runaround Pond Road going to the right. Turn right onto Runaround Pond Road. The boat access is 1.0 miles down this road on the right. There is room for many cars.

Nequasset Lake

Woolwich

MAPS
   Maine Atlas: Map 6
   USGS Quadrangle: Bath

INFORMATION
   Area: 392 acres; maximum depth: 63 feet
   Prominent fish species: brown trout, smallmouth bass, largemouth
   bass, white perch, and chain pickerel

From the Nequasset Lake boat access, one can paddle in both directions. We first paddled north up the inlet, Nequasset Brook. The wide
channel starts out lined with pickerelweed but soon takes an abrupt
left turn into a heavily forested area where the stream narrows a bit.
Hemlocks and maples form a beautiful canopy over the water for most
of this heavily wooded stream.

   The thirty to forty-foot-wide stream has plenty of water, with no
noticeable current. Marshy areas abound with swamp rose, pickerelweed, water lilies, ferns, and bladderwort. A variety of trees extends
along the wooded shore. There are spots that look good for camping,
back under the hemlocks and pines. The stream meanders around,
heading alternately north, west, south, and west, and then starts over
again.

   After paddling back about a mile, we came to some fields on the
left and a two-foot waterfall. It looked like one could portage up over
the falls and continue paddling. We turned around here and will leave
further exploration to you. It is definitely worth paddling up this quiet,
beautiful little stream. Great blue heron and many ducks burst from
the water as we rounded the sharp turns, and songbirds called constantly from the woods. Perhaps most numerous were the flutelike
notes of hermit thrushes, announcing their territories.

   The access stream widens from the boat landing down into
Nequasset Lake but is every bit as beautiful as the upstream portion.
There are several side channels choked with lily pads, and if the water
is high enough, check out the extensive wetland on the left on the way
down to the lake. The north end of the lake contains a fair amount of
water shield, a member of the water lily family with the stalk attached

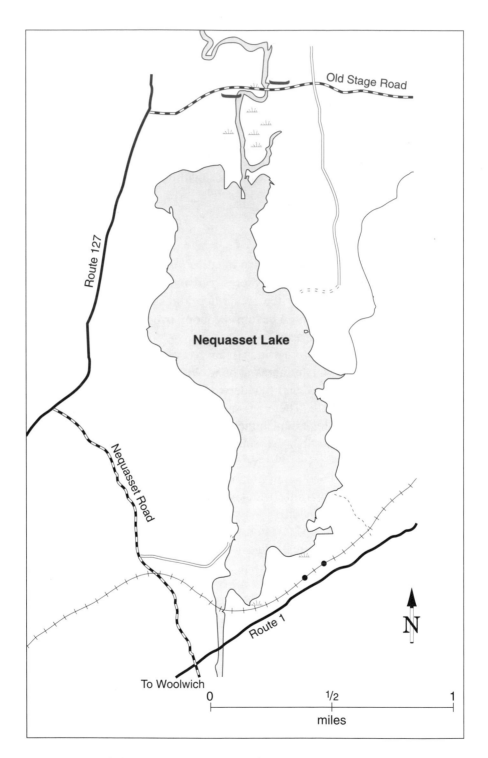

Old Stage Road

Route 127

Nequasset Lake

Nequasset Road

Route 1

To Woolwich

N

0   1/2   1

miles

at the center of a floating oval leaf. The underside of the leaf and the stems are slimy with a gelatinous film.

The shoreline of Nequasset Lake is heavily forested with mixed hardwoods and evergreens. There are many large white pines, and little development is in evidence. Large rocks protruding from the shore and the lake invite swimming. Birds are everywhere in evidence, from great blue heron, black duck, and wood duck on the stream to loons, great crested flycatchers, eastern kingbirds, kingfisher, yellowthroat, and many more along the lake shore.

Our sense is that most people using this lake are fishermen, and only a few boats were out on the lake on the July weekend when we paddled here. They were unobtrusive enough, most of them fishing quietly, but on weekends you will find more solitude paddling up Nequasset Brook. During the week, there is probably only a modest amount of boating activity, even though this lake is close to vacation heaven.

Getting There

From Bath, take Route 1 north across the bridge to Woolwich. In Woolwich, take Routes 127 and 128 north. When these split, take Route 127. Measure mileage from the split. Drive north on Route 127 for 2.0 miles; turn right onto Old Stage Road (note the green street sign). Go 0.5 mile down Old Stage Road to the bridge over Nequasset Brook. The hand-carry access is on the right just before the bridge (very limited parking along roadway), and the trailer access is on the left just after the bridge (room for several cars, but do not block the trailer access).

Brownfield Bog
Brownfield

MAPS
   Maine Atlas: Map 4
   USGS Quadrangle: Brownfield

INFORMATION
   Information on area, depth, and prominent fish species not available.
   Canoe rental and campgrounds at the Saco River bridge on Route
      160: Camp and Canoe, Woodland Acres Campground, Brown-
      field, ME 04010; 207-935-2529. River Run Canoe Rental,
      Brownfield, ME 04010; 207-452-2500.

During the summer, when the nearby Saco River is overrun with canoeists, you can paddle undisturbed on Brownfield Bog. The Brownfield Bog Wildlife Management Area, maintained by the state, contains hundreds of acres of bog to explore. When we paddled here on a warm, sunny October day, the bigtooth aspen leaves reflected golden light onto the water, along with a beautiful view of the snow-dusted White Mountains off in the distance. An extensive grassy area at the end of the road would make a scenic area for a picnic.

Oak-covered hillsides form a backdrop for Brownfield Bog. Marshy islands keep these waters calm when wind-driven waves make more open ponds unsafe.

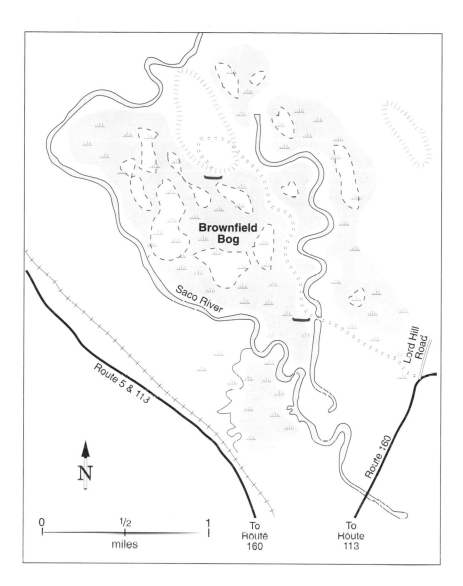

Brownfield Bog, very wild but relatively accessible, teems with wildlife. In addition to nesting waterfowl, you can expect to see deer, beaver, muskrat, turtles, and—if you paddle here early in the morning or at dusk—an occasional moose. Just about every type of bog vegetation is present as well, from pitcher plants and sundews to water lilies, sweet gale, and rhodora. Because of the huge amount of beaver activity and the extensive bog vegetation, we progressed slowly through the hidden pathways. If you need more space, just push aside the small floating islands dotting the bog. Because there is as much land as water surface area, you can paddle in the bog unaffected by wind.

If you are interested in studying trees, this area and south of here is an ideal spot to look for oaks. The hillsides surrounding the bog and the higher ground within the bog are covered with white and red oaks. Thought to have originated in Mexico and then radiated out to other areas, oaks comprise a genus with more than 500 species found throughout the warmer parts of the north temperate region. Fifty-eight species of oaks are native to the U.S., but as you would expect, the number of species present in a given area dwindles the farther you get from Mexico. For example, Texas has 29 species of oak, Illinois 20, Pennsylvania 18, New York 12, and Vermont 7. Maine has 8 species, with most of the rarer ones concentrated along the lower New Hampshire border and along the coast.

With some serious searching at Brownfield Bog and along the southern New Hampshire border, expect to find swamp white oak, chestnut oak, bear oak, black oak, and scarlet oak, along with white oak and the ubiquitous northern red oak. Only bur oak, found in the Machias region, is absent from this area. We found a thick stand of bear oak along the shore of Black Pond in Porter, the next town south of Brownfield.

Brownfield Bog typifies the kind of wilderness experience that becomes increasingly difficult to find in Maine these days. It seems that even the most remote ponds and lakes sprout cabins and camps overnight, and unfortunately more and more people adopt the sedentary TV-generation lifestyle by forsaking the traditional hand-powered Maine canoe for motorboats. Because the bog is owned by the state, it will not sprout cabins; and because it is so shallow and weedy, those addicted to throbbing horsepower will have to get their thrills elsewhere. Gazing off through fall-colored, yellow-leaved birches and aspen at the layered hillsides and mountains, we are thankful that Brownfield Bog remains wild and protected in such a heavily vacationed area.

Getting There

From the junction of Routes 113 and 160 in Brownfield, take Route 160 north toward Denmark. Cross the Saco River bridge after 0.8 mile. At 1.5 miles where the road curves right, turn left onto Lord Hill Road. Go 0.1 mile and turn left onto the Brownfield Bog access road. Notice the few large white pines and the scrubby hemlocks lining the road. There is a small shed with a list of rules at 0.8 mile. You can park here and put your boat in the water about fifty feet down the road. A more interesting place to paddle is at the end of the road another 1.5 miles into the refuge (stay left at the fork 0.3 mile from the shed).

Pleasant Pond
Fryeburg and Brownfield

MAPS
    Maine Atlas: Map 4
    USGS Quadrangles: Brownfield and Fryeburg
INFORMATION
    Area: 239 acres; maximum depth: 15 feet
    Prominent fish species: smallmouth bass, white perch, and chain
      pickerel
    Fire permits: Maine Forest Service, Saco River District 207-657-
      3552 or Southern Region Headquarters 207-287-2275

The Saco River, born among the highest peaks of the White Mountains in New Hampshire, gathers feeder streams and momentum as it roars down the steep valleys. By the time it reaches Fryeburg, though, it is a tame, meandering, marshy meadow stream, ever so popular with weekend canoeists. Hundreds of people paddle this water on summer weekends. Very few of them, however, take the time to paddle out onto Pleasant Pond, which is accessible only from the Saco River. This is their loss, because Pleasant Pond is gorgeous, with layered hills and lofty peaks of the White Mountains as a backdrop. Sitting out in the middle of the pond, gazing off at the multihued pastel layers retreating into the distance, we found it difficult to consider leaving even as the sun set over the mountains, though our delay would mean paddling back in the semidark. A magical place, indeed.

As you paddle downstream from the Route 302 access, note that the Saco's banks are lined with oaks, occasional groves of hemlocks, and scattered white pines. The banks are high, making it difficult to see out into the surrounding marsh. The current is modest in the summer and fall, but leave sufficient time to paddle back (we would allow 50 percent more time than it takes to paddle down to Pleasant Pond). Watch closely for the access stream off to the left. It's on a sharp, sweeping curve to the right. A black sign with orange letters saying No Trespassing appears in front of you; high in a tree is a broken paddle that says Pleasant on it.

Pleasant Pond is shallow and marshy, especially along the north end where the access stream enters. In addition to the huge number of oaks found in this region, the banks are often lined with silver maples.

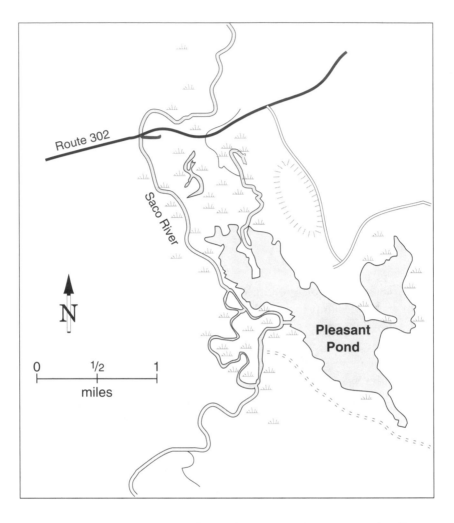

Silver maples can be distinguished from our other swamp dweller—the red maple—by the deeply cleft, five-lobed leaves with silvery undersides. Red maples have shallow-cleft, three-lobed leaves. Silver maples have the largest-winged seeds of all native maples, reaching three inches in length. These seeds are important food for squirrels, foxes, and mice, plus pine and evening grosbeaks. We saw a fat gray squirrel clambering among the silver maples searching for seeds when we visited.

It will take a few hours to explore fully all of the marshy inlets and coves of Pleasant Pond. Look for beaver, muskrat, red-winged blackbirds, turtles, and deer lurking among the shrubbery. At quieter times, especially on the north end of the pond, one might be lucky enough to see a moose browsing on the abundant vegetation.

Because of the extensive marshes, we found few areas where one could pitch a tent. It would be far easier to camp out under the oaks along the Saco River bank. Camping is free, and most of the land is unposted. Remember, though, that this is private property; please treat it with respect.

If you paddle here in the spring during high water, you probably will not be able to paddle the 1.5 miles back to the Route 302 bridge. You could take out at the Route 160 bridge, five or so miles downstream from Pleasant Pond. Given the summer crowds, probably the best time to paddle here is in the fall, when the hillsides have turned to golds, reds, and browns. We paddled here in October and saw not another soul; when we visited in June and in August, cars jammed the parking areas and canoes dotted the river. If you do paddle here in the summer, try to do it on a weekday. Because of its extraordinary beauty, however, we would paddle here even on a summer weekend if that were the only time available.

Getting There

Take Route 302 east out of Fryeburg until you reach the Saco River bridge. Cross the bridge and park in the designated area on the right-hand side. Even though there is room to park dozens of cars here, the lot is filled on summer weekends, with cars spilling out onto the adjacent road shoulders.

Kezar Pond

Fryeburg

MAPS
  Maine Atlas: Map 4
  USGS Quadrangles: Fryeburg and Pleasant Mountain

INFORMATION
  Area: 1,447 acres; maximum depth: 12 feet
  Prominent fish species: smallmouth bass, largemouth bass, white perch, yellow perch, and chain pickerel

Kezar Pond, two miles across at its widest, might not seem like a great paddling spot, especially given its relatively round shape. But initial impressions can be deceiving. We had a great time here, despite a stiff breeze from the south that made paddling difficult.

Begin your exploration at a beautiful covered bridge on the old course of the Saco River. From the covered bridge, paddle north on the stream that empties into the old course of the Saco at the bridge. This outlet stream meanders gently along with a barely perceptible current for about a mile, the sides lined with silver maple, gray birch, white pine, red maple, viburnum, and a few red oak. The water is

Marshy area at the north end of Kezar Pond.

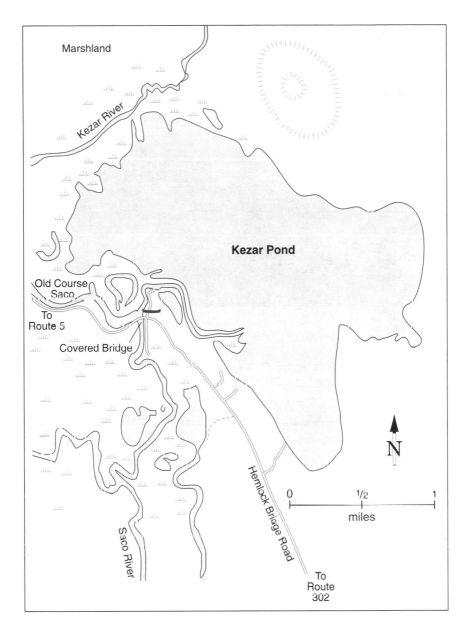

Marshland

Kezar River

Kezar Pond

Old Course
Saco

To
Route 5

Covered Bridge

Hemlock Bridge Road

Saco River

N

0   1/2   1
              miles

To
Route
302

somewhat murky, and the muddy banks extend fairly far above the
water level. You will pass one house along here, on the left.

On the main pond, you will be struck by the surrounding terrain.
Smarts Hill extends up from the northeast side of the pond, and an
extensive segment of the White Mountain range appears to the west.
From the mouth of the outlet stream—which juts out oddly into the

Hemlock Bridge, a historic wooden-truss structure built in 1857, spans the old course of the Saco River just south of Kezar Pond.

pond—you can paddle either to the right (south) or left (north). To the right you will find a few marshy coves full of pickerelweed, bulrush, and water lily, with a great blue heron more than likely fishing in the shallows. A few cottages on the southern lobe comprise the bulk of the rather modest development on Kezar Pond. After exploring this south end, we paddled across to avoid the developed areas, then around the pond counterclockwise.

An inlet stream on the eastern side of Kezar Pond provides a great little side exploration. The narrow, winding, channel—somewhat difficult to find—heads off not too far from the northernmost house along the eastern side of Kezar Pond. The channel is deep with a sandy bottom, and its sides are lined with silver maple, royal and sensitive fern, and sweet gale. Near the outlet of this creek you will also find a stand of cranberry. The large red berries in the fall dwarf the tiny oval leaves of this heath (related to blueberry and laurel).

At the far eastern tip of the pond, you can explore some other hidden coves and an inlet creek. Look to the right just as you enter the pond and you can see the creek, which is very easy to miss. We paddled a couple hundred yards up this creek—our pace quickened by the mosquitoes in this wind-shielded area—until our progress was blocked by a beaver dam. Had the mosquitoes not been there we might have pulled our canoe up over the dam and explored farther upstream, but we retreated back to the main pond and its protective wind. (Paddling in Maine one learns to love and hate the wind!)

Our favorite part of Kezar Pond was actually the northern end, extending around to the western tip. This section of the pond adjoins an area known as Swimming Bog. The shallow shoreline here is dotted with hillocks of grasses and pickerelweed. When the pond itself was filled with whitecaps, the water was fairly calm here, protected by the matrix of tiny islands. We explored lazily through and around these hillocks and the acres of pond lilies. As we snaked our way west, we kept an eye on a bald eagle we had first spotted from the eastern end of Kezar Pond (nearly two miles away) that had perched atop an old silver maple along here. As we approached, the regal bird came into ever better view, until we were almost right under it. We suspect there is a nest nearby (see page 92 for more on bald eagles).

Getting There

From the intersection of Routes 5 and 302 in Fryeburg, drive east on 302 toward Bridgton. After 5.4 miles, turn left onto Hemlock Bridge Road. Drive 3.0 miles on this road (it turns to dirt after 0.8 mile), and you will reach the Hemlock Covered Bridge and canoe access to Kezar Pond. There is room to park several cars if you turn right just before the bridge, or you can drive through the bridge and find additional parking space on the left. If you park on the right before the bridge, launch your boat and paddle to the right—not under the bridge. If you drive through the bridge and park on the left, paddle under the bridge and take the right channel to Kezar Pond.

From here you can also explore the old channel of the Saco River either up to North Fryeburg or down to its junction with the Saco River and Pleasant Pond (see section on Pleasant Pond, page 25).

Lower Range Pond

Poland

MAPS
  Maine Atlas: Map 5
  USGS Quadrangles: Minot and Mechanic Falls
INFORMATION
  Area: 290 acres; maximum depth: 41 feet
  Prominent fish species: smallmouth bass, white perch, yellow
  perch, and chain pickerel
  Camping: Paul & Gail's Campground & Marina, P.O. Box 517,
  Poland Spring, ME 04274; 207-998-5454

On the right day, with the weather just threatening enough to keep most people away, Lower Range Pond is a real treat. Good access exists at the southeast end through Range Pond State Park, and a ten-horsepower limit for motorboats keeps the place fairly quiet. The pond boasts crystal-clear water with sandy shores—superb for swimming—and the marshy coves teem with wildlife. We visited on a late afternoon midweek in August and had the place to ourselves. But you won't find much solitude here on a nice summer weekend! Judging from the size of the parking lots and restroom facilities, this place can be a real zoo.

A fair amount of development intrudes on the north end of Lower Range Pond, where the pond narrows to less than 100 feet in places. The houses along here, with their associated boats and activity, can distract significantly from your quiet paddle. For the nicest paddling, stick to the more southern end—and the marshy extension off to the southwest toward Route 26 and Middle Range Pond. By midsummer, most of this marshy cove may be too shallow and weed choked for paddling, but even in the driest conditions, a deep winding channel remains open.

During our visit, we saw quite a variety of wildlife: a pair of loons with a well-developed chick, osprey, great blue herons, black ducks, kingfishers, kingbirds, spotted sandpipers, numerous fish, fresh-water mussels, and some fascinating invertebrates: bryozoa. Bryozoa are in their own phylum (birds, mammals, and reptiles are other phyla). The bryozoan we saw here is of the *Pectinatella* genus. Individual units, or zooids, of the underwater colonies have tiny hairs

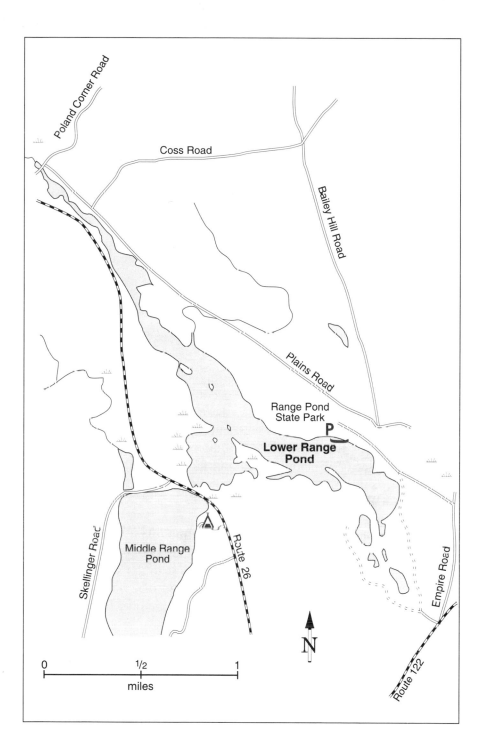

Poland Corner Road

Coss Road

Bailey Hill Road

Plains Road

Range Pond
State Park

P

**Lower Range
Pond**

Skellinger Road

Middle Range
Pond

Route 26

Empire Road

Route 122

N

0   1/2   1
miles

The sand beach and swimming area of Range Pond State Park.

or cilia that sweep through the water and capture microscopic algae, diatoms, and protozoa. *Pectinatella* colonies can grow as large as watermelons, though those we saw here were considerably smaller. The slimy, gelatinous colonies look somewhat like translucent pineapples. Look for them growing on underwater branches or rocks. Though we see bryozoa only rarely in Maine, their presence is always welcome, as they require extremely pure water and thus serve as indicators of pollution-free lakes and ponds.

Also telling of the purity of these waters is their close proximity to Maine's most famous spring-water bottling plant: Poland Spring. As you paddle around the southern tip of the pond, you can hear the hum of machinery coming from the plant just to the south—perhaps from pumping equipment. (We were assured that the small pump house near the southern tip of the pond is *not* pumping Poland Spring water from the pond.)

The trees around Lower Range Pond include white pine, pitch pine, red pine (a few), hemlock, gray birch, and red maple. Some of the pitch pines are unusually large specimens. Extensive areas of pickerelweed, water shield, pondweed, bulrushes, and grasses grow along the shallower shores. In places you will see patches of cattail, fragrant water lily, bullhead lily, and a water lily-like member of the gentian family: floating heart (with small heart-shaped leaves and small white flowers). Even with the thick aquatic vegetation, though, the bottom seems firm and sandy almost everywhere.

Lower Range Pond and its larger neighbors to the south (Middle and Upper Range ponds) are kettle ponds, formed when the last glacier receded about 10,000 years ago, leaving behind huge chunks of ice buried in glacial till. As the ice gradually melted, the deep depressions filled with water. Kettle ponds often can be recognized by their sandy shores.

Getting There

From the south, get off the Maine Turnpike (Route 495) at Exit 11. Turn right after the tollbooth, then take the first two lefts—first onto Route 202 north, then immediately onto Route 26 north. From here, drive 9.9 miles, then bear right onto Route 122 east (Poland Springs Road). Drive 1.4 miles, then take a shallow left onto Empire Road at the sign for Range Pond State Park (a hard left will take you into the Poland Spring plant—to make an appointment for a tour, call 207-998-4315). The entrance to the park is on the left in another 0.8 mile.

If you are driving from the north, get off the Maine Turnpike at Exit 12. Turn south on Route 202, then right (west) on Route 122. Stay on 122 for 3.9 miles, then take a sharp right onto Empire Road, and follow directions as above. After passing the entrance gate (entrance charge is $2.50 per adult; 50¢ for children between the ages of five and twelve; free for kids under five), the boat launch is on the left through one of the huge parking lots. Park hours are 9:00 A.M. to 7:30 P.M.

Camping is not available at Range Pond State Park, but there is a small private campground on Route 26 at the north end of Middle Range Pond, just across the highway from the inlet into Lower Range Pond (see below). While you cannot paddle between the two ponds, you can carry a canoe across the highway. (Watch out for fast traffic.)

Five Kezar Ponds
Waterford and Lovell

MAPS
> **Maine Atlas:** Map 10
> **USGS Quadrangle:** North Waterford

INFORMATION
> **Middle Pond area:** 72 acres; maximum depth: 51 feet
> **Prominent fish species:** brook trout, smallmouth bass, and chain
> pickerel

Of the Five Kezar ponds, Jewett Pond is not connected to the other four and has no public access. The other four, one unnamed, Mud, Middle, and Back ponds, are covered here. Although there are pockets of development, we include this series of small ponds for several reasons. They are still heavily forested, with a rich variety of tree species, and unusual natural features abound. After paddling up the unnamed pond, before passing under the bridge on the left into Middle Pond, keep going northwest, curving around to the right into Mud Pond.

Mud Pond is a splendid example of a peatland minerotrophic fen. Scientists recently decided to distinguish between raised peatlands

The Mud Pond fen.

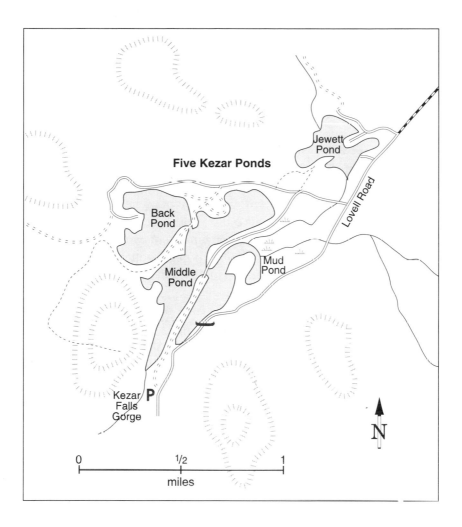

Five Kezar Ponds

Jewett Pond

Back Pond

Mud Pond

Middle Pond

Lovell Road

Kezar Falls Gorge P

N

0   1/2   1

miles

with no streams flowing through, calling them bogs, and peatlands on slopes with water flowing through, calling them fens. Minerotrophic means mineral nourished, from the flow-through of water. In contrast, the huge 4,300-acre Great Heath, twenty miles due west of Machias, is a classic domed bog with no flow-through, where almost all nutrients come from rainfall and the air. Because bogs are nutrient poor, trees and shrubs are dwarfed. The relatively large tamaracks, red maple, and black spruce of the Mud Pond fen, however, benefit from water flow-through, bringing necessary minerals and carrying away acids produced by sphagnum and plant degradation.

The shrubby environment of Mud Pond is a haven for beaver, which have opened watery paths to higher ground in order to drag succulent branches of alder, paper birch, and red maple back to their submerged food caches to gnaw on during the winter. You are sure to see them at work if you paddle quietly here in the evening. Pitcher plants and sundews, as well as many species of marshland shrubs, abound on the raised clumps of sphagnum. It is so rare that one can paddle back into such a beautiful, unspoiled peatland that this alone makes a trip to Five Kezar ponds worthwhile.

But there is one more unusual natural feature worth exploring: Kezar Falls Gorge. Paddle back out of Mud Pond, and turn right under the bridge to Middle Pond. Turn left, and paddle southwest to the out-let of the five ponds. At the end, where the pond is very narrow, pull up your boat on shore and hike the short distance to Kezar Falls Gorge. A surprising amount of water tumbles down through a steep-walled, beautifully sculpted canyon. To get a better view, climb up above on the left. You can also drive to this spot by continuing on for a short ways down the access road.

These four ponds, with relatively little boat traffic, especially in the spring and fall, can provide hours of quiet paddling. A ten-horse-power motor limit is in effect. Coupled with the outstanding natural features of a gorge and a fen, Five Kezar ponds is a wonderful place to paddle.

Getting There

From the junction of Routes 35 and 118 in North Waterford, take Route 35 south for 0.2 mile. Turn right onto Lovell Road/Five Kezars Road (right fork as you turn off Route 35). Stay straight on this road until it turns to dirt; do not take any of the turns to the right, no matter how enticingly named. After 3.2 miles, as you drive along the shore of an unnamed pond on the right, look for a small turnout on the left, big enough for two cars. Given the light traffic and width of this road, you could safely park along the road as well. The hand-carry access is down over the bank on this pond.

Horseshoe Pond

Lovell and Stoneham

MAPS
    Maine Atlas: Map 10
    USGS Quadrangle: Center Lovell

INFORMATION
    Area: 132 acres; maximum depth: 40 feet
    Prominent fish species: brown trout, brook trout, and smallmouth
      bass

Horseshoe Pond is small and shallow, but its magnificent setting, with steep hills hovering on all sides and two very different nearby hiking trails, prompted us to include it. A couple of small cabins stand on the

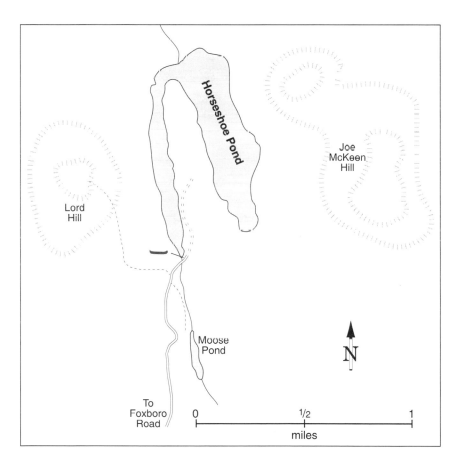

Moose teeth marks. These fresh gouges were on a red maple by Moose Pond, adjacent to Horseshoe Pond.

southern end of the pond, but the north end is protected as part of the White Mountain National Forest. The tree-covered hillsides give way to dense shrubbery along the shore. Rhodora, a type of rhododendron that boasts clusters of beautiful rose-purple flowers in late May, dominates the shoreline. There is little marshy area, but that is more than made up for by nearby Moose Pond.

The presence along the shoreline of mostly shallow-rooted trees such as spruce, red and white pine, hemlock, and paper birch indicates that the soil is not very deep in this valley. In addition to stands of pines on the hillsides, you will find lots of oak and sugar maple. An osprey, a great blue heron, and a flock of common mergansers—a colorful, fish-eating, diving duck with a narrow, serrated bill—greeted us as we paddled the narrow western arm of the pond.

Because it is small and out of the way, with the much larger Kezar Lake just five miles away taking up most of the boat traffic,

Horseshoe Pond should provide paddling solitude. A six-horsepower limit is in effect on gasoline-powered motors.

We suggest that while you are here you hike the short trail into Moose Pond. The Sucker Brook Nature Trail—part of a nature sanctuary—is owned and maintained by The Nature Conservancy, an organization that acquires land with significant national or regional natural resources. The trail begins along the road on the left, just uphill from the boat access. When we hiked here in October, a moose had made fresh tracks on the road. After a short hike into Moose Pond, we found denuded red maple and alder trunks where a moose had recently browsed on the bark. By this time it was the middle of the day, not a particularly good time for moose viewing. We suggest you hike here early in the morning or in the evening.

We did not hike the trail found immediately across the road that leads up to Lord Hill, which towers 720 feet over the west edge of Horseshoe Pond. There is an abandoned mica mine at the top, as well as a beautiful view of the pond and the Sucker Brook valley.

Getting There

Take Route 5 north out of Fryeburg to Lovell. Stay left at the junction of Routes 5 and 5A. After 0.8 mile watch for a sign to Kezar Lake and the Narrows. Turn left onto the paved road to Kezar Lake. The bridge over the narrows is 1.1 miles down this road. Continue on, marking mileage from the bridge, taking the left fork onto Foxboro Road (West Lovell Road is the right fork) 1.8 miles from the bridge. Take the right fork at 3.4 miles (New Road goes left). Turn right onto Horseshoe Pond Road (gravel) at 4.0 miles. Go downhill for 1 mile more to the boat access on Horseshoe Pond.

Virginia Lake

Stoneham

MAPS
   Maine Atlas: Map 10
   USGS Quadrangle: East Stoneham
INFORMATION
   Area: 128 acres; maximum depth: 28 feet
   Prominent fish species: white perch and chain pickerel

Surrounded by the White Mountain National Forest, Virginia Lake is a real gem, set just south of a string of peaks that stretch to 2,000 feet in elevation. The lake itself is at 820 feet. Because Virginia Lake is small, it does not see much boat traffic, aside from a few fishermen. Trout fishing here is said to be good. You can explore this scenic little lake fully in a couple of hours. There is room at the access for only a few cars; do not block the gate that leads to the one house on the lake or the boat access. Instead, after unloading drive back up the road to one of the small pullouts.

The forested shores—primarily oak—on the west, south, and east give way to marshy inlets on the north that drain the surrounding peaks. During spring high water, you should be able to paddle back into the swamp a little way. Besides the typical bog vegetation, there is an alder swamp, the summer home of an uncommon and very drab warbler-sized bird, called appropriately enough the alder flycatcher. It is an inconspicuous little bird with olive-brown back and pale-yellow belly, with two white wing bars and a small white eye ring. This fly-catcher—and the eight other similarly drab species found throughout the U.S. and Canada—sits upright on exposed branches, waiting to pounce on juicy insects that fly by. Listen for its song, a distinctive, falling, buzzy "fee-beo" anytime you are near alder stands in the spring and early summer.

When we paddled here in October, the alder flycatchers were long gone to warmer climes, those still abuzz with insects. The birches and maples along the northern shoreline had turned bright yellow and red, and the hillside oaks, with their burnished reds, stood in contrast to the dark green of scattered groves of conifers. Huge clumps of multi-colored leaves clogged the surface of the lake's south end, driven there by breezes from the north, the same ones that carry ducks and

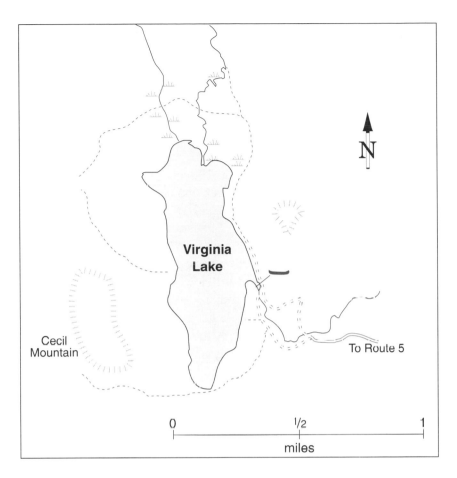

geese southward. The reflection of the brightly colored hillsides shimmered in the rippled surface of the lake. Though the paddling season would end, sadly, with leaf fall, we were reminded that one can paddle in complete solitude almost anywhere in Maine anytime after Labor Day, enjoying the cool air free of biting insects and the gloriously colored fall foliage.

Getting There

From Fryeburg, take Route 5 north through Center Lovell and North Lovell. Turn left onto paved Bartlettboro Road just as you get to Keewaydin Lake. In 0.4 mile take the left fork onto Virginia Lake Road (Birch Avenue goes right). The road forks again and the pavement ends in another 0.6 mile; take the left fork (the right fork goes to Virginia Lake Farm). The boat access is 0.3 mile down what was then a rutty dirt road. Parking is limited; do not block the gate or the boat access.

North Pond

Norway

MAPS
   Maine Atlas: Map 10
   USGS Quadrangle: West Paris
INFORMATION
   Area: 147 acres; maximum depth: 10 feet
   Prominent fish species: white perch and chain pickerel

North Pond is wild and beautiful, particularly the north and west ends. If one is looking for moose in this area, North Pond is where they should be. The heavily forested hillsides of hemlock, paper birch, aspen, white pine, oak, maple, and many other tree species should provide refuge during the day, while acres and acres of marsh vegetation should provide food by night. Although we paddled here quietly at sunset, however, we did not see any moose.

We did not spend much time paddling the southeast arm because several houses are there, standing in stark contrast to the pristine northern and western reaches of the pond. The north end is filled with twisting channels that meander their way in and out among the islands and floating chunks of marsh vegetation. One could spend several hours paddling north along the east side then down the west side, exploring each of the extensive channels reaching back up into the surrounding hills.

A fire tower rises on a hill in the north, and you can see a few farms off in the distance. Going out from the boat access, paddle by an island covered with big white pines, almost to the eastern shore, and turn north, heading for the fire tower. You can paddle up this channel all the way back to the farms on those hills. There are lots of side channels to explore as well.

While several of the low-lying islands are populated with tamarack, black spruce, and white pine, shrub vegetation predominates. Water lilies float in shallow channels lined with cattails, and members of the heath family, many of them with evergreen leaves, show up as shrubs wherever there is any soil. The heath family dominates the swamps of Maine, and North Pond is no exception. Included are those with showy flowers, such as rhodora, with its beautiful rose-purple flowers that emerge before the leaves in May; the summer-blooming

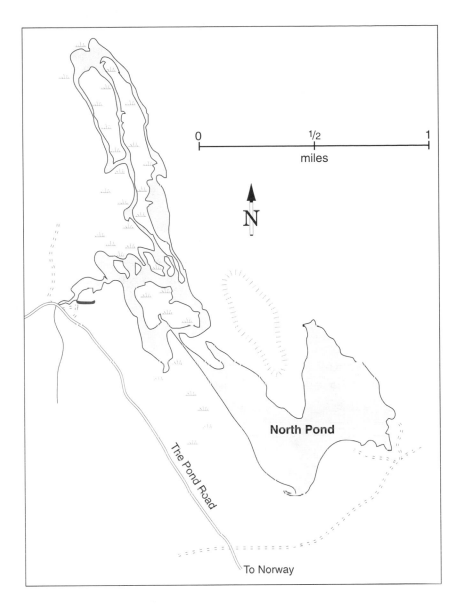

The Pond Road

North Pond

To Norway

swamp azalca, with its long, showy white flowers (near the northern limit of its range here); and the similar sheep laurel and bog laurel, with clusters of bright pink flowers. These latter two are easily distinguished by the location of their flower whorls: in bog laurel, flowers are said to be "terminal," occurring at the ends of stems, whereas with sheep laurel, there is a cluster of new leaves above the flowers.

Other members of the swamp-loving heath family include Labrador tea, with its woolly brown undersides of leaves; bog rosemary with its two-inch-long, quarter-inch-wide leaves with white undersides and its small, pink, urn-shaped flowers; and leatherleaf with its aptly named leaves and long lines of upside-down, white, bell-shaped flowers. Perhaps the best-known members of the heath family are highbush and lowbush blueberries, huckleberries, and cranberries.

Most of these plants can be found—some of them in great numbers—in and around North Pond. Although we loved exploring the channels and identifying the plants, we really wanted to see moose. Well, there is always next time....

This area of Maine is famous for its geology. Pegmatite—a very large crystal granite—is common here, and gem-quality crystals of quartz, amethyst, and tourmaline were mined from at least a half-dozen mines within a few miles of North Pond. If you are interested in collecting rocks—or seeing what others have found—visit Perhams on Route 26 in West Paris. They can give you directions to area mines.

Getting There

From Norway, take Route 117 west a short way, and turn right onto Crockett Ridge Road, which is the causeway over Pennesseewassee Lake. In about 2.6 miles, at the four-way junction, turn left onto The Pond Road. In 1.6 miles the road turns to gravel. The short access road—easy to miss—is on the right about 0.8 mile farther, just before the road takes a sharp left and goes straight uphill toward Nobles Corner and North Norway.

Dresden Bog
Dresden

MAPS
   Maine Atlas: Map 13
   USGS Quadrangle: Wiscasset
INFORMATION
   Information on area, depth, and prominent fish species not available.

Because the Dresden Bog access consists of portaging over a few beaver dams, this wonderful area, just a short distance from the state capital, receives few visitors.

Paddle down the beautiful little inlet creek, past the beaver dams that bar most people as surely as a gate. Emerging from the marshy entrance, you will be struck by the varied beauty of this place, with many islands dotting the surface, emergent vegetation covering the pond, and mature trees lining the shore.

Many wood duck nesting boxes perch along the shore and out in the water. One hundred years ago massive cutting of forests in the East and Midwest and unregulated hunting decimated wood duck populations. Concerned birdwatchers, sportsmen, and wildlife-management officials then began a program of erecting nesting boxes around swamps and rivers, resulting in a dramatic comeback for this beautiful duck. The wood duck's behavior is unusual, too: unlike most ducks, it is arboreal. When paddling wooded swamps and rivers, you can sometimes see wood ducks perched on tree branches.

Most ducks and geese nest on the ground; in this area, only wood ducks and common and hooded mergansers nest in cavities. Because common and hooded mergansers prefer wooded swamps and somewhat deeper water for diving for fish, we suspect these boxes see mostly wood ducks.

We saw several flocks of black ducks and wood ducks feeding in the marshes at the south end of this very shallow marsh. After a cursory, unsuccessful look for a passageway to Gardiner Pond, we retreated from the south end to let the ducks feed undisturbed.

The pond is surrounded by tall trees, mostly deciduous on the western shore, with many very tall white pines along the eastern shore. The whole area has dense undergrowth down to the water and

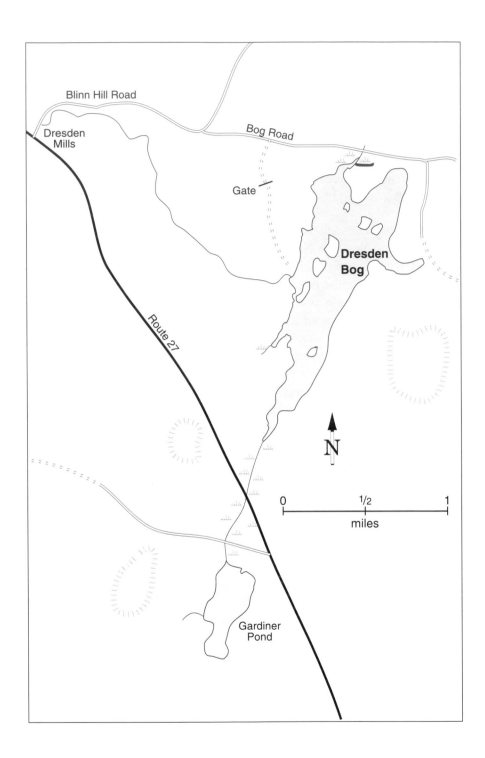

heavily vegetated islands. The water surface is covered with pickerel-weed and wild celery, whose long leaves protrude up through and then lay flat on the water surface. This is a beautiful, peaceful, interesting place to paddle and well worth a visit.

Getting There

From Augusta, go south on Routes 201 and 27 through Hallowell. When these roads split, take Route 27 left across the Kennebec River bridge. Follow Route 27 south to Dresden Mills. Just after Routes 197/127 go right, then turn left onto Blinn Hill Road (unmarked). Start marking mileage at this turn. At 1.3 miles, as the road takes a sharp turn to the left, turn right onto a gravel road. Turn right onto the carry-in access road at 1.9 miles; there is a small yellow sign on a tree at this turnoff that says State of Maine Wildlife Management Area. The gate is 0.2 mile down this road, on a curve. You had better be going slowly if it is locked, because it shows up out of nowhere and looks like it would get the better of your car in a collision.

If the gate is locked, go back out to the main gravel road, and turn right. Go another 0.3 mile until you find water on both sides of the road. Take the creek channel on the right (south) side of the road. There is room for two small cars. Do not get too comfy in your boat, though, because the first beaver dam portage is just twenty-five feet away. There were only two more such dams when we paddled here, and the lower part of the channel is free of beaver dams, sinewy, and beautiful.

The Spectacular Wood Duck

If you have yet to see a male wood duck, you are in for a treat on your paddling trips. Of all our ducks—and perhaps of all our bird species—few approach the wood duck for sheer beauty. With distinctive multicolored breeding plumage—iridescent in the sunlight—the male wood duck is quite something to behold. To get a good look at these extremely wary ducks, though, requires some very quiet paddling. Look for them in marshy areas, as you paddle around the grassy islands and meandering inlet channels. Most of the time, you will glimpse wood ducks only as they fly away.

Along with its gorgeous plumage, the wood duck, *Aix* *sponsa,* is unusual for several other reasons, most notably its nesting habits. Unlike most ducks, wood ducks nest in trees, using abandoned woodpecker holes, cavities hollowed out by decay, and—more recently—artificial nesting boxes. Sharp down-curving claws on the toes help the bird cling to the tree trunk. The duck can also walk or run overland far better than most other ducks. We remember being quite surprised canoeing on Umbagog Lake one time to see a female wood duck with a string of chicks swim to the shore and then run into the protective vegetation—it seemed so unducklike! When danger threatens, wood ducks can dive underwater and even swim underwater for a fair distance.

Wood ducks pair up in the fall or winter in the Southeast, where New England's wood ducks overwinter. During spring migration, the male follows the female to the area—usually the same pond—where she was raised. In early spring, the female selects a suitable nesting cavity, which may be from four to fifty feet up in the air and over either water or land (it can be up to a mile from water).

The hen lays ten to fifteen eggs. When the young hatch—all within a few hours of each other—they stay in the nest for only a day. Then, after checking carefully for signs of danger, the mother flies down to the water or ground below and calls to the chicks. They climb up to the entrance and, without hesitation, jump out of the nest. Claws on the toes of the chicks enable them to cling to the inside of the nesting cavity when leaving. Their short, stubby wings and downy feathers slow the chicks' descent, and remarkably, even when jumping from a nest fifty feet above ground, they seldom get hurt. They may bounce on the ground and be stunned for a moment, but a few seconds later, they get up and cluster around their mother.

The chicks can swim right away, but sometimes they must walk up to a mile overland to reach water, a most perilous time for the young. Many are lost to predators before reaching water. In the water, large fish (bass, northern pike, pickerel) and snapping turtles prey on the young. Wood-duck chicks grow quickly during the summer and can fly by the time they reach eight to ten weeks of age.

The male wood duck molts during the summer, losing his beautiful breeding plumage until fall. In the nonbreeding, or eclipse, plumage, the male resembles the female (if you get a close look, the male retains his red eyes and bill, and the female has distinct white eye rings). For a two- to three-week period during molting, the male cannot fly. The female also goes through a molt a little later than the male, but her plumage does not change significantly in appearance.

In the fall, wood ducks congregate in large numbers, especially in the evening. Sometimes hundreds or even thousands of wood ducks fly to the same roosting pond each evening and leave at daybreak to feed on nearby ponds and streams. By midautumn, most of New England's wood ducks have migrated south. They usually travel in small, loosely aggregated flocks.

While wood-duck populations remain relatively strong today, the species was hunted almost to extinction around the turn of the century. Efforts began to protect it through state legislation after the U.S. Biological Survey reported in 1901 that wood ducks faced possible extinction. At that time the newly formed National Audubon Society and a few other organizations began a long, slow effort to get federal legislation enacted—which was considered necessary to assure survival.

The first national legislation protecting waterfowl passed in 1913 (the Weeks-McLean bill); the Migratory Bird Treaty Act, signed into law in 1918, afforded even greater protection. This treaty extended protection of wood ducks and other migrating birds to Canada, gave the federal government greater authority to regulate hunting, and prohibited the sale of wildfowl. The hunting season on wood ducks was closed completely by the U.S. and Canada until 1941, when the species had recovered enough to open a limited fall season.

The recovery of wood ducks in the Northeast was set back by the 1938 hurricane, which blew down many old trees that had provided nesting cavities. To provide more sites, the first artificial nesting boxes were put up in Great Meadows National Wildlife Refuge in Massachusetts, and the idea soon spread around the country. Today, tens of thousands of wood duck nesting boxes appear throughout the East. You are likely to see these boxes as you paddle around the ponds, lakes, and marshes of Maine.

The biggest threat to wood ducks today is loss of suitable nesting habitat. Wood ducks need remote ponds and marshes to raise their young, and these areas are increasingly threatened by development.

Duckpuddle Pond
Nobleboro and Waldoboro

MAPS
   Maine Atlas: Maps 7 and 13
   USGS Quadrangle: Waldoboro West

INFORMATION
   Area: 293 acres; maximum depth: 23 feet
   Prominent fish species: smallmouth bass, white perch, and chain
   pickerel
   Camping: Duckpuddle Campground, P.O. Box 176M, Nobleboro,
   ME 04555; 207-563-5608. Located on Pemaquid Lake.

As you paddle out from the boat access toward Duckpuddle Pond, you
are greeted by alders, pickerelweed, rushes, grasses, a sea of water
lilies ... and mosquitoes. The passageway out to the pond is narrow
and filled with aquatic plants. When we visited in mid-July, the water
was cloudy from a huge pondwide algae bloom; we were unable to
locate the source of the nutrient influx that might cause such a bloom,
given that there is only scattered development on the pond.

Trees around this shallow pond include white pine, hemlock,
paper birch, sugar and red maple, and red oak, with oak predominat-
ing along the northern shore. There are several marshy coves to
explore, but save time to paddle down the beautiful outlet stream—
about a four-mile round trip.

water lilies

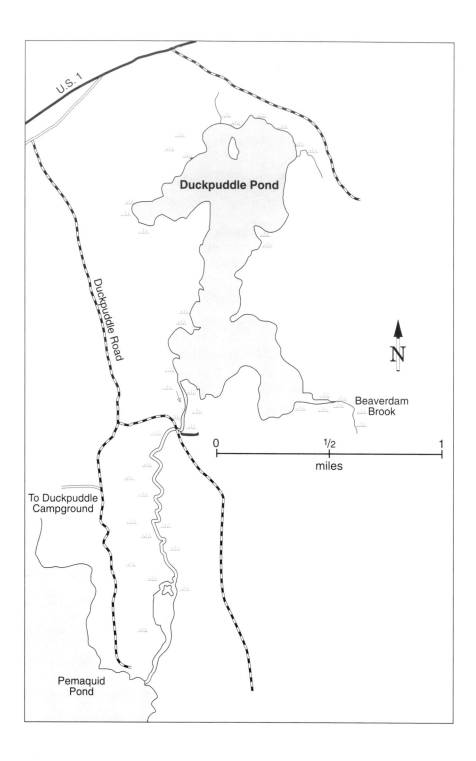

U.S. 1

Duckpuddle Pond

Duckpuddle Road

Beaverdam
Brook

N

0   1/2   1
miles

To Duckpuddle
Campground

Pemaquid
Pond

The two-mile-long marshy connecting stream between Duckpuddle and Pemaquid ponds contains a large variety of marsh plants, providing outstanding habitat for beaver, deer, and other wildlife.

Start east from the access and stay to the right around the peninsula, covered with large white pines, that separates the two lower bays. The eastern bay is marshy, and a stand of pickerelweed hides an inlet on the lower eastern shore. Paddle right through the center of the pickerelweed, back into Beaverdam Brook, threading your way through the sweet gale and other bog plants. Although the passage is narrow, you can paddle back in quite a way, especially if you are willing to portage over the beaver dams of this appropriately named stream.

If portaging is not your cup of tea, paddle back to the boat access, go under the large culvert, and paddle down the two miles to Pemaquid Pond. The channel on this connecting stream is wider and does not require portages. The vegetation and channel width change several times, making this a very quiet, interesting place to paddle.

In places the channel to Pemaquid is wide and covered with pickerelweed, bullhead lily, and fragrant water lily. In other areas it is narrow, and alders, sweet gale, buttonbush, and other shrubs line the waterway. Beautiful pink swamp roses are everywhere, and a variety of songbirds calls from the undergrowth. Monster beaver lodges poke up here and there, some with tons of cuttings protruding up through the water surface just in front of the lodge. The beavers seem just barely able to keep the alders from closing the channel.

The channel winds around the valley, drifting past many wood duck nesting boxes. Note in the quieter stretches the patches of yellow-flowered bladderwort, a fully aquatic carnivorous plant whose bladders ingest microscopic organisms. The largest patch seems to be near Pemaquid Pond, just before a large grove of tamarack.

There is one house along the shore in this two-mile stretch, but we saw no one else on our weekend visit. The outlet stream down to Pemaquid Pond, with its great blue herons and loads of other wildlife, is a genuinely wild place to paddle right in the middle of one of the most heavily used recreational areas on the eastern seaboard.

Getting There

Take Route 1 west from Waldoboro. After the junction with Route 32, continue on Route 1 for 3.5 miles, then turn left onto a paved loop road (returns to Route 1) at the sign for Duckpuddle Campground. Turn left off the loop road after 0.4 mile onto Duckpuddle Road (there is another campground sign here). Stay on Duckpuddle Road (still paved) and turn left after another 1.3 miles. The boat access is on the left 0.3 mile down this road, just after the bridge. There is room for several cars on the right.

Dyer Long Pond and Musquash Pond

Jefferson

MAPS
  Maine Atlas: Map 13
  USGS Quadrangle: North Whitefield
INFORMATION
  Area: 392 acres; naximum depth: 16 feet
  Prominent fish species: largemouth bass

True to its name, Dyer Long Pond is long, extending in a northeast-southwest orientation. From the access point on the southern tip, paddling around to the right, we could find no way to go farther south to Musquash Pond, where there is also boating access reachable by a four-wheel-drive trail. The marshy southern and northern ends and the coves of Dyer Long Pond provide interesting areas to explore; towering white pines dominate the shoreline around the rest of the pond. Several cottages are hidden among these pines; they start almost immediately on the western shore but do not occur on the eastern shore until halfway up the pond. Several scattered cottages and a couple of trailers appear on both shores on the northern half. Although there is little boat traffic, paddling here will not be a wilderness experience.

Much of the shoreline is covered with granite boulders, deposited by glaciers 10,000 years ago as they gouged out the lake bed. The large boulders deposited just under the water's surface by the same glaciers do not enhance the pond's scenic character. Instead, they scrape the boat bottoms of unwary paddlers. Go slowly near the shoreline, especially where boulders jut out to form a point.

We saw an osprey, loons, and several beavers when we paddled here in the early evening. At the marshy southern access point, the adjacent landowner has erected thirty songbird nesting boxes on poles out in the water. After a few minutes there, we understood why. Obviously, the owners try to encourage tree swallows to feed their ever-hungry young with the ever-present hordes of mosquitoes. Our boat launch occurred in record time, and within minutes we were out on the water and insect free.

Normally, tree swallows do not nest colonially, as do purple martins. Instead, they chase other tree swallows away. That is why people who want to encourage bluebird nesting always put nesting boxes up

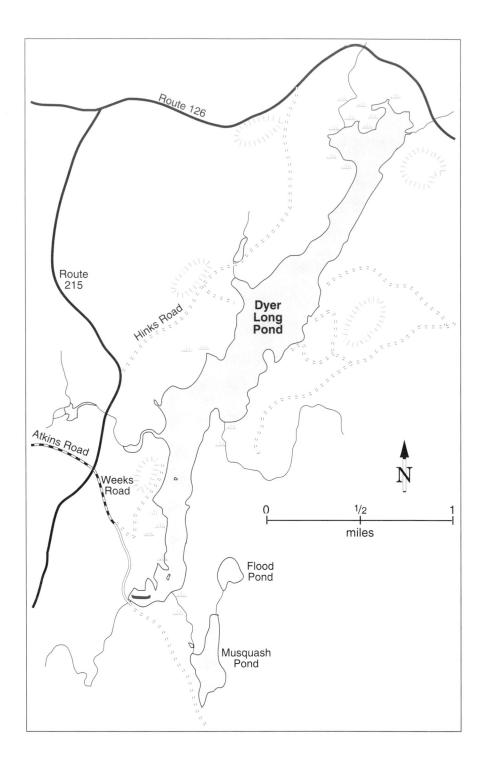

Route 126

Route
215

Hinks Road

Dyer
Long
Pond

Atkins Road

Weeks
Road

N

0   1/2   1
miles

Flood
Pond

Musquash
Pond

in pairs. The first box gets occupied by the more aggressive tree swallows who chase away other tree swallows, leaving the other box free for bluebirds, whom the swallows ignore. Apparently, these tree swallows have not heard of this theory, because every box had nesting tree swallows. Perhaps the sheer volume of pesky insects overwhelmed the swallows' aggressive territorial tendencies (if they spend all their time chasing insects, they have less time to chase each other).

Getting There

From Augusta, take Routes 17 and 32 east. When they split, take Route 32 south, and after a short way turn right onto Route 215 south. Route 215 joins 126 west for a short distance, then turns off to the left (south) again. Continue on 215 for another 2.1 miles from here. At the crossroads, where Atkins Road goes to the right and Weeks Road to the left, turn left onto Weeks Road, one of the narrowest blacktop roads you will ever see. The pavement ends in 0.3 mile; continue straight (right) at the fork here for another 0.5 mile to the bridge over the outlet of Dyer Long Pond.

Park in the open area on the right just before the bridge, but do not block the easily missed road that heads back into the woods. The carry-in access is just a short way back up the road away from the bridge.

Lower Togus Pond

Augusta

MAPS
   Maine Atlas: Map 13
   USGS Quadrangle: Togus Pond

INFORMATION
Information on area, depth, and prominent fish species not available.

There is quite a surprise waiting for you on Route 105. First is the contrast between the development on Togus Pond and the lack of it across the road on Lower Togus Pond. Perhaps more surprising, though, is that such a wild and beautiful place as Lower Togus Pond exists within the corporate limits of Maine's capital city.

Lower Togus Pond is long and narrow, with no development until you get to the very lowest section. Because it is so shallow and weedy, there is little boat traffic. There are several islands and lots of coves, but what really draw and hold one's attention are the literally hundreds of acres of fragrant water lily, especially in the extensive coves along

Acres of fragrant water lily welcome paddlers to the protected coves of Lower Togus Pond. The aromatic white flowers appear midsummer and last into fall.

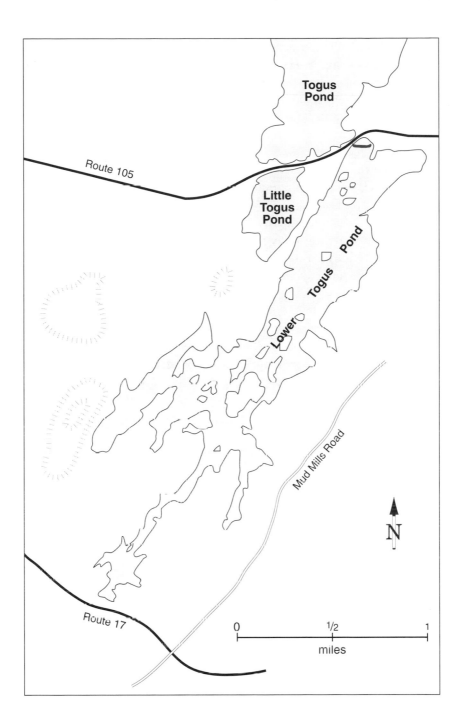

Togus
Pond

Route 105

Little
Togus
Pond

Togus Pond

Lower

Mud Mills Road

N

Route 17

0   1/2   1
                  miles

the western shore. Some of these patches extend unbroken for 100 yards and more. There are sundews and pitcher plants everywhere on the hummocks, and every native variety of bog vegetation certainly must be present.

In the spring, try to stay clear of the many wood duck nesting boxes as you thread your way back into the recesses of these coves. Big fish and beaver both slap the water as you glide by, and two cormorants let us cruise close enough to catch the gleam in their eyes. We also saw several great blue heron fishing the shoreline and turtles sunning on nearly every log. Some beaver lodges extend six feet or more above the water line.

This is an extraordinarily beautiful canoeing spot, which would take the better part of a day to explore fully. It is a place that can be paddled on windy days, because the acres of water lilies damp the swells, and the numerous islands block the wind.

Getting There

From Augusta, on the rotary where Routes 202 and 105 divide, follow Route 105 east. After dividing, Route 105 heads south for just a few blocks and then takes a sharp left turn to the east. The boat access is 5.8 miles from the split, along the roadway that separates Togus from Lower Togus Pond.

Stevens Pond
Liberty

MAPS
    Maine Atlas: Map 14
    USGS Quadrangles: Washington and Liberty

INFORMATION
    Area: 336 acres; maximum depth: 43 feet
    Prominent fish species: smallmouth bass, largemouth bass, white perch, and chain pickerel (brown trout have been introduced recently)

The town of Liberty maintains a park on Stevens Pond, so on warm summer days, especially on weekends, bathers crowd the boat access near the outlet dam. Stevens Pond serves as a major tributary to the St. George River, and with the popular Lake St. George just upstream, the motorboat traffic pretty much stays busy elsewhere. Most fishermen here use canoes or rowboats; occasionally a small outboard will risk continual fouling from the ubiquitous aquatic vegetation. Fortunately, the fish dislike their noise as much as we do, so these fishermen keep their motors off. Even though others may intrude on your solitude occasionally, Stevens Pond is a wonderful place to paddle, especially midweek.

Heading out from the boat access, stay to the left; it is more interesting and avoids most of the development, which is screened by the first large island, and there are extensive marshes to explore down the eastern shore. Beautiful granite boulders extend down into the water from the island.

Very tall white pines dominate the shorelines of both the mainland and the large island. They seem to thrive on the thin soil above the hard granite outcroppings. In contrast, hardwoods need more soil for their taproots, which generally go straight down. This explains, at least in part, the dearth of very large hardwoods along most of these granite-laden shorelines, while at the same time the white pines and other conifers can grow to great size there. One wonders, however, how such a thin layer of soil can support such towering trees. Perhaps they wedge their roots into the fissures in the underlying rocks.

Curving around to the left, you come to a boggy island with a sizable population of a rare pink orchid, the rose pogonia. Borne on ten-inch stalks, the delicate pink flowers bloom in late June. This sight is a

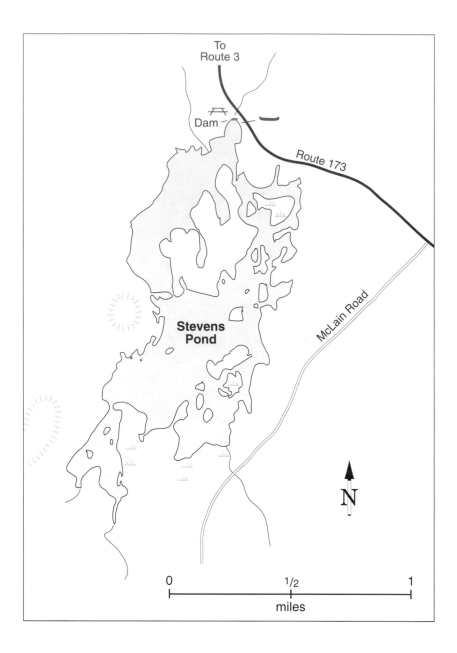

rare treat; please be very careful not to injure these gorgeous flowers. You will also see an unusually large number of pitcher plants in flower if you paddle here in the early summer. Each tuft of sphagnum along here seems to harbor a patch of tiny sundews, their sticky leaves waiting to latch onto unwary insects. Like the pitcher plant and other

Rose pogonia.

carnivorous plants, the sundew absorbs nitrogen and other nutrients from captured insects it dissolves with enzymes.

Have you ever noticed the huge eyes on deer flies before you swatted them? They are sight predators, which explains their pesky daytime presence. More than a few of them buzzed around our heads in the narrow passages of the marsh. At times, we wished that some of those people around the boat access had paddled out here to help share the burden. Nonetheless, we were completely alone in our explorations on a warm, sunny weekend in June.

The extensive patches of lily pads extending out into the middle of the lake indicate that most of the pond is fairly shallow, and except by the boat access, there is little sign of human presence.

Getting There

From Augusta, take Route 3 east. At the junction with Route 220, turn south on Route 220. Go 1.1 miles to the junction of Routes 220 and 173 south and go left on 173. Start marking mileage here. Continue on Route 173 as it goes right in 0.8 mile. The boat access is on the right at 1.3 miles from the junction with Route 220.

Hutchinson Pond and Jimmie Pond
Manchester and Farmingdale

MAPS
  Maine Atlas: Map 12
  USGS Quadrangles: Augusta and Winthrop
INFORMATION
  Hutchinson Pond area: 100 acres; maximum depth: 24 feet
  Prominent fish species: largemouth bass and chain pickerel
  Jimmie Pond area: 107 acres; maximum depth: 75 feet
  Prominent fish species: brook trout, smallmouth bass, largemouth
  bass, and chain pickerel

From the access point on Bog Farm Road, one can paddle upstream into Jimmie Pond with comparative ease. Or one could paddle downstream into Hutchinson Pond with comparative difficulty. Which way should you go?

There is no development on Hutchinson Pond and very little on Jimmie Pond because both supply water for the town of Hallowell, but these two ponds are quite different. With the exception of the small southern arm, Jimmie Pond is deep, lacks marshy areas, and supports a cold-water fishery; it has access points on both the south and north. In contrast, Hutchinson Pond is shallow, marshy, supports a warm-water fishery, and is relatively inaccessible. The question becomes: How hard do you want to work in order to see the beautiful, seldom visited, wild Hutchinson Pond?

The southern arm of Jimmie Pond is small, shallow, and boggy on all sides. Resist the temptation to rush on through to the larger, less interesting, main pond. Immediately after getting in your boat, note the dead tree with an osprey nest in it on the far side, and check the boggy areas for sundews and pitcher plants. Diverse species of bog plants inhabit this area, and shrubs dominate the shoreline, with large deciduous trees and a few scattered pines farther back. A beaver announced the displeasure of our company with a tail slap as we paddled by, and a loon swam before us in the channel between the two sections of Jimmie Pond.

The main Jimmie Pond, in contrast, has almost no boggy areas to speak of and is relatively deep. A tall mixed canopy marches down to the shoreline on all sides, and, aside from one island, there is little to

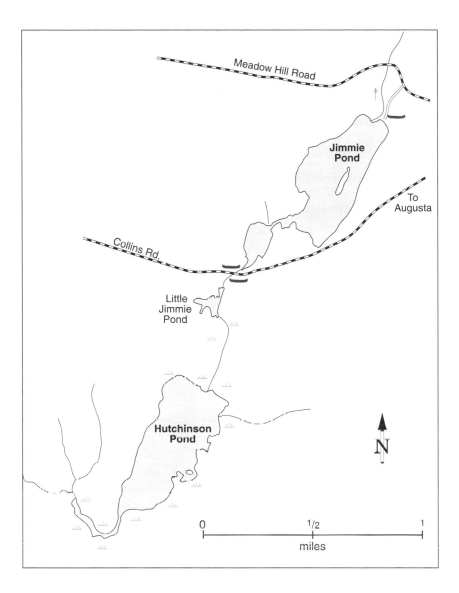

explore. It is still a picturesque little pond, well worth your visit, especially if you fish.

Hutchinson Pond, on the other hand, gets very little attention because of difficult access. First, before going to Hutchinson (notice we did not say paddling), ask permission at the house by the access to launch your boat from their grass on the downstream side of the bridge. The sign out front says Ed Rowe, Coleman Repair. They are very friendly and actively encouraged us to paddle down to Hutchinson Pond.

As you look down the narrow channel leading to Hutchinson, note the first of several beaver dams. It seemed as though all we did was portage over these amazing little engineering wonders when, in truth, we had to go over only six in a half-mile. Of course, the same six dams impeded our progress on the way back.

The channel after the last dam is beautiful. It is crowded with vegetation, and you have to thread your way through. Along the way, note the several lodges of the perhaps overly diligent waterway engineers. Extensive marshy areas occur on all sides of Hutchinson Pond, and there is a lot to explore, which you should be able to do in solitude. On the northeast shore look for the only bog-free area. A huge, beautiful granite boulder creeps up the shoreline to a great little campsite. One gets the impression that you could spend a few days here and not see another soul.

In retrospect, the trip was definitely worth it. Beware, though, of leeches. We found three leeches in the bottom of the boat, having dropped off our legs. One tenacious little leech that escaped detection was removed at a gas station a half-hour later. Funny how they can hide under sandal straps.

Getting There

From Augusta, take Route 201 south to Hallowell. As you come into town, the buildings come right to the road. Take an immediate right on Winthrop or Central Street (or any of the next few through streets to the right). Go sharply uphill for two or three blocks to Middle Street. Turn left onto Middle Street. Keep going up Middle Street until it makes a sharp right turn where it merges with Litchfield Road. Start marking mileage here.

From the junction of Litchfield Road and Middle Street, the road goes over the interstate at 0.4 mile. Note the Rollins Furniture Company on the left and a crossroads sign on the right. Make an immediate right turn at 0.7 mile onto Bog Farm Road. At 2.1 miles go sharply left with the main road. Fork left at 3.0 miles, turning onto Collins Road. The carry-in boat access is on the right just before the bridge. Be careful here, because there are blind curves on both sides of the bridge, and people speed here.

An alternative access exists at the pumping station at the north end of Jimmie Pond. Heading from the Collins Road access back toward Hallowell, take the first left (where you forked left onto Collins Road) onto Meadow Hill Road. The pumping station road is on the left less than a mile down this road.

Turner Pond

Palermo and Somerville

MAPS
   Maine Atlas: Map 13
   USGS Quadrangle: Razorville
INFORMATION
   Area: 193 acres; maximum depth: 7 feet
   Prominent fish species: largemouth bass and chain pickerel

Turner Pond is a rare, undeveloped gem with few visitors. Islands of all sizes dot the surface of this long and narrow pond, making it seem much larger than its 193 acres. There is one very smooth, gigantic boulder out in the middle, just inviting you to climb on it. Flat spots tucked up under the pines on both the mainland and the islands appear to be made just for picnicking. Here are two locations in particular: Leaving the boat access, travel up the right shore past the first peninsula; there is one on the right-hand shore opposite the large island. Farther up the pond on the left-hand side is a beautiful little spot on an island.

We saw a newborn, fuzzy black baby loon swimming with its parents. The attentive parents called frequently as we tried to give them a wide berth, and they herded the little one between them. In contrast to the total chaos that erupts when one comes suddenly upon a mother merganser with a dozen babies in tow, the loons beat a much more dignified retreat. We had hoped to see one of the parents give the young loon a piggyback ride, but we will have to wait for another time. They probably have the fishing pretty much to themselves here.

mergansers

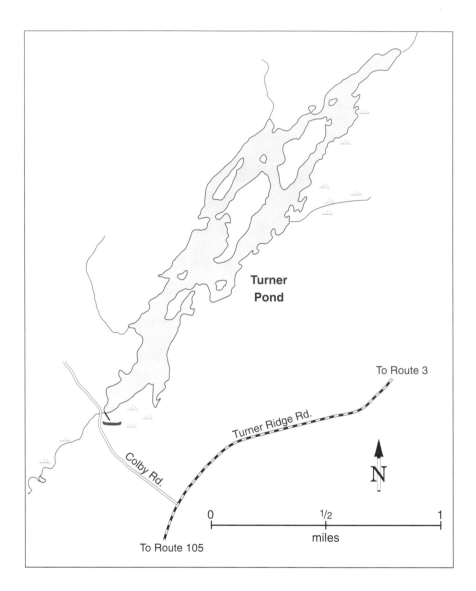

Turner
Pond

To Route 3

Turner Ridge Rd.

Colby Rd.

N

0   ½   1
          miles

To Route 105

Explore the numerous coves for wildlife, and enjoy the water lily-filled passages between islands. Many different tree species occur here, enhancing the scenic quality of the pond, and because the entire pond is so shallow, marshy areas filled with all of the typical bog vegetation are abundant. Because of the numerous coves and islands, it takes quite a bit of time to explore all of Turner Pond. Just when you think you have gotten to the end, you pass around yet another large island and emerge out onto another stretch of open water.

One of the many islands on Turner Pond. This large granite boulder provides a pleasant place to swim.

Back at the boat access is an old dam and the Turner Mill site, filled with rusting machinery. Also, as you walk down the access road to the water, note that the property immediately joining the road on the left side is private. Please stay off it.

Getting There

From Augusta, take Route 3 east. After passing out of Kennebec County and into Waldo County, watch for a Fish Cultural Station sign on the right at the top of a rise. The sign is horizontal and brown. Just after this sign, turn right onto Turner Ridge Road, which is paved. Go 4.7 miles, and turn right onto unpaved Colby Road. The road is hard to see as you approach it. Once on Colby Road, go 0.6 mile to the boat access. There is plenty of parking along the widened road here. It is a short walk down to the water, which you can see off to the right.

Alternatively, you can take Route 105 east from Augusta through Windsor. Turn left on Turner Ridge Road in Somerville, then left on Colby Road, and follow directions as above (we did not check distances, so use the *Maine Atlas*).

Branch Pond
Palermo

MAPS
  Maine Atlas: Map 13
  USGS Quadrangle: Palermo

INFORMATION
  Area: 322 acres; maximum depth: 38 feet
  Prominent fish species: brown trout, white perch, and chain pick-
  erel

Branch Pond is a small shallow pond, dotted with islands and fes-
tooned with marshy channels and coves to explore. Although the boat
access is an easy one from a paved road, it is also at a private gristmill
owned by the Dinsmore Grain Company. If you wish to paddle here,
you must ask permission to launch your boat at the Dinsmore Grain
Company General Store, just across the street from the boat access.
We were told that no one yet has been refused permission to launch
here, but the owners would probably deny access to power boats with
anything but the smallest motors.

Retaining access to this delightful spot and many others hinges
on our willingness to treat others' property with respect. We should
clean up after ourselves and after the thoughtless litterbugs who unfortunately frequent these sites. We always have a trash bag handy and
have put much more into it than we care to remember.

Right at the boat access is a small dam and the Dinsmore mill
site, which until relatively recently still milled grain, although the
lumber mill has been shut down for quite some time. The owners have
kept the property in good shape, and there is hope that the mill can be
restored.

Going out from the boat access, travel up the right (east) side of
the pond, as there is much more to explore on this side, and a few cottages intrude on the left side. You can weave in and among the numerous islands, and there are coves and small streams with lots of interesting plants and wildlife. We saw a pair of loons with a small, black
chick in tow, as well as many ducks feeding in the shallows.

We paddled here during a warm rain that was not heavy enough
to keep either us or a fishing osprey off the pond. Because it lacks a
state-maintained public access, Branch Pond does not suffer from

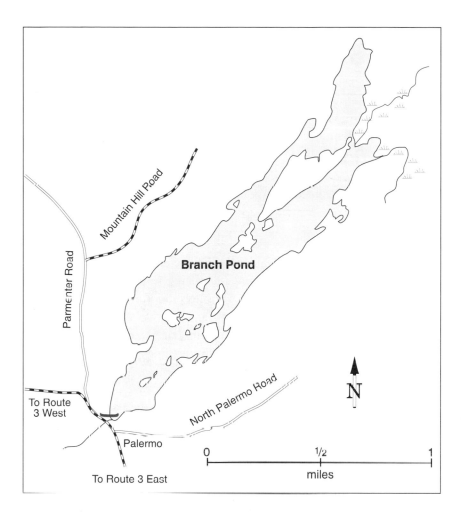

overuse. We hope the people who own the Dinsmore Grain Company will generously continue to allow quiet water paddlers access to this beautiful spot.

Getting There

Take Routes 9, 3, and 202 east from Augusta. Start marking mileage when Routes 9 and 202 split off in South China. Stay on Route 3 and go 4.3 miles to the turnoff to Palermo on the left, marked by a Coastal gas station. The Dinsmore Grain Company boat access is 0.7 mile down this road on the left. Be careful not to block the fire-company hydrant, where they draw water from the pond to fill their pumpers.

Bunganock Pond

Hartford

MAPS
    Maine Atlas: Map 11
    USGS Quadrangle: Canton

INFORMATION
    Area: 51 acres; maximum depth: 12 feet
    Prominent fish species: largemouth bass, yellow perch, and chain
      pickerel

The outlet stream that flows under the bridge at Bunganock Pond sees hardly any visitors and is far more interesting to the quiet-water paddler than Bunganock Pond itself. Although the pond is undeveloped, with only one visible cabin, it is small and relatively round with not a lot of interesting features. We paddled the complete shoreline in less than an hour and then spent our remaining time paddling down and back on the meandering Bunganock Stream.

Many large white pines hug the shoreline of Bunganock Pond, along with maples, paper birches, and other deciduous trees. Explore

Fragrant water lilies and pickerelweed abound in the shallow, marshy areas of Bunganock Pond.

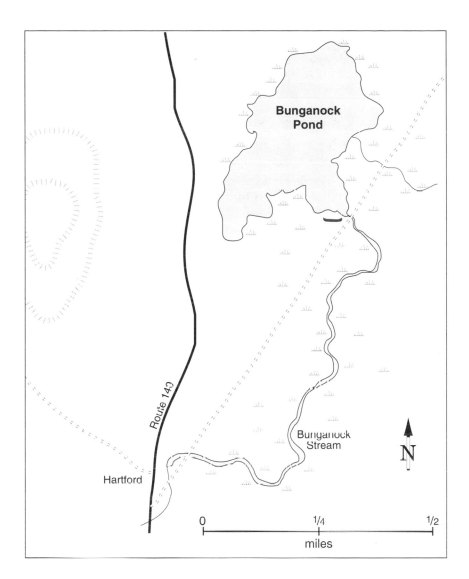

Bunganock
Pond

Route 140

Bunganock
Stream

N

Hartford

0   1/4   1/2
miles

the marshy coves, and enjoy the view of forested hills to the west. The pond is shallow, as evidenced by the abundance of pond vegetation, especially water lilies. Most floating-leaved pond vegetation, such as fragrant water lily, bullhead lily, water shield, and bladderwort, cannot grow in more than about four feet of water, though some less common aquatic plants can tolerate deeper water.

Although we paddled here in July, the water level was relatively high. We suspect that late in the summer or during dry years, the outlet stream may be somewhat less navigable. Indeed, even getting into the outlet stream is difficult. We just slid the boat down through the overgrown road bank next to the bridge, then followed the path it made. The first hundred feet of the stream are the most difficult, and we had to get out of the boat three times to make it over beaver dams and shallows before the channel widened out to an easily paddlable thirty feet. If your boat floats in this widened channel, there is probably enough water for you to paddle all the way to the end.

This place is filled with wildlife, marsh vegetation, and solitude. We saw eastern kingbirds, great blue heron, song sparrows, and painted turtles poking their heads up through the floating vegetation. The turtles would dive down through the tea-colored water as we approached. Fragrant water lilies and bullhead lilies are abundant, along with pickerelweed and grasses lining the shore. Sweet gale and other shrubs crowd the shore in places, and such water-tolerant trees as tamarack and red maple encroach on the banks wherever the ground rises slightly above the marsh.

At bends in the stream, occasional large granite boulders stand like sentinels guarding the passageway. In those areas, beware of submerged boulders. We had little trouble if we stayed in the middle of the channel near visible boulders.

The stream snakes around the large pine island in the middle of the marsh, and it looks like it disappears at a dwarf-tamarack and red-maple forest. Instead, the stream takes an abrupt right turn and continues on for another few hundred yards before it takes a sharp left-hand turn down a narrow rocky channel. At this point you have reached the road at Hartford Center; do not bother with the narrow channel as it is filled with submerged rocks.

Getting There

Take Route 4 north out of Lewiston. Turn left onto Route 219 in North Turner. At the junction of Routes 219 and 140 north, turn right onto Route 140. Drive 0.5 mile, and turn right by a sign that says Deaf Child; go through a sand pit on a very straight dirt road. Continue 0.8 mile to the boat access, where there is room to park three or four cars. It is difficult to turn around on this narrow road; have someone guide you as you make a multipoint turn.

Parker Pond
Mount Vernon and Vienna

MAPS
  Maine Atlas: Maps 12 and 20
  USGS Quadrangles: Fayette and Farmington Falls
INFORMATION
  Area: 1,610 acres; maximum depth: 76 feet
  Prominent fish species: salmon and smallmouth bass

Even though Parker Pond has some shoreline development, we include this large, scenic pond because there is so much to explore and because much of the development is hidden from view by the numerous islands dotting the western shore. Even if you paddle past these islands, most of the houses are well back from shore, hidden by trees.

After leaving the boat access, head to the right. What appears to be a peninsula is really a series of islands. On the far side of these islands is a huge flat rock that provides an excellent spot for swimming and picnicking. After exploring these islands, head for the northwest cove around to the right. A series of beautiful pine-covered islands, extending down the whole western side of the pond, guard this cove and the western cove. Many are suitable for picnicking and swimming.

Well out from shore a series of large boulder formations extend up from the water's surface; these would make an ideal location for swimming or picnicking when biting insects seem to patrol every patch of vegetation. The water is quite clear, giving good views of the rocky floor of the pond. We suspect that the large boulders gleaming up at us everywhere except in the center of the pond help to keep the motorboat traffic down.

We saw osprey, loons, fifteen ring-billed gulls resting on a bare rock formation, kingfishers, and dozens of swallows. Besides the beautiful white pines covering the islands, balsam fir, hemlock, red and sugar maple, paper birch, red oak, and gray birch line the western shore.

Because of all the coves, bays, inlets, peninsulas, and islands, it will take all day to explore this scenic pond. A word of caution, though: This is a large pond, subject to wind. If the wind is out of the north or west, you should be able to paddle along the north shore and

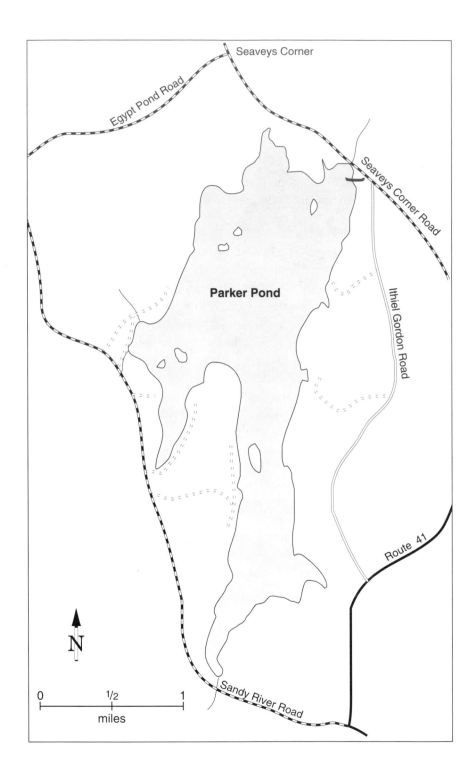

Parker Pond

Egypt Pond Road

Seaveys Corner

Seaveys Corner Road

Ithiel Gordon Road

Route 41

N

0   1/2   1
miles

Sandy River Road

down among the protected islands ringing the western shore. If the wind is out of the south, however, it may be difficult just to get your boat into the water.

Getting There

Take Route 17 west from Augusta to Readfield where it joins Route 41. When Routes 17 and 41 split, take Route 41 north. Start measuring mileage from the public boat-access sign on Route 41 on Echo Lake in West Mount Vernon. Continue north on Route 41 for 3.7 miles, then turn back sharply to the left onto Seaveys Corner Road in Mount Vernon; both roads are very narrow here, with buildings coming right to the edge of the road. Ithicl Gordon Road enters from the left at 1.4 miles, and the boat access to Parker Pond is on the right at 1.5 miles.

Sandy Pond
Freedom

MAPS
    Maine Atlas: Map 22
    USGS Quadrangle: Unity
INFORMATION
    Area: 430 acres; maximum depth: 11 feet
    Prominent fish species: largemouth bass

This is a nice little pond located right in the town of Freedom. It gets used by fishermen in small boats and canoes, but you should have it pretty much to yourself during the week. There is little development, except at the boat-access area and on the opposite end of the pond. As you leave the boat access in the northeast cove, curve to the right to explore the extensive marshy area along the north central section of the pond. The floating islands in this marsh extend well out into the pond and will take a long time to explore fully. The rest of the shoreline lacks marshy areas, although aquatic vegetation occurs everywhere in this very shallow pond.

Acres of cattails, marsh grasses, and boggy islands provide extensive exploration opportunities. Protruding logs in various stages of decay drip with sphagnum, sundews, and basking turtles. Bullhead lilies and pickerelweed fill the channels. When we paddled here, an osprey with a fish in its talons was having better luck than the rod-and-reel set.

turtles

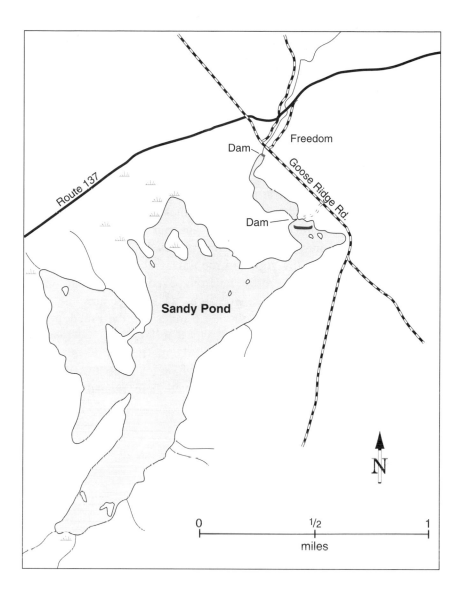

Some beautiful little islands appear just where the pond widens, about a half-mile from the boat access, and the first one looks like a great spot for a picnic. When we were there, several herring gulls were ensconced on its shores, trying to keep out of the wind. We were much less successful and had to use the islands and the marshy areas to shelter us from the wind-driven swells.

Beautiful layered hillsides surrounding the pond fade into the distance, and large trees dot the shoreline and cover the hills, making this a picturesque spot and a pleasurable place to paddle. The far, southwest end of the pond has some development, and we worry about the pond's ultimate fate. As we paddled, we listened to the ominous sound of chain saws on the surrounding hills. Paddle here now while this little gem is still relatively untrammeled.

Getting There

From Unity take Route 139 east, which joins Route 220 immediately. When Route 139 goes left at Thorndike, follow Route 220 south. At the flashing red light at the junction of Routes 220 and 137, turn right onto Route 137 toward Freedom, and start marking mileage. As you come down a hill into town, note the Agency Liquor Store sign on Knowlton's Store on the right. Immediately across the street just before a white house at 1.2 miles, take the paved diagonal road on the left. At the top of the hill at the stop sign at 1.5 miles, turn left. Note the large white church on the right at 1.6 miles and the Freedom Fire Company on the right at 1.7 miles. At 1.8 miles, there are two dirt roads on the right in quick succession. Take the first of these back to the boat access. Don't be surprised when you see a large brown garage and, possibly, a Knowlton's tank truck parked there. Indeed, this is the boat access.

Carlton Pond and Carlton Bog

Troy

MAPS
    Maine Atlas: Map 22
    USGS Quadrangle: Unity Pond
INFORMATION
    Area: 430 acres; maximum depth: 8 feet
    Prominent fish species: chain pickerel

The state of Maine preserves and maintains Carlton Pond and Carlton Bog as a waterfowl-production area. We found it suitable not only for waterfowl but also for paddlers. Indeed, Carlton Pond remains one of our favorite places to explore. Because development has not intruded on the vast marshes here and to the immediate north, this is an excellent place to look for moose. In the spring and at other times of high water, one can paddle almost the entire bog area, and it would take most of a day to explore every nook and cranny. Because it has a maximum depth of only eight feet, the entire pond, except for a few narrow channels, is literally choked with nearly every species of aquatic vegetation found in this part of Maine.

Typical bog vegetation covers the higher ground in and around this gigantic marsh. Hummocks seem to float everywhere, covered with sweet gale, rhodora, blueberries, sheep laurel, and lots more. Pitcher plants, sundews, and sphagnum moss abound. The sphagnum provides habitat for an orchid, rose pogonia, that was in bloom in large numbers in late June.

The sphagnum provides more than a soft, mossy pad for sundews, pitcher plants, and orchids. It exchanges some of its hydrogen ions for water-borne metal ions, thereby acidifying its immediate vicinity. This process makes the habitat unsuitable for most other plants that might crowd it out, except those that can tolerate an acid environment. When many layers of sphagnum accumulate, the bottom layers, which are devoid of oxygen, cannot decay much, and peat develops.

When we paddled here, waterfowl were very much in evidence. There were no loons, cormorants, or diving ducks, probably because of the shallow water, but dozens of dabbling ducks bobbed on the surface, occasionally dipping for a mouthful of aquatic vegetation. We

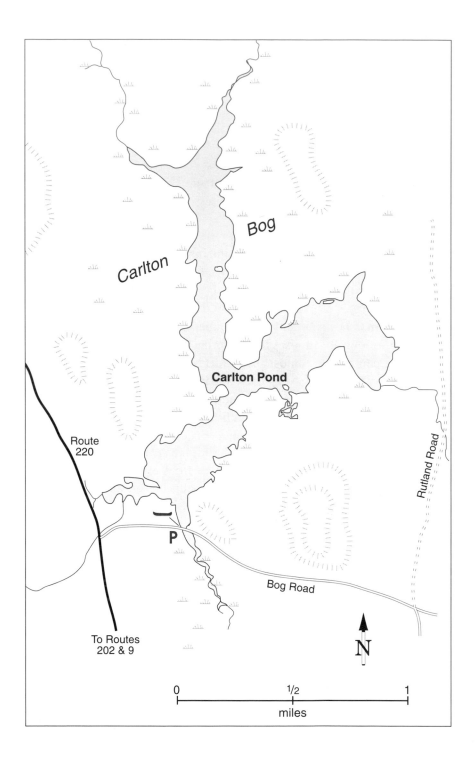

Carlton

Bog

Carlton Pond

Route
220

P

Bog Road

Rutland Road

To Routes
202 & 9

N

0	1/2	1

miles

tried not to get too close, but when we did, the ducks would leap into the air with a single wingbeat, helicopter style. This takeoff contrasts with the way heavier loons and cormorants run across the water's surface to get up enough speed to become airborne.

When you see a duck on land, note its horizontal profile; the profile of a perching cormorant is vertical. Cormorants and loons have their feet set well back on their bodies to enhance their underwater swimming capabilities as they chase fish. Their resulting streamlined horizontal profile in the water, along with their heavy bodies, makes it difficult for them to get vertical for liftoff. On the other hand, puddle ducks, which only bob their heads and necks underwater to gobble up plants, have their legs set at midbody. Consequently, all they have to do to get vertical is stretch their necks upwards.

You will also have to share this bog with a few mosquitoes. Fortunately, there were few out on the water. Back on land, though, we must have set a record for getting the boat loaded up.

Getting There

From Unity, take Routes 202 and 220 east. Follow Route 220 when it turns to the left just out of town at Greens Corner. This turn is easy to miss. After about 1 mile, Route 220 takes a right turn at Smarts Corner, and less than a mile later at the bottom of a steep hill it takes a left turn at Cooks Corner. Start marking mileage at this point. After topping a rise, notice a concrete bridge with steel guardrails and a gravel road leading off to the right just before it. This is Bog Road at 1.2 miles. Turn right and go 0.3 mile to the carry-in access on the left; park on the right.

From I-95, get off at the Newport exit, Exit 39. At the end of the exit ramp, turn west onto Routes 11 and 100. After about 2 miles, go straight onto an unmarked, paved road as Routes 11 and 100 veer to the right. At the stop sign, turn left onto Route 220. Pass a Citgo station and an iron bridge. When Routes 220 and 69 east divide, go right onto Route 220 and start marking mileage. Bog Road is on the left at 7.7 miles, and as before, the boat access is 0.3 mile down Bog Road.

Douglas Pond
Palmyra and Pittsfield

MAPS
  Maine Atlas: Map 21
  USGS Quadrangle: Pittsfield

INFORMATION
  Information on area, depth, and prominent fish species not available.
  Camping: Ringwood Campground, Palmyra, ME 04354; 207-487-3406. This small campground on Douglas Pond is located off Route 152 opposite Spring Road.

Douglas Pond is a natural pond enhanced by a small dam on the Sebasticook River. Much of the pond is part of the Madawaska Marsh Game Management Area, set aside primarily as duck and fish breeding habitat. Because this water is popular with fishermen, you will not paddle alone here, but few people actually paddle back into the marsh itself, where you will find acres of solitude.

From the boat access, paddle left, going under the interstate. The river here is narrow, with large deciduous trees lining the banks, including red and sugar maple, elm, red oak, and mature paper birches. Look for the drooping branches of a grove of hemlocks hanging out over the water on the left. As the channel widens, an alder swamp appears on both sides. Notice the large beaver lodges just past the interstate.

There are acres and acres of cattails, rushes, and pickerelweed as the channel broadens out into the shallow pond. Except perhaps in late summer, you should be able to paddle way back into the marsh, where you are likely to see wood duck, muskrat, pickerelweed, arrowhead, great blue heron, and red-winged blackbirds—to mention only a few.

If you are looking for exercise, you can paddle up the Sebasticook River as far as you like. Except during flood stages, the current is modest to nearly undetectable. We paddled about a mile above the Route 2 bridge and saw Canada geese, kingfishers, great blue herons, green-backed herons, two loons, and many other birds.

Douglas Pond, given its proximity to I-95, Waterville, and Bangor, is one of the most accessible of Maine's quiet-water lakes. As you enter the marsh, the interstate noise gradually fades into the distance

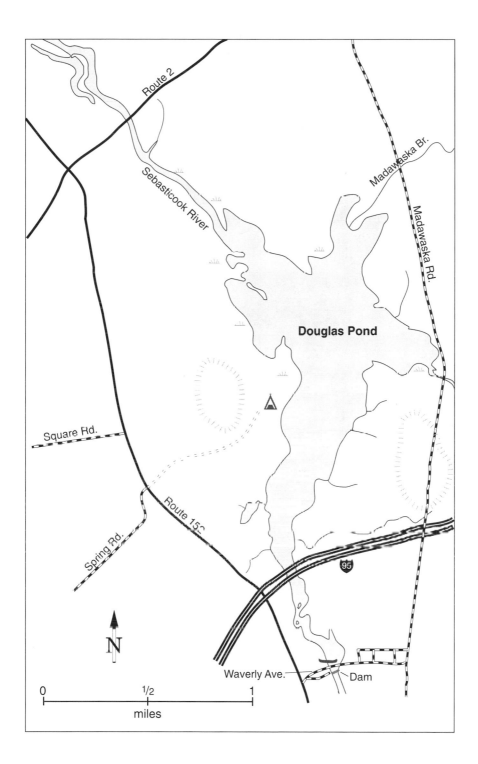

Route 2

Sebasticook River

Madawaska Br.

Madawaska Rd.

Douglas Pond

Square Rd.

Route 15?

Spring Rd.

95

N

Waverly Ave.

Dam

0   1/2   1

miles

as your focus turns to the sounds of birds, insects, and frogs, while your eyes feast on the vast beauty of the Madawaska Marsh. It is hard to believe that such a wonderful place, teeming with fish and wildlife, exists right under the road that whisks the trailered boats to more exotic destinations.

Getting There

From the Exit 38 ramp of I-95, follow signs to Pittsfield and to Routes 11 and 100. In 0.8 mile, turn left onto Route 152 north. After another 0.7 mile, turn right onto Waverly Avenue. The boat launch is 0.2 mile down on the left.

# Downeast Region

Silver Lake

Bucksport

MAPS
  Maine Atlas: Map 23
  USGS Quadrangle: Bucksport
INFORMATION
  Area: 630 acres; maximum depth: 33 feet
  Prominent fish species: smallmouth bass, pickerel, and white
    perch

Even though Silver Lake lies in close proximity both to Bangor and to the vacation meccas of Acadia, Blue Hill, and Camden, it remains relatively untrammeled and, as far as we could tell, seldom visited. When we paddled here on a warm, sunny Sunday in August, there was only one other canoe, which is surprising, given the natural wonders we found.

We saw at least three and probably four bald eagles at close range: two immatures, which superficially resemble golden eagles, and one or two different adults with their characteristic white heads and tails. A group of seven loons swam together, and the far eastern cove harbored dozens of feeding wood ducks. Right at high noon, when you would least expect it, a doe and her spotted fawn came down to the shore of the northern arm to take a lengthy drink, seemingly oblivious to our presence, while two adult and one juvenile osprey took serious exception to our presence within fifty yards of their nest on a utility pole.

We saw muskrats swimming out to harvest aquatic plants, young ungainly great blue heron learning to fish the shallows, and several beaver lodges with masses of fresh cuttings. Most grassy areas near

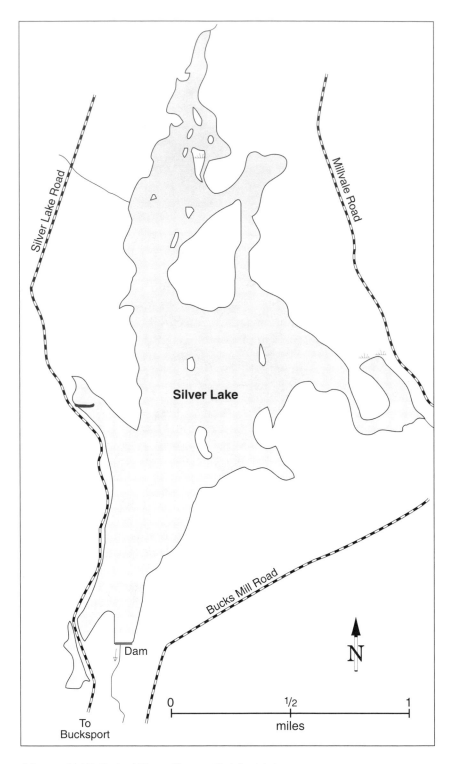

Silver Lake

Silver Lake Road

Millvale Road

Bucks Mill Road

Dam

To
Bucksport

0   1/2   1

miles

N

shore harbored large numbers of frogs, and we found piles of mussel shells where raccoons frequent the shoreline on nightly feeding forays.

Although a few houses can be seen in places from the water, there is no shoreline development. A power line cuts up diagonally along the northwestern shore, providing aeries for two pairs of ospreys. There is an excellent camping spot along the northwest shore, under a grove of large conifers. An elegant hand-carved sign contains the plea: Please carry in, carry out. Cut no live trees.

The coves are marshy, sporting luxuriant growths of pickerelweed, cattails, bulrushes, arrowhead, horsetails, bladderwort, and bur reed. The shoreline is densely packed with shrubs, while white pine, aspen, paper birch, red maple, and red spruce dominate the canopy. The northern reaches harbor dozens of islands, ranging from a few feet to a half-mile in length. A few of the smaller islands are floating, and many are covered with sphagnum, sundews, and pitcher plants. Others are covered with sweet gale, bog rosemary, and other typical marsh plants, and there are substantial stands of tamarack on many. The intricate pattern of islands and waterways can lead to hours of paddling in quiet seclusion.

Getting There

From Bangor, at the stoplight at the junction of Routes 395 and 15, go south on Route 15 for about 13.2 miles and turn left onto Town Farm Road. Take Town Farm Road to the junction with Silver Lake Road in 2.2 miles. Turn right onto Silver Lake Road, and go 1.7 miles south to the boat access on the left.

Alternatively, from Bucksport, at the junction of Routes 1, 3, and 15, where Routes 1 and 3 turn south to cross the Penobscot River, drive west on Route 15. After 0.5 mile, turn right on McDonald Street, which goes steeply uphill. McDonald Street turns into Silver Lake Road, and the boat access is 2.1 miles from the junction with Route 15.

Bald Eagle
Our National Bird Back from the Brink

Without a doubt, the bald eagle is our most dramatic and recognizable raptor. With its unmistakable white head and tail, contrasting with a dark-brown body, an adult bald eagle flies over the nation's waterways on powerful wings. In flight, its large size stands out—it soars with wings straight out, spanning up to eight feet. From beak to tip of tail, eagles measure from thirty-four to forty-three inches; males weigh eight to nine pounds, while the larger females weigh ten to fourteen pounds.

Adults do not attain their distinctive plumage until reaching four or five years of age. Until that time they may be mistaken for golden eagles, as they are mostly dark brown with some white mottling on the underside and tail. As they mature, the head and tail become progressively whiter. At close range, the adult's large yellow beak and piercing yellow eyes convey a fierce strength. Our country's founders evidently felt this image symbolized what our young nation stood for, selecting *Haliaeetus leucocephalus* as our national symbol. Appropriately, this is the only eagle found exclusively in North America.

Bald eagles range throughout Maine and can be seen in all

but the most populated areas in the southern part of the state. They mate for life, although when an adult dies its mate will usually succeed in finding a new partner. Eagles locate their nests generally in trees at the water's edge. Pairs return to the same nest for years, adding to it annually. An old eagle nest may be six feet in diameter, more than eight feet deep, and weigh more than a ton. The largest nest ever found was nine and a half feet in diameter and twenty feet deep. Because eagles often build nests in dead trees, the huge mass of the nest eventually topples the tree.

Bald eagles usually lay two eggs several days apart. Incubation lasts thirty to thirty-six days, during which time the male and female share in nest sitting. The young hatch several days apart; the earlier born, larger chick may outcompete its younger sibling for food. If food is scarce, the younger chick usually dies, a strategy that improves the chances of fledging at least one chick. Because eagles live long lives—as long as thirty years in captivity but usually much less in the wild—they really only need to fledge a few chicks to replace themselves, thus maintaining a stable population.

After ten to twelve weeks of a diet consisting mostly of fish, chicks reach the fledgling stage, when they begin to fly. For the next seven or eight weeks, they increasingly gain independence, eventually leaving the nest to migrate to coastal areas where the water does not freeze. In years past, when eagles were plentiful, they congregated in great numbers off both coasts and in the Mississippi drainage each fall. Eagles still congregate by the thousands in mid-November along a ten-mile stretch of the Chilkat River in Alaska, to feed on hordes of dead and dying salmon.

While bald eagles occur frequently in Maine today, just a few years ago only a few remained. Maine's population of eagles plummeted to a low of twenty-one breeding pairs in 1967, producing just six chicks. In the late 1960s and early 1970s, incubation success was very low because toxins in the eagles' bodies resulted in thin egg shells that broke during incubation. Long-lasting chlorinated hydrocarbons—such as DDT and its breakdown products, left over from its use for controlling mosquitoes—reached high concentrations in eagles and other species at the top of the food chain.

Eagle populations have rebounded to about 4,000 nesting pairs in the U.S. outside Alaska, 150 of them in Maine (as of 1993)—with the greatest concentration around remote lakes in the eastern and northern regions. Despite the gains, however, the nesting success rate of bald eagles in Maine remains below 1 fledged chick per nest (115 fledged in 1993). Because some pairs fledge two chicks, this means that many fail to produce a single surviving chick. Experts in the Maine Department of Inland Fisheries and Wildlife blame the low nesting success rate on various toxins in the eagle's food chain: mercury, probably from coal-burning power plants in the Midwest, deposited in Maine by acid rain; DDE, a breakdown product from DDT that still remains in Maine's environment more than twenty years after DDT was banned; dioxins, released by the paper industry; and PCBs, released from various industrial operations and found in older electrical transformers.

Because populations have risen gradually during the past twenty years, aided by reintroductions in many areas in the country, the U. S. Fish and Wildlife Service removed the bald eagle from the Endangered Species List in 1994. The bird is still listed as threatened, however, and is fully protected from hunting or trapping.

We feel privileged to paddle on lakes with resident bald eagles, keeping ever watchful for their glorious presence. Some people have accused them of being opportunists, and indeed we have watched a few chase smaller osprey laboring with heavy fish, circling to gain altitude before flying off to their aeries. In one case, after the osprey dropped its hard-won catch, a bald eagle snatched it, flying off gracefully with its ill-gotten goods. In our view, this is not a case of good and evil; instead it represents the triumph of bald-eagle adaptation, ensuring its survival.

Humans still shoot eagles and build high-tension lines that electrocute them—although designs and devices exist that reduce eagle mortality from these high lines—and many eagles die from flying into human-made structures (towers, smokestacks, power lines, and buildings). But the biggest threat to the eagle's continued survival comes from an expanding human population, one that spews forth toxic chemicals into the environment and develops the shoreline of every lake in sight. If we wish to continue to enjoy this majestic creature as it patrols the waterways of America—and keep it from returning to the Endangered Species List—we must take steps to keep some of its habitat undeveloped and unadulterated by the toxic wastes of a consumer society. The eagle represents an enduring wildness that we must protect for future generations to enjoy.

Wight Pond
Penobscot

MAPS
　　Maine Atlas: Map 15
　　USGS Quadrangle: Penobscot
INFORMATION
　　Area: 135 acres; maximum depth: 21 feet
　　Prominent fish species: largemouth bass, chain pickerel, and white
　　perch

Wight Pond has no development along its shoreline, which is amazing, given its close proximity to Penobscot Bay and millions of tourists. The pond is long and narrow and has much to offer. If you are there in late summer, start by checking out the outlet stream by the boat access for cardinal flower, a brilliant red member of the lobelia family. We visited here with a naturalist, formerly with the New England Wildflower Society, who said this was the largest and most spectacular concentration of cardinal flowers she had seen.

　　Paddling out from the boat access, pass through acres of aquatic vegetation, including pickerelweed, arrowhead, bullhead and fragrant

Alex glides by a painted turtle perched on a log. Turtles bask in the sun's warmth to raise body temperature and boost metabolism.

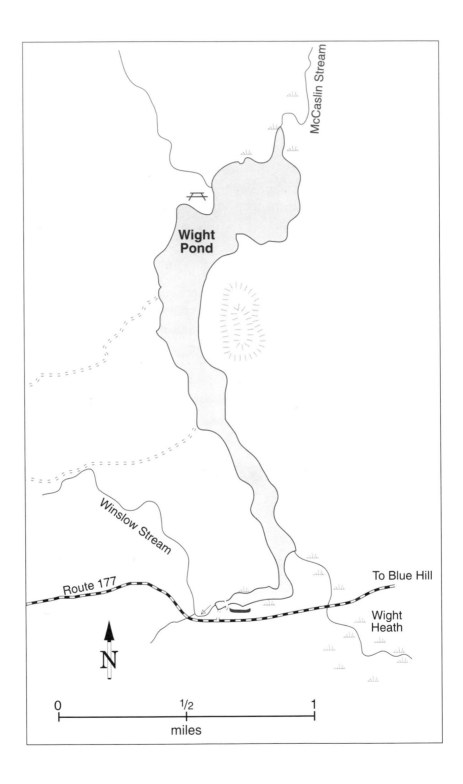

McCaslin Stream

Wight
Pond

Winslow Stream

Route 177

To Blue Hill

Wight
Heath

N

| 0 | 1/2 | 1 |

miles

water lilies, bulrushes, bur reed, and purple bladderwort. We managed to paddle right up to a painted turtle which was out sunning on a log. It never moved as we floated on by.

Passing out into the main part of the lake, the aquatic vegetation disappears at the same time the shore becomes lined with large rocks. Seemingly everywhere were piles of empty mussel shells, indicating, we suspect, the dining locations of hungry raccoons. Up at the north end of the lake on the left is a great picnic spot for humans as well.

The shoreline is typical of most ponds in this area, and it is lined with a large variety of trees, shrubs, and ferns. The predominant tree species include white pine, red oak, red spruce, red maple, and balsam fir.

On the northeast corner of the lake is an inlet that weaves back through the marsh for about a half-mile. We scared out black ducks and a bittern from the reeds. Besides the wildlife and two fishermen, we had this pond to ourselves on a beautiful Saturday in mid-August.

Getting There

From Blue Hill take Route 177 north, measuring mileage from the point where Routes 15, 172, and 176 split off. At 3.6 miles, Route 177 takes a sharp turn to the left, toward Penobscot. The Blue Hill–Penobscot town line is at 5.4 miles. The access point on the right is at 5.8 miles, and it is easy to miss. The turn is just past an S-curve warning sign.

Mount Desert Island
Long Pond, Seal Cove Pond, Eagle Lake, and Jordan Pond
Bar Harbor and Mount Desert Island

MAPS
   Maine Atlas: Map 16
   USGS Quadrangles:
      Long Pond: Southwest Harbor and Bartlett Island
      Seal Cove Pond: Bartlett Island
      Eagle Lake: Southwest Harbor, Seal Harbor, Salsbury Cove, and Bar Harbor
      Jordan Pond: Southwest Harbor

INFORMATION
   Physical information:
      Seal Cove Pond area: 283 acres; maximum depth: 44 feet
      Eagle Lake area: 436 acres; maximum depth: 110 feet
      Jordan Pond area: 187 acres; maximum depth: 150 feet

   Prominent fish species:
      Long Pond: salmon, smallmouth bass, and chain pickerel
      Seal Cove Pond: brook trout, brown trout, smallmouth bass, and perch
      Eagle Lake: salmon, lake trout, and brook trout
      Jordan Pond: salmon, lake trout, and brook trout

   Camping: Superintendent, Acadia National Park, Route 233, Bar Harbor, ME 04609; 207-288-3338. There are two national-park campgrounds on Mount Desert Island with about 540 campsites, plus another ten private campgrounds with about 1,500 campsites. Still, these campgrounds are all frequently full, and reservations are advised.

   Canoe and kayak rentals: Acadia National Park has two canoe and kayak rental locations: at the north end of Long Pond (207-244-5854), and at Bar Harbor (207-288-0342). There are also several private canoe and kayak rental stores, including Acadia Bike and Canoe (207-288-9605) and Acadia Outfitters (207-288-8118).

Known primarily for its craggy shorelines, deep harbors, sailboats, tide pools, lobsters, and coastal vacationing, Mount Desert Island also offers some surprisingly nice fresh-water lake and pond canoe-

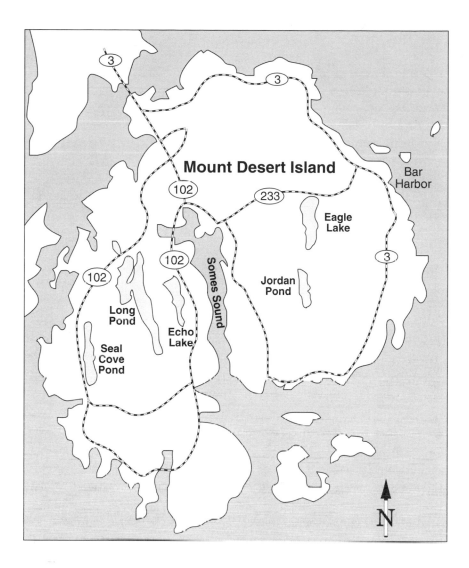

ing. The island extends roughly fifteen miles north to south and twelve miles east to west, and is one of Maine's most popular vacation spots. Acadia National Park, comprising about half of this rocky island, is the oldest national park east of the Mississippi and the second most visited in the country, with more than four million visitors per year. Nestled among the majestic granite peaks of the island are four fresh-water lakes and ponds that we highly recommend for paddling. We describe each, following some general information about the island.

Geologic History

Several important geologic events shaped Mount Desert Island. First, volcanic activity deep underground 350 million to 400 million years ago extruded molten rock into the thick layers of rock that had originally formed as sea-bottom sediment. This bubble of magma never made it to the surface of the ground to erupt as a volcano, cooling instead underground. Because the rock cooled slowly, it formed coarse crystals, distinctive of the resultant pink granite. Following this period, the entire region uplifted as North America collided with Europe and Africa.

Over several hundred million years, the overlying rock gradually eroded away exposing the pink granite below. Finally, during the last million years, glaciation scoured the granite, rounding off mountain peaks and gouging the deep valleys and cliffs so characteristic of the island. The last glacier left Mount Desert Island only 13,000 years ago—a mere wink of an eye in geologic time. One of the deep glacier-carved troughs on the island connects with the ocean, making it a fjord—the only true fjord in the United States outside of Alaska. This is Somes Sound, with steep rock faces extending deep into the salt water. Several other glacial troughs, sealed off from the sea, form fresh-water lakes and ponds, and these provide excellent canoeing today.

Lake and Pond Canoeing on Mount Desert Island

One can paddle on at least five lakes and ponds on Mount Desert Island. We've paddled four of these: Long Pond, Seal Cove Pond, Eagle Lake, and Jordan Pond. We didn't paddle on Echo Lake because Route 102 runs right along the eastern shore. Except for continuous road noise, it should be quite nice, and there is a very good (if occasionally crowded) public swimming beach.

Long Pond

Long Pond, stretching about four and a half miles from north to south, is the largest fresh-water lake on the island. Quite a bit of development exists at the northern end, so on a nice summer weekend you will share the pond with lots of motorboats, water-skiers, jet skis, and the like. There can also be lots of paddlers here. At the north end of the pond, just across the road from the boat access, a National Park Service facility rents canoes and kayaks. Nearly the entire western shore

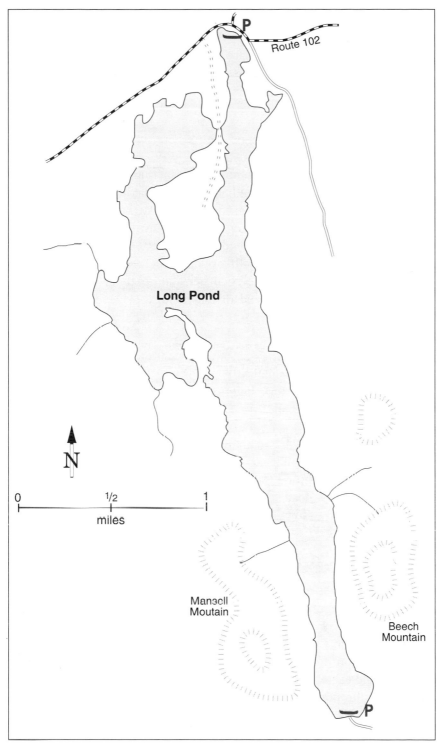

Route 102

Long Pond

N

0   1/2   1

miles

Mansell
Moutain

Beech
Mountain

P

P

of the lake is part of Acadia National Park, as is the eastern shore near the southern tip.

Long Pond runs generally north-south, with the north end divided into an eastern and western section by Northern Neck. The eastern arm of the pond, with the boat access, is more developed than the western arm. In fact, the western arm has some surprisingly isolated and wild coves where you can get away from most of the activity. We passed a few northern fen ecosystems here, with sphagnum moss, pitcher plants, sundews, tamarack, cranberry, leather leaf, and other species one sees much more commonly farther north in Maine.

The long, narrow, southern half of Long Pond suffers from winds that commonly blow from south to north, as we can attest. The water can get quite rough, so use care paddling here in windy conditions. The south end of the pond provides dramatic views, with mountains rising on either side, tall rock cliffs overlooking the water, and jagged, wind-sculpted white pines perched here and there. Numerous trails radiate out from the south end of the pond; a parking area leads to carry-in boat access.

Getting There

After getting onto the island, drive south on Routes 102 and 198 to Somesville. At the 102 fork south of Somesville (where Pretty Marsh Road starts), take the right fork and stay on Pretty Marsh Road for 1.4 miles. The boat access is on the left, and the boat-rental facility is just to the right. To reach the southern access on Long Pond, go through Somesville as above, but stay to the left on 102 toward Southwest Harbor. Stay on 102 for 5.0 miles, and turn right onto Seal Cove Road. Follow Seal Cove Road for 0.5 mile, then turn right onto Long Pond Road, which you follow for 0.7 mile to the boat access.

Seal Cove Pond

Seal Cove Pond is much smaller and more remote than Long Pond. It is also very different ecologically. Most of the pond is very shallow, and the extensive marshy areas—thick with fragrant water lily, bulrushes, horsetails, and pickerelweed—provide superb wildlife habitat. We saw wood ducks, cormorants, loons, great blue heron, and a mature bald eagle. There are just a few houses (along Route 102) visible from the pond, and the entire eastern shore is within Acadia National Park.

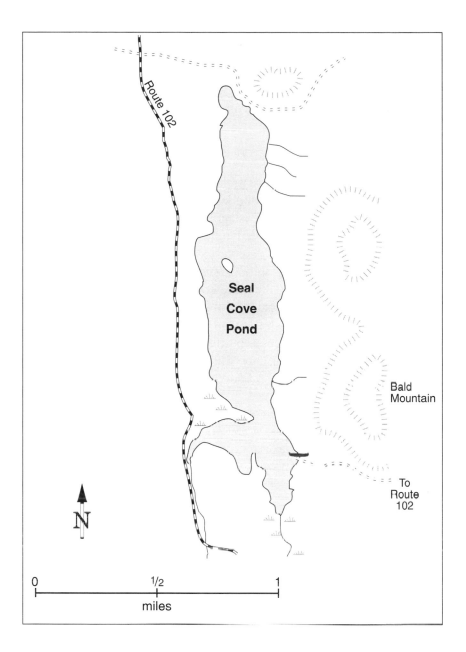

Route 102

Seal
Cove
Pond

Bald
Mountain

To
Route
102

N

0   1/2   1
miles

Getting There

See directions above for Long Pond (northern access). From the north
end of Long Pond (at the boat access), continue on Route 102 (Pretty
Marsh Road) for another 6 miles. Then turn left onto Seal Cove Road,
about 0.2 mile after crossing a small bridge over the Seal Cove Pond

outlet. Follow Seal Cove Road for 0.5 mile, turn left and drive another 0.8 mile (passing a road to the left leading to Bald Mountain), then turn left onto Western Mountain Road, following signs for the Seal Cove Pond boat access. The boat access is 0.7 mile down Western Mountain Road. There is parking for only about five cars here.

Eagle Lake

Eagle Lake, the second largest fresh-water body on Mount Desert Island, remains undeveloped and very attractive. Because the lake serves as a water supply for the island, the northeastern tip is off-limits, and swimming is not permitted in the lake.

The shores of Eagle Lake are very rocky. In places massive slabs of the characteristic pink granite extend down into the water. Along other sections of shoreline, the granite is broken down into a coarse, chunky gravel—stuff that could cut deep scratches in your canoe. A few—but not many—marshy areas occur along the western shore where you'll see pickerelweed, bulrushes, and a few other wetland plants, but mostly this is an unproductive (oligotrophic) lake. Where they have succeeded in gaining a foothold in the rocky soil, you'll see white and red pine, cedar, spruce, and fir.

From the lake you can enjoy spectacular vistas of Pemetic Mountain to the south and Cadillac Mountain to the east. Carriage roads and trails extend around the lake and connect to Jordan Pond, the West Face Trail up Cadillac Mountain, and a beautiful area between Eagle Lake and Jordan Pond known as The Bubbles.

Getting There

Take Routes 102 and 198 south after getting onto the island. Turn left onto 198 where it splits off at the north end of Somes Sound. Stay on 198 for 1.4 miles, then bear right onto Route 233. Stay on 233, and the boat access is on the right in 3.6 miles.

Jordan Pond

Despite its small size, Jordan Pond is probably the best-known pond on Mount Desert Island. The dramatic scenery around the pond, the trail and carriage-road network, and—probably most significantly—the Jordan Pond House restaurant at the southern end all contribute to its reputation. The original Jordan Pond House dated to 1847, when the Jordan

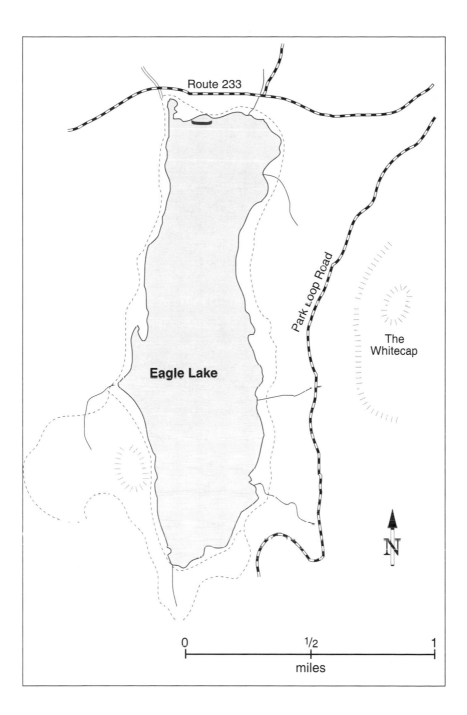

Route 233

Park Loop Road

Eagle Lake

The
Whitecap

N

0   ¹/₂   1
miles

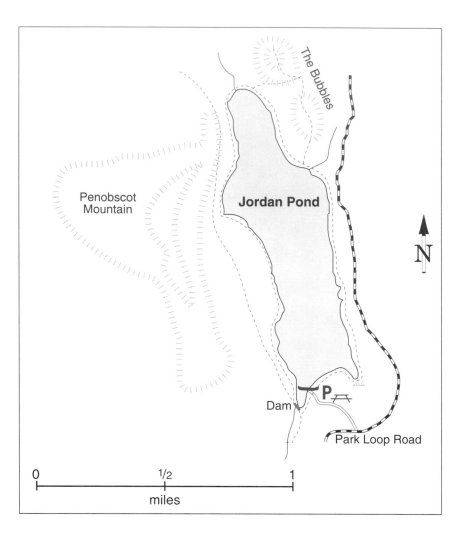

Penobscot
Mountain

Jordan Pond

The Bubbles

N

Dam

P

Park Loop Road

0   1/2   1
miles

family of Seal Harbor built the house at a mill near the pond's outlet. The house became a restaurant in the early 1870s and was operated by Mr. and Mrs. McIntire for more than fifty years starting in 1895. John D. Rockefeller, Jr., purchased the property and gave it to the National Park Service to ensure its continuation. In June 1979 the original house burned, but it was rebuilt as it stands today. From the restaurant you can enjoy elegant dining in view of the spectacular pond.

Paddling on Jordan Pond is somewhat limited. Because the pond serves as a public water supply, the park restricts boats at the south end to a narrow strip up the center of the pond, designated by buoys. Where you can paddle along the shore, it is beautiful, but with little

*Jordan Pond on Mount Desert Island offers a civilized paddle in
Acadia National Park, one of America's most popular parks.*

variation and no coves or marshy areas to explore. On the plus side,
though, the park restricts motors to ten horsepower here.

Jordan Pond is extremely deep. There are places where it drops to
more than 100 feet just a few yards from shore, and the maximum
depth is 150 feet. The cold, well-oxygenated waters provide fairly
good habitat for cold-water fish.

Getting There

To reach Jordan Pond, get on the Park Loop Road either at the north
end near the Acadia National Park Visitors Center, or from Route 233
near the north end of Eagle Lake. Drive south on the Loop Road, and
get off at the sign for Jordan Pond (5.1 miles below Route 233). There
is a parking area and picnic area near the boat access, as well as the
easy half-mile Jordan Pond Nature Trail, with interpretive signs. The
Jordan Pond House restaurant is close by.

Jones Pond
Gouldsboro

MAPS
   Maine Atlas: Maps 16 and 17
   USGS Quadrangle: Winter Harbor
INFORMATION
   Area: 467 acres; maximum depth: 48 feet
   Prominent fish species: smallmouth bass, chain pickerel, and sup-
   posedly a few lunker brown trout

Just a few miles, as the gull flies, from heavily visited Mount Desert
Island, Jones Pond is much less well known, at least to tourists. The
town of Gouldsboro maintains a recreation area on the pond that is
heavily used by local residents. On a nice summer weekend, you can
expect to see a lot of people. In addition, scattered houses intrude on
the shoreline all around the pond. Though paddling here will not be a
wilderness experience, enjoying the water and wildlife in the early
morning or before or after the main summer season can prove quite
rewarding. The pair of nesting loons we saw here suggests that it
never gets too crowded, because repeated human disturbance drives
loons away.

Several attractive islands add scenic character to Jones Pond, and
beautiful mosses and lichens festoon the huge granite boulders on the
far shore. The pond is surrounded by a mature mixed canopy with a
well-developed understory. While there is good diversity in the understory, sweet gale dominates the shoreline. Where it is plentiful pinch
off a few leaves and enjoy the pungent aroma.

According to local fishermen, there are supposed to be some
huge brown trout lurking in the depths of Jones Pond, as well as a
healthy population of smallmouth bass. Because of the pond's close
proximity to salt water, large numbers of gulls, both herring and great
black-backed, appear, along with double-crested cormorants, great
blue herons, and belted kingfishers. We heard and saw yellow and
chestnut-sided warblers, American redstarts, and song sparrows along
the shoreline. At the base of the southeast arm, you will see lots of
beaver activity.

The town park at the boat access has several picnic tables, grills,
benches looking out over the lake, and a small building with bath-

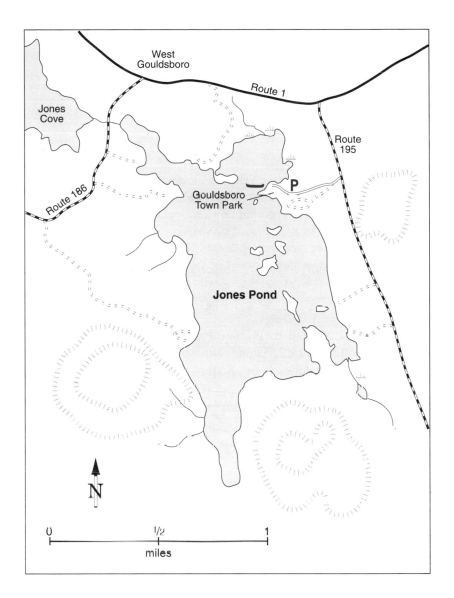

rooms, screens, and a wood stove. The immediate vicinity is covered with blooming wildflowers in the spring.

Getting There

From Ellsworth, drive east on Route 1. Turn right at the junction with Route 195 in Gouldsboro. Go 0.4 mile and turn right. Take another immediate right through the gate into the Gouldsboro Town Park. The boat launch is 0.3 mile down this road.

Donnell Pond
Franklin and T9SD

MAPS
  Maine Atlas: Map 24
  USGS Quadrangle: Sullivan
INFORMATION
  Area: 1,120 acres; maximum depth: 119 feet
  Prominent fish species: salmon, lake trout, brook trout, white
  perch, yellow perch, and chain pickerel
  Bureau of Public Lands, Maine Department of Conservation, State
  House Station 22, Augusta, ME 04333; 207-289-3061
  Fire permits: Maine Forest Service, Down East District (207-434-
  2621) or Central Region Headquarters (207-827-6191)

Don't be too discouraged by the development along the western arm
of Donnell Pond. Past Little Island, Donnell Pond is largely undeveloped and a superb paddling spot on all but the busiest summer weekends—when motorboats, jet skis, and water skiers can be oppressive.
To enjoy fully the beauty of Donnell Pond, paddle here on weekdays,
or after Labor Day—the autumn is our favorite time for canoeing—
when the bugs and most of the people are gone.

A deep, rocky pond covering more than a thousand acres, Donnell Pond is not very productive biologically (which keeps the water
exceptionally clear). Granite boulders, bedrock, and sand beaches
define much of the shoreline, with thick woodland extending back
from the shore. The pond nestles beneath several mountains that rise
up a thousand feet from the water's surface. About a mile east of the
boat access you will come to a cluster of islands. Great slabs of
exposed granite bedrock extending down into the water dominate the
largest of these, which is appropriately named Mile Island. This is a
superb picnic spot.

Geologically, Donnell Pond lies in the center of a massive
granitic intrusion that extends over a seventy-square-mile area. The
granite, rich in quartz and feldspar, weathers into a coarse, well-
drained, acidic soil. This soil leads to generally dry conditions and
vegetation prone to fires. Researchers believe that fires contributed to
the exposed "balds" on Schoodic and Black mountains. A number of
plant species are at the northern limit of their ranges here, including

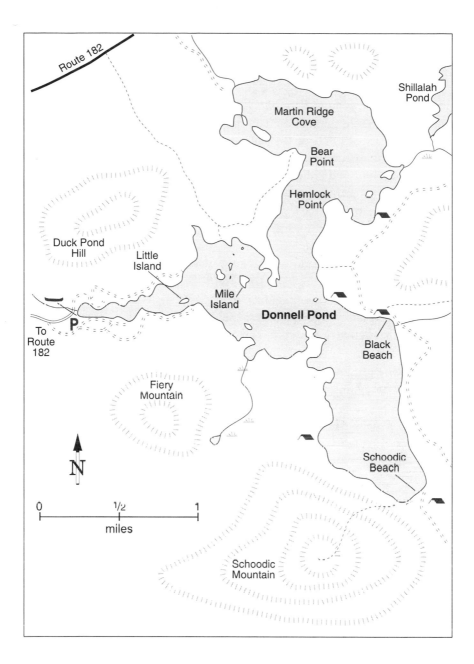

bayberry, common juniper, golden heather, and highbush blueberry. The Schoodic and Black mountain balds support a number of rare plant species.

As many as three pairs of loons nest here, and osprey have nested in a dead spruce along the pond in recent years. Bald eagles, though frequently seen here, do not now nest near the pond. For anglers, Donnell Pond's deep, clear waters offer cold-water fishing opportunities. The pond harbors salmon, white perch, lake trout, brook trout, yellow perch, chain pickerel, alewives, and smelt, though it is not known as an easy place for fishing. Salmon are stocked annually to supplement the native landlocked population; lake-trout stocking was stopped in 1989.

At the south end of the lake, roughly three miles from the boat access, is Schoodic Bay and the Schoodic Beach day-use area. Coarse, pebbly granite sand comprises this broad natural beach. There are picnic tables and outhouses here, plus a camping area just to the east with multiple campsites. Rising from the pond to the south is Schoodic Mountain (1,069 feet); a trail extends up the mountain from the day-use area. An equally nice beach and camping area, Black Beach, can be found on the east side of the pond where Redman Brook flows in. Several other individual campsites, with picnic tables and pit toilets, are scattered around the pond (see map).

We are lucky that Donnell Pond is still as nice as it is. A land speculator, Patten Corporation, purchased much of the surrounding land in the late 1980s and planned to develop it with hundreds (or thousands) of vacation homes. Fortunately, conservation groups and the state of Maine got wind of the impending loss, and in 1988 the state acquired approximately 7,000 acres around the pond, including roughly two-thirds of the shoreline and land to the east and south, through a complex five-way land swap. In fact, this land transaction was one of the catalysts for the formation of the Northern Forest campaign by several environmental/outdoors organizations in the Northeast, including the Appalachian Mountain Club.

While Donnell Pond narrowly escaped large-scale development that would have ruined its beauty and tranquillity, any warm, sunny, summer weekend will remind paddlers that the pond still sees heavy use by motorboaters. To remain a nice place for paddling, Donnell Pond needs a local initiative to restrict motorboat access. When we visited here the boat ramp was in poor shape and really suitable only for hand-carried boats (which is great), but not much "improvement" would be needed to make the ramp readily accessible to big trailered boats—which could be devastating to Donnell Pond and the wonderful campsites situated around its shores. We would love to see a local group petition the state for restrictions on boat access or use at Donnell Pond. Restricting the access to carry-in boats only would be our first priority, then we'd hope to see a horsepower restriction on the pond and a prohibition on personal watercraft (jet skis). Ultimately, an outright ban on gasoline-powered boats would be our goal, but we recognize the unlikelihood of that happening.

Hiking opportunities abound at Donnell Pond. As noted above, a trail to Schoodic Mountain begins at Schoodic Beach at the south end of the pond, and a network of trails from Black Beach on the eastern shore leads to Black Mountain and Wizard Pond, east of Donnell Pond. Near Wizard Pond is a twenty-one-acre stand of old-growth red spruce. In addition to these maintained trails, many old logging roads crisscross the public lands east of the pond.

Camping is exceptional around the pond. Currently, there are no "fire-safe" campsites on Donnell Pond. If you want to build an open fire, you must obtain a fire permit from the Maine Forest Service (no fire permits are required for camp stoves). We expect permitted campfire sites to be built in the future, though the fire risk in this area means campers should be extremely careful with open fires. Always extinguish fires completely after use, and do not leave fires unattended.

Getting There

To reach Donnell Pond from points west and south, take coastal Route 1 west from Ellsworth toward Sullivan. Turn left (northeast) on Route 182 a few miles outside of Ellsworth. Drive on 182 for approximately 7.3 miles (1.4 miles past the fork where Route 200 south splits off from 182), and turn right onto an unmarked, paved side road. After 0.2 mile take the right fork. This road turns to gravel after another half-mile, and 1.4 miles from Route 182 you will reach another fork. Take the left fork here, reaching the boat access in another 0.2 mile. There is parking space for about a half-dozen cars by the boat access.

Scammon Pond
Eastbrook

MAPS
   Maine Atlas: Map 24
   USGS Quadrangles: Eastbrook and Molasses Pond
INFORMATION
   Information on area, depth, and prominent fish species not available.

Scammon Pond is a beautiful place to paddle and well worth exploring. There is no development, as it is maintained by the state as the Lyle Frost Wildlife Management Area. It is also unlikely that you will see many boaters here, given that the pond is shallow, weed filled, and dotted with stumps and boulders. We would love to have seen the size of the glacier that deposited the huge granite boulders lining the shore. It is really hard to paddle here and not run into an occasional submerged stump or granite boulder. We recommend that you go slowly and enjoy the birds, plants, and animals of this quiet and scenic spot.

Aquatic vegetation, stumps, and granite boulders keep motorboats out of Scammon Pond.

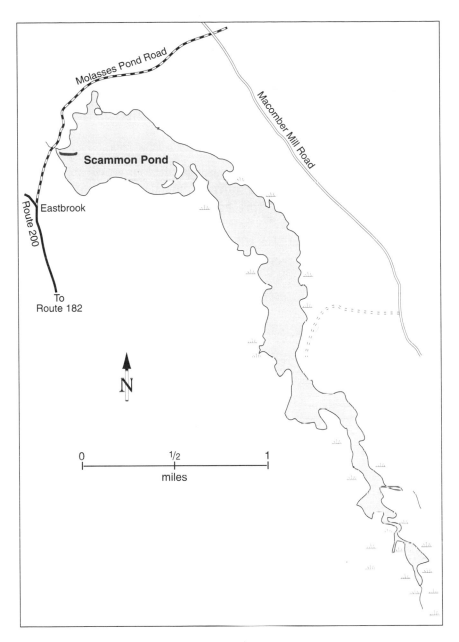

There are a few enormous, flat-topped boulders protruding from the water that would make great picnic spots. On hot, sunny days, a better picnic spot would be under the pines on the points on either shore where the pond narrows, about a mile from the boat access.

The shore is lined with trees of many species, and the understory is quite dense. Aquatic vegetation is everywhere, including acres of fragrant water lily, and we found lots of sundews growing on exposed stumps and on the hummocks. This boggy area is ideal habitat for carnivorous plants, and pitcher plants were also in abundance.

Although pitcher plants digest unlucky insects that enter the water-filled tubular leaves, for some mysterious reason they do not digest the larvae of one species of mosquito. Why does this mosquito lay its eggs in pitcher plants when there is obviously stagnant or slow-moving water in every conceivable location in Maine? It is probably because there are no dragonfly or other predacious insect larvae, or small fish or bladderworts in the pitchers, to eat the mosquito larvae. In the competition for space, this mosquito seems to have done well. We think anyone who paddles in Maine in the spring will agree the next target for plant geneticists should be to develop a strain of pitcher plants that produces enzymes capable of surmounting all mosquito larvae's defense mechanisms.

Ducks are everywhere, feeding among the aquatic plants, and we saw several osprey fishing. Ravens, cedar waxwings, and swallows cavorted over the water, while several great blue herons fished the shoreline. We thought we heard young birds calling from a great blue heron rookery, but we could not locate the nests among the dense rows of trees lining the shore.

The upper end of the pond contains several mammoth beaver lodges. Keep an eye out for muskrats harvesting grasses in the shallows. As you pass into the upper reaches of the pond, it narrows considerably, and you have to wend your way through meandering channels filled with pickerelweed and dense patches of water lily. After paddling about three-quarters of the way to the end of the pond, you will have to portage over a beaver dam to gain access to the rest.

Getting There

From Ellsworth, take Route 1 east for a few miles until Route 182 goes left. Take Route 182 to the junction with Route 200. Go left on Route 200 to the town of Eastbrook. At the fork in town, go right on a paved road (Molasses Pond Road) for 0.3 mile to the boat access on the right. There is a little concrete dam at the end of the parking area, making it quite easy to lower your boat into the water.

Carnivorous Plants
The Tables Get Turned

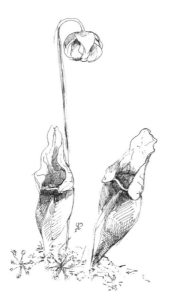

Carnivorous plants are fascinating—and a common sight as you paddle through the marshy sections of Maine's lakes and ponds. Their specialized adaptations make them one of nature's true wonders and make us wonder how their meat-eating habit evolved.

For many people, evolution brings to mind Darwin's finches of the Galapagos Islands. Supposedly, a few ancestral birds landed on the Galapagos Archipelago. Their offspring then radiated out among the widely scattered islands and encountered different types of seeds. In order to be successful seed predators, the birds on one island developed larger beaks and bodies to accommodate larger seeds, while another set of birds on a different island developed smaller beaks and bodies to feed on smaller seeds. When altered bird forms encountered each other later, their body morphologies were driven further apart by the need not to compete for the same food resources. Careful observations in this decade have lent credence to this theory, as one well-studied species of Darwin's finch evolved a different beak size as a direct result of changing seed resources. This is an example of divergent evolution, where an ancestral species evolved into several separate species, each with specialized adaptations.

Having published in 1875 a volume entitled *Insectivorous Plants*—a book that catalogued the known information on carnivorous plants—Darwin also figures prominently in this field. In contrast to the divergent evolution of Darwin's finches, however, carnivory in plants apparently resulted from convergent evolution: the taking on of similar traits among unrelated species. Carnivory in plants exists in many different, completely unrelated plant families on nearly every continent. These plants have two characteristics in common: They live in mineral-poor soils and so supplement the meager available soil nutrients with those from animals, and they use modified leaves to trap food.

Two main capture strategies have evolved: active and passive. Most people would recognize the active capture strategy of the Venus flytrap, a plant that grows in sandy soils in a narrow band along the coastal border of North Carolina and South Carolina. The plant's modified leaves form a bi-lobed trap. When an insect lands in the trap and touches the protruding hairs, the sides slam shut, sandwiching the hapless insect. The plant then secretes enzymes to aid digestion, a strategy common to most but not all carnivorous plants. (Unfortunately, this fascinating plant is threatened with extinction because of collection.)

Few other carnivorous plants have developed active capture strategies, but one that has grows abundantly—sometimes forming dense mats—in the quiet, shallow marshes and bogs of Maine: bladderworts of the genus *Utricularia*. Bladderwort leaves, described more fully below, consist of minute bladders that, upon stimulation, inflate and ingest insect larvae and other organisms, to be digested by the plant's enzymes.

Passive capture strategies have taken two main paths among the remaining carnivorous plants of Maine. Pitcher plants—*Sarracenia purpurea*—collect rainwater in their funnel-shaped modified leaves. Insects, attracted to nectar secreted around the top of the pitcher, fall in. Stiff, downward-pointing hairs in the plant keep most insects from climbing back out. Eventually the insects drown, and a combination of plant and bacterial enzymes reduces the insects to absorbable nutrients.

Another passive-capture plant uses sticky surfaces to ensnare insects. Sundews (genus *Drosera*) form tiny rosettes that protrude from a central root.

Stalked glands of two types cover the surface of the modified leaves. One type secretes a sticky substance that glistens like dew in the sun, giving the plant its name. Entrapped insects, drawn initially by the nectarlike secretions, get digested by enzymes secreted by the second set of glands.

Each of the plants described above—bladderworts, pitcher plants, and sundews—captures its intended victims in a different way, but they all do so because, in the nutrient-poor marshes and bogs of Maine, absorbing nitrogen and other minerals from insects and other prey gives them a selective advantage over other plants.

Do not be fooled by the black, fertile-looking soils of marshes and swamps. Black dirt like this in Iowa means fertile soil, but in bogs it usually means black carbon from undecomposed plants. The tea-colored water, laden with organic acids from decaying vegetation and supplemented by acid rain, effectively washes out the minerals necessary for plant growth. Although the two primary nutrients supporting plant growth—carbon dioxide and water—remain plentiful, nitrogen, phosphorus, potassium, and other important elements get leached out or bound up in the underlying layers of sphagnum and peat. Carnivorous plants,

with their diet of insects and other organisms, supplement the lost nutrients, making them effective competitors in the bog ecosystem.

Bladderworts: Bladderworts grow in quiet, shallow waters or in shoreline muck. Keep an eye out for small yellow or purple snapdragonlike flowers, leading on short stalks to their carnivorous underwater bladders. The vast majority of the plant lives underwater in dense, feathery mats, bearing hundreds of tiny (0.02 to 0.1 inch long), bulbous traps that are the plant's leaves. The bladders have two concave sides and a trapdoor. When an insect larva or other small organism bumps into the door's guard hairs, the bladder's sides pop out, creating suction, the door swings open, and water along with the hapless critter get sucked in. All of this occurs in about 1/500 of a second, followed by slow digestion by plant enzymes.

In most ponds, mosquito larvae form the bulk of the bladderwort diet, but the plant also ingests other insect larvae, rotifers, protozoans, small crustaceans, and even tiny tadpoles. As the animal is digested, its remains get absorbed by plant tissues, causing the trap's sides to go concave again, readying for its next meal. If the prey is small, chances are that new prey will be captured before the first is fully digested. If it is large, such as a tiny tadpole, the door will close around the organism, and part of it will get digested. The next time the hairs get triggered, the plant ingests more of the organism, eventually sucking it all in.

Several species of bladderwort grow in Maine, including two with purple flowers, one aquatic and one terrestrial, and possibly as many as ten species with yellow flowers, mostly aquatic but including at least two terrestrials. We usually notice the presence of these plants when we see their snapdragonlike flowers protruding a few inches above the water's surface. Their dense underwater mats attest to their successful adaptation to nutrient-poor waters. If you lift a mat out of the water and listen carefully, you may hear crackling as the bladders suck in air instead of their intended prey.

Pitcher Plants: Although seven other species of *Sarracenia* pitcher plant exist in North America, the northern pitcher plant, *Sarracenia purpurea,* has the widest distribution, growing from British Columbia to Nova Scotia, southward through the Great Lakes region and down the eastern coastal plain, crossing the Florida panhandle to the Mississippi River. Initially green

in the spring, the pitcher plant's funnel-shaped leaves turn progressively more purple, becoming deep maroon in the fall, and then return to green again in the spring. During midseason, the red veins of the hood stand in stark contrast to the mostly green pitchers. Flowering occurs in June and July in Maine, and single reddish flowers, borne on stout stalks, tower about a foot over the cluster of pitchers.

In contrast to most other species, the northern pitcher plant does not have a hood to keep rain out. The curved pitchers recline, allowing rain to fall freely into the open hood. Because of this dilution of the pitcher's contents, insects drown well before digestion occurs. The stiff, downward-pointing hairs in the plant's throat keep insects from climbing back out, and the relatively narrow funnel leaves little room for airborne escape. The upper pitcher walls sport a waxy coating, making for slippery footing. A combination of plant and bacterial enzymes degrade the unlucky insects, and their nutrients pass easily through the unwaxed surface of the lower pitcher.

Amazingly, several different types of organisms can live in the pitchers, unharmed by the digestive juices. One harmless genus of mosquito, *Wyeomyia,* lives its aquatic life cycle in the pitcher, and other insects are able to escape by walking up the waxy cuticle and out over the downward-pointing hairs.

Pitcher plants usually grow near water, often with their roots submerged. Inexorably, plant material accumulates and marshes start to fill in. As shrubs and small trees begin to grow on the elevated ground, the pitcher plants get crowded out. Fortunately, with all the remaining water in bogs and marshes in Maine, pitcher plants will remain for us to enjoy for quite some time.

Sundews: The best way to find sundews is to look for the glistening drops at the ends of their traps. Because they are so small—the smallest plants may be only an inch across—sundews are easily overlooked. Four species occur in Maine, but two grow only in the most northern reaches. We describe the most common species here: roundleaf sundew (*Drosera rotundifolia*).

This remarkable plant grows mainly in sphagnum bogs, from Alaska to northern California, across the Canadian Rockies and plains, through the Great Lakes, north throughout Labrador, south to Chesapeake Bay, and down through the Appalachians. The same plant grows in Europe as well, where Darwin studied it in detail, devoting much of his book *Insectivorous Plants* to this one species. The entire plant averages about three inches across and about an inch high, and all of its leaves are modified into sticky traps. A short leaf stalk ends in a flattened oval pad covered with red, stalked glands. The longer glands secrete a sticky fluid, while the shorter glands secrete digestive enzymes. Insects, attracted to the nectarlike secretions, become trapped. Slowly, imperceptibly, the pad edges roll over slightly, placing the insect in contact with the digestive juices.

The usually white but sometimes pink flowers hover well above the plant's leaves, borne on a slender stalk. Although they are easy to miss, a little careful looking on sphagnum mats will show up many of these reddish rosettes. You should also see several small insects in various stages of digestion. And you, too, can wonder about how these plants developed the incredible ability to supplement the meager amount of available nutrients with those from insect prey.

Bog Brook Flowage
Beddington and Deblois

MAPS
Maine Atlas: Map 25
USGS Quadrangles: Northeast Bluff and Lead Mountain

INFORMATION
Information on area, depth, and prominent fish species not available.

Bog Brook Flowage can only be described with superlatives. Completely undeveloped, seldom visited, and maintained as a Maine Wildlife Management Area, it would take an entire day to explore every nook and cranny of this small, three-mile-long lake. Numerous side channels and coves extend, seemingly in every direction, away from the open water in the main channel.

True to the area's name, bog shrubbery dominates the shoreline, including bog rosemary, sweet gale, rhodora, cranberry, leather leaf, and Labrador tea. While exploring the coves, you will have to thread your way through numerous small islands of these plants. Large

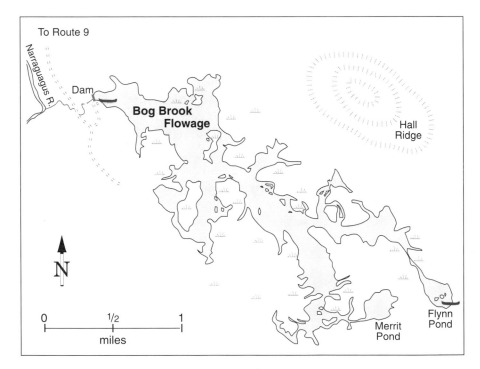

John breaks in a new sea kayak paddling over this beaver dam between Flynn Pond and Bog Brook Flowage.

patches of bullhead lilies and other aquatic vegetation poke up through the shallow water of the coves. Keep an eye out for small yellow, snapdragonlike bladderwort flowers, leading on short stalks to carnivorous underwater bladders that suck in and digest (all too few) mosquito larvae.

The vast majority of the plant lives underwater in dense, feathery mats, bearing hundreds of tiny (0.02 to 0.1 inches long), bulbous traps that are the plant's leaves. When an insect larva or small animal bumps into the trigger hairs, a small door opens and the concave sides of the trap inflate, sucking in water along with the hapless animal. Ingestion occurs in about 1/500 of a second, followed by several days of digestion by plant enzymes. If you lift a mat out of the water and listen carefully, you may hear crackling as the bladders suck in air instead of their intended prey. In most ponds, mosquito larvae form the bulk of the diet, but the plants also ingest other insect larvae, rotifers, protozoans, small crustaceans, and even tiny tadpoles.

As you paddle up the left side, look for osprey nests, two of which are almost on the water. A great blue heron rookery occupies another extensive patch of dead trees. If you paddle here in the spring or early summer, enjoy these wonders with binoculars, as paddling too close may interfere with nesting or interrupt feeding the young. Large numbers of black ducks and wood ducks feed in the shallows. There are a couple pairs of nesting loons as well.

As you paddle through boggy areas, keep an eye out for bobolinks, one of the few birds that is black underneath and brightly colored on the back, in this case yellow and white. The black tern, another rare marsh bird that is also black underneath, inhabits these wetlands as well. We also saw upland sandpipers, increasingly rare in the East, strolling about the blueberry fields on the way in. Northern harriers cruise these same fields, tilting back and forth, patiently waiting to pounce on rodents that do not have the good sense to be under cover in the middle of the day.

Getting There

Take Route 9 (Air Line Road) east from Bangor; drive seemingly forever (almost to Calais on the New Brunswick border). After Route 193 turns off to the right, continue on Route 9 for 1–2 miles and, just after crossing the Narraguagus River, turn right on a gravel road. Note your mileage here. Stay on the main road. Bear right at a fork in 2.0 miles. You should pass an open gate in 4.2 miles, then cross over a creek in 5.5 miles. A few hundred yards past the bridge, turn left and drive up a slight rise where you can park and carry your canoe down to the water.

There is another access on Flynn Pond at the southeast tip of Bog Brook Flowage. While we found that access eventually, it was exceedingly difficult and required miles of driving through a myriad of blueberry fields.

Great Pond

Great Pond

MAPS
    Maine Atlas: Map 34
    USGS Quadrangle: Great Pond

INFORMATION
    Area: 679 acres; maximum depth: 34 feet
    Prominent fish species: brown trout, smallmouth bass, yellow
    perch, and chain pickerel; brook trout in the streams
    Fire permits: Maine Forest Service, Downeast District (207-434-
    2621) or Central Region Headquarters (207-827-6191)

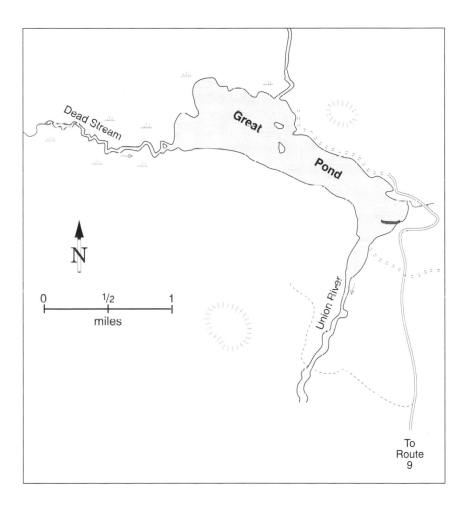

Great Pond is the site of the Dow Pines Air Force Recreation Area, but when we paddled here there were few visitors in evidence. We saw one other boat, but most of the time we paddled in complete solitude. Great Pond also marks the beginning of the West Branch of the Union River trip. The West Branch starts just around a bend to the left from the Dow Pines access site. If you paddle down this stream, it is unlikely that you will be able to paddle back up against the substantial current at the pond outlet. Supposedly, the river turns to flatwater shortly after leaving the pond, but we did not explore this.

The hillsides and islands here are covered primarily with deciduous vegetation, with only a few scattered pines, making us wonder about the name of the recreation area. It is a scenic spot, with two nice tree-covered islands.

The best time to paddle here is in the evening or very early morning, especially up the Dead Stream inlet at the west end of the lake. We paddled here during a beautiful sunset on a warm, calm evening, when the water's surface was like glass. At nearly every bend in the meandering stream we came across beavers, who protested our presence with loud tail slaps. Several waited until we got right up to them before sounding the alarm and diving for cover, splashing us with water. We had such a good time that we waited until well after sunset to paddle back, our way lighted by alpenglow on the hillsides, and we arrived back at the boat access well after dark.

Unless you get caught up watching the antics of the resident beaver population, it should not take more than a few hours to explore all of Great Pond. We also do not know how to predict when the recreation area might be overrun with air force personnel; we paddled alone here on the Saturday of Labor Day weekend. But Great Pond is so easy to get to, with paved roads the whole way from nearby Bangor, that it is well worth visiting some late afternoon.

Getting There

From Bangor, take Route 9 east for about 26 miles to the junction with Route 179, just after crossing into Aurora Township. From this junction, stay on Route 9 for 1.6 miles, and turn left onto Great Pond Road. Follow this paved road for 7.2 miles to the Dow Pines boat access. Park near the boat access so you do not block any drives or entrances.

Mopang Lakes

Deveraux Twp.

MAPS
  Maine Atlas: Maps 25 and 35
  USGS Quadrangles: Peaked Mountain and Quillpig Mountain
INFORMATION
  Second Mopang area: 145 acres; maximum depth: 20 feet
  Prominent fish species: white perch and chain pickerel
  Fire permits: Maine Forest Service, Downeast District (207-434-
    2621) or Central Region Headquarters (207-827-6191)

Mopang Lake and Second Mopang Lake are among the many great paddling lakes in Washington County, Maine. This county, also known as Sunrise County, feels the morning rays of sun before anywhere else in the United States. The larger lake is somewhat bell shaped, with a sizable peninsula (almost an island) near the south end and numerous islands and large boulders near the north end. Typical Maine trees populate the shore: red spruce, northern white cedar, white pine, hemlock, some red pine, paper birch, and maple. The shoreline overflows with sweet gale, leather leaf, rhodora (a beautiful pink wild azalea that blooms in May), alder, and highbush blueberry. Mopang Second Lake resembles its larger neighbor, but has a more remote feeling to it.

In the spring, one can paddle upstream from Second Mopang into Mopang, especially if you have a small canoe. Pick your way carefully between the rocks as you paddle up the briskly flowing small connecting creek. We only paddled in one direction, upstream; going downstream, you would go too fast with the current and almost certainly scratch your canoe. The alternative is to carry your canoe either through the water or through the brush and trees beside it. Several very nice campsites hide along the southeastern end of Second Mopang, where there is also a hard-to-find and rough access road.

Near the outlet from Mopang Lake, along the south shore, a white pine sports a large nest in a fork near the top. Though we did not see any birds when paddling here, this is almost certainly an osprey nest. We saw two species of terns here: the more prevalent common tern (which is no longer very common throughout most of its range) and the distinctive black tern, which, as its name suggests, is nearly solid black, with a white undertail patch and dark, silvery

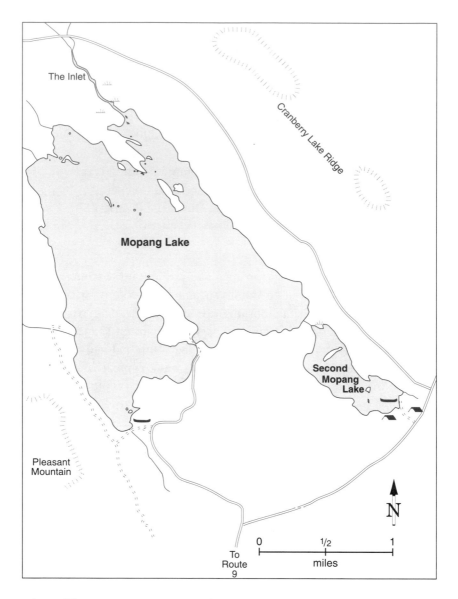

wings. The common tern nests in small colonies on some of the large protruding boulders in the northern half of the lake. During nesting season, keep your distance so as not to disturb this graceful black-capped, red-billed bird. At the north end in the marshy inlet, you may see wood ducks, mergansers, and other waterfowl. Like all lakes and ponds in the region, you are almost certain to see (or hear) the resident loons. We noticed at least three pairs on the two lakes.

A very coarse pegmatite granite dominates the rocky shoreline. This mostly black-and-white granite has very large and easily visible

common tern

crystals of biotite mica, feldspar, and quartz. The large size of the crystals indicates that the granite formed deep underground where the molten magma cooled very, very slowly.

For camping, one of the nicest places on the main lake is the neck connecting the large peninsula near the southern end. Sandy coves occur on both sides of this neck, with pleasant tenting sites under the tall conifers and several trails for exploring the area and observing the numerous wildflowers: painted trillium, pink lady's slipper, wild sarsaparilla, and bunchberry, to mention a few. A permit is required for open fires.

Getting There

To reach the larger Mopang Lake, take Route 9 (Air Line Road) east from Bangor. After passing the junction with Route 193 south, drive another 6.6 miles. Then turn left onto a gravel forest road with signs identifying this as Champion Paper land. In 1.3 miles take the left fork, and in another 1.2 miles you will reach the boat access, with a wide beach area for boat launching.

To reach Second Mopang Lake, follow directions as above, except bear right at the fork you reach 1.3 miles from Route 9. Then drive 1.7 miles, and turn left onto a somewhat hidden, unmarked, and unmaintained dirt road (if you come to a major gravel road going off to the left, you have gone about 0.2 mile too far). Do not try to drive this way if your vehicle has low ground clearance. Driving into Second Mopang you need to stay to the right at one fork, and you will reach the lake 0.3 mile from the main gravel road.

Rocky, Round, and Second Lakes
T18 ED BPP

MAPS

    Maine Atlas: Map 26

    USGS Quadrangles: Long Lake and Whiting

INFORMATION

    Area: 1,555 acres; maximum depth: 37 feet

    Prominent fish species: white perch and chain pickerel, with a few large smallmouth bass, and a few salmon in the winter; small brook trout in the Southern Inlet

    Bureau of Public Lands, Maine Department of Conservation, State House Station 22, Augusta, ME 04333; (207-454-7708.)

    Fire permits: Maine Forest Service, Downeast District (207-434-2621) or Central Region Headquarters (207-827-6191)

Which one of these three lakes you choose to paddle depends on what type of trip you have in mind and to a certain extent on the weather. Rocky Lake and its inlet and outlet streams include lots of interesting water to paddle. Round Lake is privately owned and has little to offer compared to the other two lakes, but we include it here because it is part of the East Machias River trip (see description under Pocomoonshine Lake); it provides an alternate access both to Rocky Lake and to Second Lake. Although we did not paddle Second Lake, we include a short description here because it is four-fifths owned by the state of Maine and has no development. Most of this section describes Rocky Lake.

First, Rocky Lake: This is a big, long lake, about four and a half miles long. The southern two-thirds is owned and maintained for recreation by the state of Maine. Several access points allow flexibility in planning a trip—an important point when north or south winds roll deep swells and whitecaps up or down this north-south oriented lake. In calm or modest wind conditions, by all means paddle Rocky Lake.

Start from the main access point at Mud Landing. As you leave the inlet at the end of Mud Landing, the left (southeast) shore sports an extensive stand of white cedar that provides an important wintering yard for deer. The water is quite shallow, and true to the lake's name, rocks are everywhere: lining the shore, protruding from the water, and lurking just beneath the surface. These rocks keep down the number of high-speed boats. Generally, you will see only other paddlers and a few fishermen with small outboards. One can still have a true wilder-

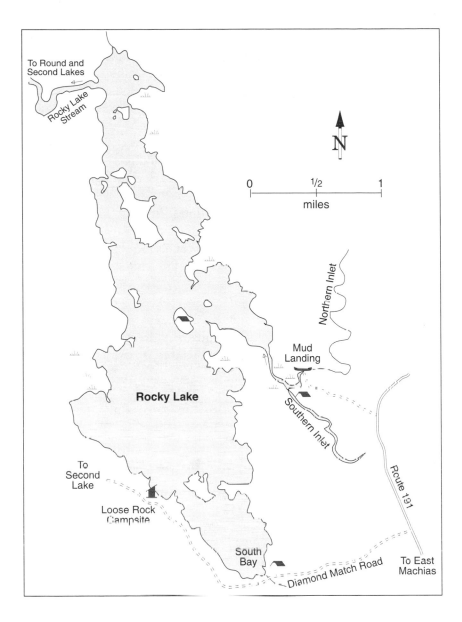

ness experience here, and it is a great location for looking at plants and wildlife.

You can camp at both access points: Mud Landing and South Bay. Along the southwestern shore at Loose Rock, you will find a third official campsite with picnic table, outhouse, and lean-to. In addition to the official campsites, several informal campsites exist on islands and at various points along the shore. You do not need a campfire permit at the Mud Landing site, but you do at all other locations.

If you have enough time, explore Rocky Lake Stream at the northwest end of the lake. Paddling down Rocky Lake Stream, you will come to Northern Stream, which enters from the right (north). Take a side-trip up Northern Stream, or continue downstream to the East Machias River, where you can turn left and paddle downstream to Second Lake, a distance of about nine miles from Mud Landing. Not having paddled all the way to Second Lake, we are not sure about water conditions, especially at Munson Rips; paddling back upstream may be difficult. However, if you leave a car at Second Lake, you can make this a one-way trip.

We paddled on Rocky Lake three times: in May, July, and September. In May, a severe wind and driving rain kept us from leaving the inlet at the end of the Mud Landing boat access. In July, the wind barely rippled the water, but in September the whitecaps broke over the bow as we dipped through two-foot swells that almost—and should have—kept us off the lake. If the wind keeps you off the main lake or if you want some solitude, by all means paddle from Mud Landing to the right up the Northern Inlet or to the left up the Southern Inlet. This will take you back into remote, marshy areas, filled with plants and wildlife.

If you paddle up the Southern Inlet, you will have to portage over a beaver dam almost immediately. After we crossed the dam it was smooth sailing up the meandering stream—though, as you know, beavers are always at work, and other dams may appear. The whole area is quite boggy, mainly with shrub vegetation, but it contains occasional stands of dwarfed red maple and some good-sized tamarack. Alder, paper birch, aspen, and red maple dominate the shoreline farther back, and white pine, spruce, and many other tree species appear back in the woods. We paddled more than a mile into the marsh until our way was blocked by a second beaver dam. We turned around here, but you certainly could go farther.

We also paddled up the Northern Inlet some distance, until we reached the first beaver dam. We leave it to you to explore this area more fully.

If the wind blows from the south, as it often does during the summer, you can launch from the southern tip of Rocky Lake and hope the winds abate for your return (the launch site is called South Bay; see directions below). Alternatively, you could put in at Round Lake on the East Machias River and paddle to Rocky Lake on streams generally unaffected by wind. From the Round Lake boat access at the outlet, paddle about a mile down the East Machias River; then turn left and paddle up Rocky Lake Stream. After about another mile, Northern Stream enters from the left and may be paddled as well. Except for the first hundred feet after the Round Lake boat access, none of this water has any current to speak of, and most of the time it is hard to tell whether you are paddling upstream or down. This route takes you through undisturbed wilderness, with loads of beaver activity, thick marsh vegetation, extensive alder swamps, and excellent moose habitat.

Coming out of Round Lake, instead of turning into Rocky Lake Stream, if you continue down the East Machias River you will come shortly to Second Lake, which has a couple of informal campsites. In the area just above Second Lake, bald eagles have nested over the years. When we paddled here in July, we started our trip at Pocomoonshine Lake, traversing the upper portion of the East Machias River trip, taking out at Rocky Lake (see Pocomoonshine Lake for further information). Second Lake can be reached by the Diamond Match Road with a several-hundred-foot portage down to the lake (see directions below).

Getting There

From East Machias, at the junction of Routes 1 and 191, turn onto Route 191 north. After about 7.5 miles, look for a blue sign on the right that says Rocky Lake Unit; if you turn left here onto a dirt road, it will take you 1.7 miles (go right at the fork at 1.6 miles) to a campsite and a primitive, muddy boat-launch area on the very southern tip (South Bay) of the lake. A fire permit is required here. This road, the Diamond Match Road, continues on to Second Lake and ends in a small parking area with a several-hundred-foot portage down to the lake.

To get to Mud Landing on the Northern Inlet to Rocky Lake, continue on Route 191 to the next blue sign, at 8.7 miles from Route 1 in East Machias. Turn left onto a 0.7 mile-long dirt access road that ends at Mud Landing. There is a campsite here at the top of a knoll on the left under some tall white pines. No fire permit is required.

Directions to Round Lake: From Mud Landing, go back out to Route 191 and turn left. Take an immediate left onto a good gravel road heading north. After six or seven miles, watch for two small bridges in quick succession and a road turning back to the left. Follow the signs to Hatts, some very nice people from Machias who own a cottage on the southern tip of Round Lake. Go past all of the cottages to the end of the road at the East Machias River.

Rocky Lake II
Whiting, Marion Twp.

MAPS
> **Maine Atlas:** Map 26
> **USGS Quadrangles:** Long Lake and Whiting

INFORMATION
> **Area:** 1,126 acres; maximum depth: 33 feet
> **Prominent fish species:** brook trout (primarily in the winter) and yellow perch
> **Fire permits:** Maine Forest Service, Downeast District (207-434-2621) or Central Region Headquarters (207-827-6191)

Why someone would give two lakes within eight miles of each other the same name—Rocky Lake in this case—is beyond us. To keep them separate, we affectionately call them Rocky I and Rocky II. Maybe affectionately is the wrong word given the large number of submerged rocks and the general shallow character of both. This lake—Rocky II—is east of Machias. Rocky I is north of Machias (see preceding section).

Bunchberry, Cornus canadensis, *a member of the dogwood family, is a low-growing spring wildflower that blooms in profusion in the woods around Rocky Lake.*

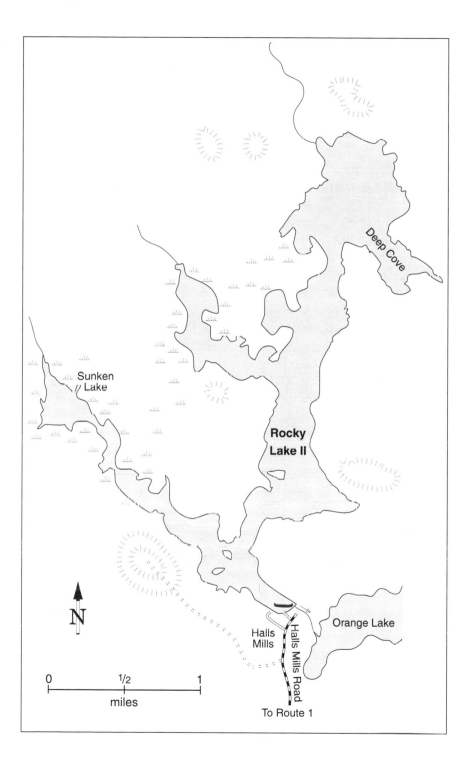

Deep Cove

Sunken
Lake

**Rocky
Lake II**

N

Halls
Mills

Halls Mills Road

Orange Lake

0   1/2   1
miles

To Route 1

The boat access from Halls Mills is on the very southern tip of the lake. As we paddled up this southern arm (albeit during a dry summer), almost every single paddle stroke struck the mud bottom of this heavily vegetated, marshy lake section. We tried to paddle up the northwestern arm to Sunken Lake but had to turn back at about the halfway point because of shallow water. If you are here when the water is a little deeper, it would be well worth the trip up this, the most interesting arm of the lake. The Department of Inland Fisheries and Wildlife claims this waterway is normally at least a few feet deep.

As you look up the waterway with binoculars you will see among the lily pads and pickerelweed a series of evenly spaced beaver lodges. Evidence of beaver cuttings is everywhere, and back up in this remote area would be a good place to look for moose. In this area we saw osprey fishing, one with a fish in its talons, and a pair of Canada geese with a raft of downy goslings.

As you go up the main section of Rocky II, the water is much deeper, accommodating at least one pair of nesting loons. The coves, however, particularly the large one on the left, are shallow and thick with aquatic vegetation. There are a few cottages scattered along this part of the lake, but one gets the impression that Rocky II does not see much traffic.

The best time to paddle here, it would seem, is in the spring when the water is high. That would provide the best chance of getting up to Sunken Lake to look for moose in the early morning or evening hours.

Getting There

Take Route 1 east out of Machias. Start measuring mileage at the junction of Routes 1 and 191. Drive 7.4 miles on Route 1 and turn left onto Halls Mills Road. After 1.9 miles, turn left just before the bridge, just past a green cottage which sits nearly on the road. The boat access is 0.1 mile down this dirt lane.

Chain Lakes (First, Second, and Third)
T26 ED BPP

MAPS
Maine Atlas: Map 35
USGS Quadrangles: Wesley and Clifford Lake

INFORMATION
First Chain Lake area: 336 acres; maximum depth: 31 feet
Second Chain Lake area: 589 acres; maximum depth: 30 feet
Third Chain Lake area: 157 acres; maximum depth: 33 feet
Prominent fish species: white perch, yellow perch, and chain
pickerel
Fire permits: Maine Forest Service, Downeast District (207-434-
2621), St. Croix River District (207-738-2601), or Central
Region Headquarters (207-827-6191)

First, Second, and Third Chain lakes provide very good canoeing, particularly the northern sections between Second and Third lakes and above Third Lake. Because the nicest areas lie some distance from the boat-launch area, we recommend this trip primarily for paddlers seeking exercise or planning to camp. From the boat access on First Chain

*Rhodora, a member of the heath family, puts on a dazzling display of
showy purple flowers before leaf emergence in the spring.*

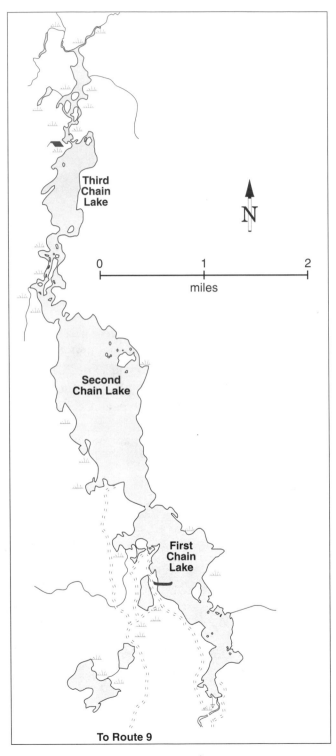

Third
Chain
Lake

N

0   1   2

miles

Second
Chain Lake

First
Chain
Lake

To Route 9

Lake, you will probably want to head north into Second Lake, but if you don't have a full day available, you might want to explore just the southern part of the lake. A few houses stand near the outlet, but there are also some interesting islands to explore, and the shallow water here will discourage most motorboaters. Development is moderate on First Chain Lake.

Second Chain Lake has less development than First Lake, and the *Maine Atlas* shows one primitive campsite along the western shore. A few marshy coves, where you're likely to see great blue herons, wood ducks, moose, and beavers, break up the generally wooded shoreline. According to the *Maine Atlas,* a carry-in access exists halfway up the western shore, but we did not investigate it.

Those interested in wildlife and a wilderness feel should paddle on through Second Lake, into the boggy channel between Second and Third lakes. By the most direct route, this channel is about a mile in length, but if you paddle around islands and explore all the inlets and coves, you could easily paddle two or three times that distance. Watch for the unique northern pitcher plant and the many different heaths that grow here (rhodora, bog laurel, bog rosemary, leather leaf, highbush blueberry, and lowbush blueberry).

A quiet paddle through the marshy connector stream between Second and Third Chain lakes.

Third Chain Lake is also very pretty. There are a few rustic cabins along the western shore near the south end, but that's all. Farther north are some absolutely gorgeous lichen- and moss-covered boulders that extend down into the water. A beautiful campsite perches on a large boulder at the north end of this lake. In all, the Chain Lakes extend about seven miles from northern to southern tips, exclusive of the slowly meandering Chain Brook Stream, which you can explore for another mile or so.

Getting There

Take Route 9 (Air Line Road) east from Bangor. The turnoff to Chain Lakes is on the left approximately 22.2 miles past the junction of Routes 9 and 193 south. If you pass the turnoff (easy to do), you will quickly reach the Wesley–T31 MD BPP Township line. If you miss the turn to Chain Lakes and get to the junction of Route 192, or if you are driving west from Calais or north from Machias, drive west on Route 9 for 3.1 miles from the junction of Routes 9 and 192; the turnoff to Chain Lakes is on the right, just 0.2 mile past the township line between Wesley and T31 MD BPP.

After turning off Route 9, drive north on the gravel road passing a Champion Paper sign. After 0.5 mile, bear right at the fork. Continue for another 1.3 miles and bear right, then bear right again after another 0.1 mile. You will pass a small pond on your left and reach another fork in 0.3 mile. Bear left around the pond and aim for the water; you should find one of two potential boat access points, both of which have ample parking for several cars.

Clifford Lake and Silver Pug Lake
T26 ED BPP and T27 ED BPP

MAPS
　　Maine Atlas: Map 35
　　USGS Quadrangle: Clifford Lake

INFORMATION
　　Clifford Lake area: 954 acres; maximum depth: 50 feet
　　Prominent fish species: smallmouth bass (not many, but trophy
　　　size), white perch, and chain pickerel
　　Fire permits: Maine Forest Service, St. Croix River District (207-
　　　738-2601) or Central Region Headquarters (207-827-6191)

Clifford Lake is a beautiful spot: remote, undeveloped, and small enough that you don't feel too exposed in an open canoe. The lake has a horseshoe configuration, with the west arm connected by a stream to Silver Pug Lake. Clifford Lake has many attractive islands and granite boulders along the shore. The surrounding hillsides are covered with a variety of conifers, including spruce, red and white pine, and hemlock. During our first ten minutes on the East Arm, we saw five loons; as we traveled about the two lakes we saw several more. Unfortunately, because of the overcast and rainy weather, we missed the pair of nesting bald eagles that were in the process of fledging one young eagle in the summer of 1993. Eagles routinely return to the same nest year after year, enlarging it each spring. The nest is on the connector stream between Clifford and Silver Lakes (the locals call this Silver—rather than Silver Pug—Lake).

Both Clifford and Silver Pug are shallow, harboring warm-water fish species, primarily smallmouth bass that hide out among the numerous rocks. Hemlocks with lacy branches hang out over the water. Lime-green lichens festoon the dead trees along shore. Occasional maples and other deciduous trees break the monotony of the conifer-covered hillsides.

We also saw several cormorants; ring-necked, wood, and black ducks; great blue herons; and lots of songbirds. Numerous coves, begging for exploration, line the shore, and you can paddle all the way up to the small dam at the north end of Clifford Lake. This is a wild place that seems to get few visitors, and it will provide hours of paddling in solitude.

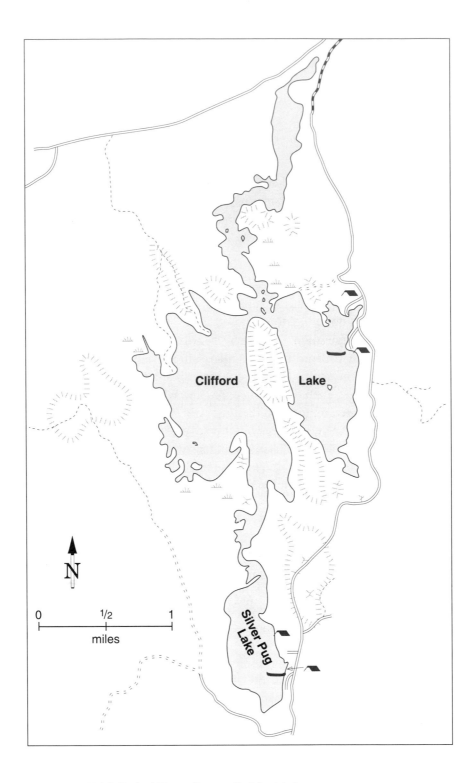

Clifford Lake

Silver Pug Lake

N

0   1/2   1
miles

cormorants

Getting There

From Calais, take Route 9 west to Crawford. From the Crawford picnic area on the East Machias River, go 1.1 miles farther on Route 9, and turn right onto a gravel road at the Wesley town-line sign. The rest of the mileage is given from this junction. At about 4.3 miles up this road you will reach the south end of Possum Pond, with a primitive campsite off to the left, set among hemlock, spruce, and red pine. At 4.6 miles, there is a campsite with a roofed shelter. At 4.8 miles, a road takes off to the left around the southern shore of Silver Pug Lake. At 5.2 miles and for the next few hundred yards, there are a couple of boat-access points and campsites, set among a picturesque grove of small paper birches. The campsite here is a permitted site, meaning you don't need to get a fire permit. For other sites, fire permits must be obtained.

The turnoff to the boat access on Clifford Lake is at 8.4 miles. There is a picnic table, a shelter, and a very nice boat-launch area. Camping is available here as well.

Nicatous Lake

T40MD, T41MD, and T3ND

MAPS

Maine Atlas: Map 34

USGS Quadrangles: Gassabias Lake, Spring Lake, and West Lake

INFORMATION

Area: 5,165 acres; maximum depth: north part, 38 feet; central part, 40 feet; south part, 56 feet

Prominent fish species: smallmouth bass, white perch, and chain pickerel

Fire permits: Maine Forest Service, St. Croix River District (207-738-2601) or Central Region Headquarters (207-827-6191)

Nicatous Lodge, Box 100-SC, Burlington, ME 04417; 207-732-4771. Eight guest cabins.

Nicatous Lake is much more accessible than many of the other large lakes in this region of eastern Maine. But it suffers from the same drawback: because the glaciers crept down out of the north in this region, most large lakes point north-south, meaning that none is paddlable when the wind is blowing strongly from the north or south. Under these conditions, it is best to retreat to the nearby smaller bodies of water, such as Great Pond, Bearce Lake, Folsom, Crooked, and Upper ponds, or Bog Brook Flowage.

The northern and middle sections of Nicatous Lake are the most interesting. There are many, many islands, several campsites, and little development away from the boat access. In contrast, the southern end below the Narrows widens out and consequently has more open water—and more development. In all, the lake is more than nine miles long. It would take several days to explore the entire shoreline and all of the islands.

One gets the feeling that this lake does not get much motorboat traffic, especially on the north end. It is in a beautiful setting, with forested hillsides all around.

Paddling out from the boat access, we were struck by the granite boulders lining the shore and by the white cedars that dominate the shoreline. There are lots of sugar maples here, as well as paper birch, hemlock, spruce, and white and red pine. The islands are heavily forested with tall, mature trees. Most are dominated by conifers, some

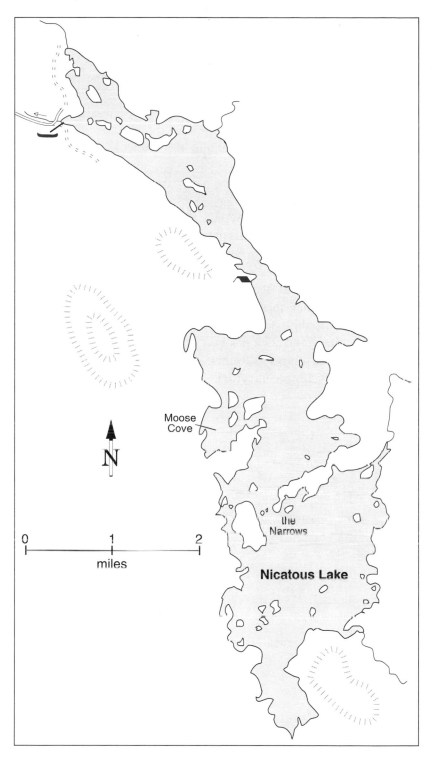

Moose
Cove

the
Narrows

Nicatous Lake

0   1   2
miles

N

with dense stands of red pine, with a few paper birch and red maple thrown in.

In addition to exploring the islands, paddle quietly down into Moose Cove to look for wildlife. Although there are several marshy areas in various coves, this one is the most extensive.

Several campsites are on the lake; one of the nicest is on a little peninsula on the western shore, just above the Nicatous Club. Sparse vegetation should allow the breeze in to keep the bugs down.

Getting There

From I-95, take the Howland/West Enfield exit (#54). Drive east on Routes 155 and 188. Follow Route 188 when Route 155 splits off. Stay on the main road, following the signs to Nicatous Lodge, as this leads directly to the boat access on Nicatous Lake. From the end of the pavement, the boat access is another 5.6 miles. As you come around a sharp corner, there is the lake and the boat access. There is no sign, but the public access is the second dock on the right after turning the corner. The dock has two iron wheels out in the water for cranking it back up onto shore in the winter. Park over to the side near the access (the road is plenty wide).

Third Machias Lake

T5ND BPP

MAPS

Maine Atlas: Map 35

USGS Quadrangles: Dark Cove Mountain, Fletcher Peak, and Monroe Lake

INFORMATION

Area: 2,612 acres; maximum depth: 31 feet

Prominent fish species: smallmouth bass, white perch, and chain pickerel; eel in the fall at the outlet

Fire permits: Maine Forest Service, St. Croix River District (207-738-2601) or Central Region Headquarters (207-827-6191)

Paddling out from the boat access and indeed throughout most of the southwest arm of Third Machias Lake, one is taken by the number of beautiful, enormous granite boulders deposited at random by retreating glaciers. Many of them protrude well out into the lake, making this a very picturesque spot. Most of the shoreline is covered with conifers that retreat up the hillsides into the distance, although there is a well-developed understory right at the water's edge, consisting of small paper birches, red maples, and a variety of shrubs.

Staying to the right as you leave the small arm at the boat access, note the extensive sand beach around to the left. Paddling out among the boulders and islands, you may notice that Little Ship Island is indeed bigger than Big Ship Island and that White Birch Island is covered with red pines. The large cove off to the right just after Norway Island is guarded by tons of large granite boulders. A small amount of marshland gives way to scrub vegetation on the shore, followed by a uniform stand of pines on higher ground.

After threading our way through the islands at the top of the southwestern arm, we turned right (south) into the eastern arm and paddled down to campsite 6 on the western shore. A road leads to this spot, but there are few amenities. The other campsites are much nicer, particularly those on the island and peninsula that separate the north and south ends of the lake. There is also an official campsite across from Prune Island, just north of the outlet of Wabassus Lake.

Another interesting area on Third Machias Lake is the inlet in the far northwest, Fourth Lake Stream, which drains Fourth Machias

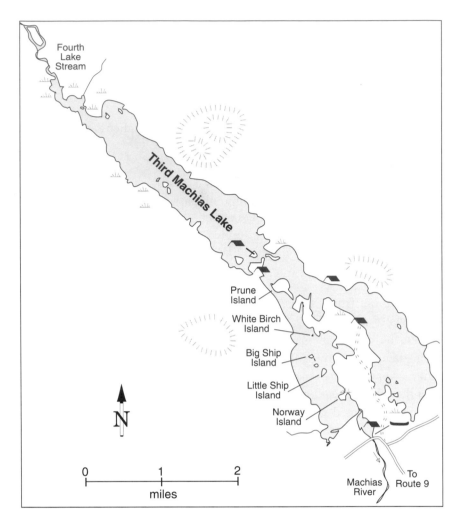

Lake. You can paddle back almost a mile before boulders and riffles block your way. This is a peaceful, marshy area, filled with beaver lodges and recent cuttings. Although we did not see any moose here in the midafternoon, this would be a good place to look for them. Indeed, we did watch a cow moose feeding in the water in a similar marshy area on Fourth Machias Lake. In the spring it is possible to paddle down from Fourth Machias Lake, through Third Machias Lake, all the way to the town of Machias.

While paddling here, we saw few other people and lots of red-breasted mergansers, ring-necked ducks, loons, and other birds. In the early morning and evening you should have no trouble finding beaver willing to slap their tails on the water as they dive out of sight. This is a beautiful, wild place one could easily spend several days exploring.

Because they live in low-nutrient soils, pitcher plants trap insects for food. Insects fall into the leaf "pitchers," where rainwater mixes with digestive enzymes. Downward-pointing hairs keep them from climbing out.

Getting There

From Machias, take Route 192 north and turn left onto Route 9. Measuring mileage from this junction, there is a T30 town-line sign at 10.3 miles just after crossing the Machias River, followed by a sharp curve to the left. Just as you start into this curve at 10.9 miles, turn right onto a wide gravel road. Set your trip odometer here and follow it carefully, as there are several confusing turns and lots of logging roads along the way.

At 9.0 miles, just after cresting a rise, take the right fork. Careful, this is easy to miss. At 9.1 miles, jog right, go across the Machias River bridge, and take an immediate left. At 13.5 miles, turn left off the main road and go steeply downhill. At 14.1 and 14.2 miles, two roads enter from the right. Continue straight, and you reach the boat access on the right just before the bridge at 14.3 miles.

Don't be concerned if there are several cars parked at the boat access. Chances are that most of them belong to people who have put in below the bridge to do the Machias River trip.

Fourth Machias Lake
T5ND BPP and T42MD BPP

MAPS
> **Maine Atlas:** Map 35
> **USGS Quadrangles:** Dark Cove Mountain, Duck Lake, Fletcher Peak, and Gassabias Lake

INFORMATION
> **Area:** 1,539 acres; maximum depth: 26 feet
> **Prominent fish species:** white perch, yellow perch, and chain pickerel
> **Fire permits:** Maine Forest Service, St. Croix River District (207-738-2601) or Central Region Headquarters (207-827-6191)
> The Pines, P.O. Box 158, Grand Lake Stream, ME 04637; 207-796-5006. Lodge with guest rooms plus cabins.

Fourth Machais Lake represents the essence of eastern Maine's wild lake country. Remote, marshy, nestled beneath gentle mountains, and filled with wildlife, it receives few visitors. Although getting there is not easy, it is well worth a visit. One could explore the whole lake and its tributaries in one long day, but a leisurely two-day exploration allows more time to absorb the beauty of this setting and to enjoy its abundant wildlife.

In the evening and early morning, explore for moose in the extensive marshes surrounding the five inlet streams. The largest expanse of marsh surrounds Dead Stream, which flows from the southeast into the upper arm of Fourth Machias Lake. Occasional tamarack dot the otherwise flat terrain of this broad valley. When we paddled here in mid-June, we went back in about a mile, past a pair of Canada geese with their fluffy yellow goslings, to find a cow moose wallowing in the water, buried up to her nose. She was doing the same thing with her long ears that we were doing with our hats: shooing away hordes of black flies. We even forgot for a moment the accumulating bites on the backs of our necks as we glided silently past the cavorting moose.

On higher ground, away from the huge expanses of marshland, you will find large stands of white and red pine, with a few spruce thrown in. Paper birch and red maple grow along the shore, along with scattered hemlocks. Tamarack, black spruce, northern white cedar, and red maple grow on the higher hummocks in the swamps.

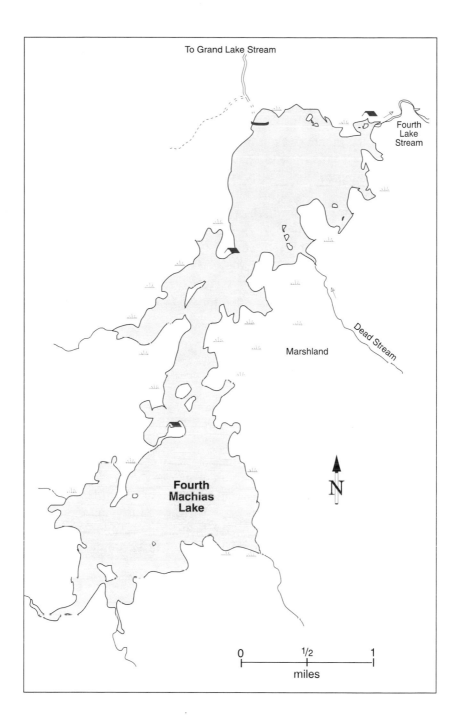

To Grand Lake Stream

Fourth Lake Stream

Dead Stream

Marshland

N

Fourth Machias Lake

0   1/2   1

miles

Because of the extensive marshes surrounding Fourth Machias Lake, there is little high ground to support campsites. You are no longer allowed to camp near the boat access. The only suitable campsites we found are on peninsulas on the right-hand side at the beginning and end of the connector between the upper and lower arms of the lake. According to the topographic map, there is supposed to be a campsite at the mouth of Fourth Lake Stream, but we did not look for it. Of course, if you want to enjoy a respite from the bugs, you can stay at The Pines, a lodge a short way back down the road on Sysladobsis Lake.

In the spring during high water, you can paddle Fourth Lake Stream down into Third Machias Lake. From there you can continue on the Machias River trip, eventually taking out at Machias. We looked at this stream in the middle of June in a high-water year and decided there was not quite enough water to avoid the rocks. If there were more water, however, we were not sure we could paddle back up the stream to Fourth Machias Lake. In a low-water year in September, the stream was down to a trickle.

Getting There

From Calais, take Route 1 north through Princeton. Turn left onto a good paved road at the sign for Grand Lake Stream. Continue on through Grand Lake Stream, staying on the pavement. Start marking mileage when the pavement turns to gravel. At 0.3 mile take the right fork, following the sign for Elsemore Landing (on Pocumcus Lake). At 11.5 miles, a major road goes off to the right, down to The Pines (on Sysladobsis Lake); stay left here. Beaver had flooded the road at 11.9 miles when we were here. As the main road curves to the right at 12.4 miles, turn left and reach the boat landing at 12.6 miles.

Pocumcus, Junior, and Sysladobsis Lakes
T5 ND BPP and T5 R1 NBPP

MAPS
    Maine Atlas: Map 35
    USGS Quadrangles: Dark Cove Mountain, Scraggly Lake, Bottle Lake, and Duck Lake

INFORMATION
    Physical information:
        Pocumcus Lake area: 2,201 acres; maximum depth: 44 feet
        Junior Lake area: 3,866 acres; maximum depth: 70 feet
        Bottle Lake area: 281 acres; maximum depth: 42 feet
        Sysladobsis Lake area: 5,376 acres; maximum depth: 66 feet
    Prominent fish species:
        Pocumcus Lake: white perch, salmon, and smallmouth bass
        Junior Lake: salmon, smallmouth bass, perch, and chain pickerel
        Bottle Lake: brook trout, salmon, smallmouth bass, perch, and chain pickerel
        Sysladobsis Lake: salmon, smallmouth bass, perch, and chain pickerel
    Fire permits: Maine Forest Service St. Croix River District (207-738-2601) or Central Region Headquarters (207-827-6191). Fire permits required for all campsites except Elsemore Landing.
    Outfitting: Sunrise County Canoe Expeditions, Inc., Cathance Lake, Grove, ME 04638; 207-454-7708
    Maine Wilderness Camps, RR 1, Box 100, Springfield, ME 04487; 207-738-5052

The loop comprised of Pocumcus, Junior, and Sysladobsis lakes in the heart of eastern Maine's lake country offers one of the best extended quiet-water loop trips in the state, especially when one detours for a few days into Scraggly Lake. These lakes flow into the St. Croix River, which forms the southeastern border between Maine and New Brunswick. Because you can end up where you started, the trip requires just one car. But be aware that these are large lakes; under breezy conditions, large waves can build up quickly, making paddling difficult and, at times, quite dangerous. Always keep your plans flexible and be ready to change them if the conditions prevent you from

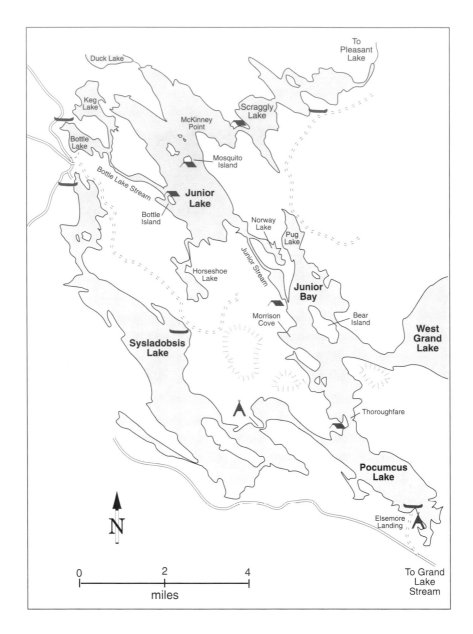

Duck Lake

To
Pleasant
Lake

Keg
Lake

Scraggly
Lake

McKinney
Point

Bottle
Lake

Mosquito
Island

Bottle Lake Stream

**Junior
Lake**

Bottle
Island

Norway
Lake

Pug
Lake

Junior Stream

Horseshoe
Lake

**Junior
Bay**

Morrison
Cove

Bear
Island

**West
Grand
Lake**

**Sysladobsis
Lake**

Thoroughfare

**Pocumcus
Lake**

Elsemore
Landing

N

0   2   4
|———————|———————|
miles

To Grand
Lake
Stream

paddling on the big lakes. We recommend traveling in parties with at least two canoes for safety.

The ease of this loop trip depends somewhat on water levels. With relatively high water levels (usually up until midsummer), you can paddle from Junior Lake into Sysladobsis Lake via Bottle Lake Stream, Bottle Lake, and a half-mile carry into Sysladobsis. But with lower water levels the closest take-out on Bottle Lake may be inaccessible. In that case, the carry would require either disembarking on someone's waterfront yard (Bottle Lake is more heavily developed than any other part of this trip) or making a much farther carry from the official boat access at the north end. So from midsummer through fall, you might want to plan a different up-and-back trip, rather than making a loop of it. Here we give the description of a loop trip that takes anywhere from two (if you really push it) to five days.

Elsemore Landing on Pocumcus Lake to Junior Lake

Elsemore Landing, near the south end of Pocumcus Lake (pronounced po-COM-ses, and referred to locally as Compass Lake) has a state-run campground where you can leave a car and launch your canoe. Midweek, the campground is pretty nice; on a busy weekend, though, it can become a rowdy madhouse (we returned from a multiday trip on Fourth of July weekend to find cars, RVs, tents, and barbecue grills packed like sardines). During the summer season, a campground host lives in a trailer to the right as you enter the camping area and can tell you the best place to leave your vehicle.

Pocumcus Lake is about five miles long and a mile across at its widest point. Deer Brook Cove, about two miles up on the left shore, is a wonderful cove filled with boggy islands and marshy shorelines to explore. We watched a cow moose browsing on underwater vegetation near the north end of this cove, observed lots of beaver activity, and paddled by a week-old loon chick riding on its parent's back near the entrance to the cove. On the sphagnum islands and floating logs, look for the small reddish leaves of sundew, one of several carnivorous plants found in the area. On a windy day, this cove provides a nice respite from the main lake.

To reach Junior Lake, paddle north through the Thoroughfare. Along the western shore, north of the Thoroughfare, are several interesting islands and a deep cove. To the east you will see the quarter-mile-wide outlet from this lake system into West Grand Lake, which is really too big a lake to paddle enjoyably, except in very calm conditions. Head north between Morrison Cove and Bear Island into Junior Bay.

Near the north end of Bear Island on the western shore, Junior Stream drains Junior Lake. You'll find a great campsite here, with picnic tables, outhouses, and plenty of flat tenting locations. This is a permitted campsite, meaning that you don't need a fire permit. (See Introduction (page ix) for an explanation of fire-permit regulations.) If you camp here, spend a few hours around daybreak exploring the Junior Bay and Pug Lake shoreline or Junior Stream and Norway Lake; moose frequent these shallow waters and marshy coves. Also watch for otters, deer, loons (seemingly everywhere), and bald eagles.

With favorable weather, you can make the Junior Stream campsite a lunch stop and continue on to Junior Lake, where you will find some island campsites. We chose to continue on when paddling here—and regretted it. Most of the morning we had had a light tail wind, and we wanted to keep taking advantage of it. But by early afternoon, when we got out onto Junior Lake, the wind had picked up considerably. Our two laden canoes (one with precious cargo of four- and seven-year-old daughters) bobbed in the increasingly rough water as we made our way for an island campsite near the center of the lake. We got there all right, but just in time, as the winds picked up even more, increasing the waves to two feet.

Though we did not realize it at the time, the island we chose is named Mosquito Island—with good reason. Two stagnant lagoons on the small island, one at each end, breed a crop of healthy and hungry mosquitoes that become all too apparent as soon as the wind dies down. Bottle Island, where we also camped, farther to the south and a bit west, is far better during mosquito season. Another campsite is found on McKinney Point. On one of the islands just north of McKinney Point, a bald-eagle nest perches in a tall white pine. Be careful not to get too close. Eagle nesting success has been poor in recent years due to dioxin pollution from Maine's paper mills (see page 93); this magnificent raptor needs all the help and protection we can give it.

This island area near McKinney Point has a very wild and remote feel to it. Huge granite boulders dot the undeveloped shoreline. Watch out for boulders lurking just beneath the water's surface; we hung up our canoes pretty thoroughly a few times. From the eastern arm of Junior Lake, you can make a wonderful trip into Scraggly Lake to the east (see the following section). The deep coves extending to the north and Duck Lake extending to the northwest, offer hours—and miles—of exploration.

Another interesting side trip from Junior Lake is on the western shore, south of Bottle Island and the mouth of Bottle Lake Stream: Horseshoe Lake. From a campsite on Bottle Island (the nicest campsite, with a picnic table, is on the north end), paddle south about a mile to the entrance to Horseshoe Lake. The channel into Horseshoe narrows to just a few yards across in places, and a few spots swarmed with mosquitoes, but we loved this little out-of-the-way alcove. On the western shore, just before the channel widens to form the lake, look for a floating bog. The thick mat of sphagnum moss floats on the water and harbors fascinating plants, including pitcher plant, sundew, bog laurel, leather leaf, and two species of orchid: rose pogonia and calopogon, both in full bloom with pink blossoms at the beginning of July—a real treat to be enjoyed from your canoe, never picked! We watched a deer drink at Horseshoe Lake, and it looked like a great area for moose. There is said to be another eagle nest near Horseshoe Lake, though we did not find it.

Junior Lake to Sysladobsis Lake

To the northwest of Bottle Island is the access stream into Bottle Lake, where you can portage into Sysladobsis Lake. The two-mile marshy stream was beautiful when we visited in 1993, with cattail, pickerelweed, bullhead lily, and many, many stumps of trees from when the area was dammed. Enjoy this area while it is still relatively undeveloped. As part of a land settlement in 1979, the federal government returned extensive tracts of land to the Passamoquoddy and Penobscot Indians land they claimed had been taken from them illegally. Facing financial difficulty a decade later, the Indians sold large tracts to developers, who in turn are subdividing it into forty-acre tracts. Cottages are beginning to appear on Bottle Lake Stream and parts of

Paddling across Junior Lake.

Junior Lake in an area that until recently was almost totally undeveloped. Fortunately, Maine has fairly strong regulations controlling development next to water, requiring significant setbacks and stringent septic design for all development, even summer cottages.

Just before you paddle into Bottle Lake proper, a channel to the right leads into Keg Lake, which we didn't explore but is supposedly quite nice. Bottle Lake's heavy development provides a glimpse of what much of this area might look like in ten years if the recent pace of development continues. While not as thickly developed as many lakes farther south and west in Maine or in other New England states, Bottle Lake represents the kind of place we prefer to paddle through as quickly as possible.

A developed boat launch exists at the north end, but if you are paddling onto Sysladobsis Lake, a small cove extending to the south provides much closer access. As mentioned above, however, this may not be easily reachable at very low water levels. To find the portage, paddle around a small peninsula (almost an island) and behind a boathouse (gray when we visited). Though not marked or maintained, we are told this is an acceptable access for the half-mile carry to or from Sysladobsis. From the boathouse, walk south on the dirt road a few hundred feet, then bear right. In a few hundred yards, cross a larger gravel road and continue south for another few hundred yards until you see an access stream on the left. You can launch into this access stream or carry down the dirt road next to it and launch on the main lake.

Sysladobsis, or Dobsy, as it is locally known, is a big lake, stretching about nine miles from northwest to southeast and extending about a mile and a half across at its widest. You will become well aware of its size with even a modest breeze from the north or south. We had to buck a strong breeze paddling south from the access at the northern tip.

There is some development along the shores, but nothing like Bottle Lake. Dobsy is still clear and clean. Summer residents pump their drinking water right out of the lake, and anglers catch good-size salmon regularly. You can explore the few coves and inlets along the lake if the weather conditions permit leisurely paddling. We paddled a few hundred yards up Sysladobsis Creek, which drains Upper Sysladobsis Lake, but low water and rapids eventually blocked our way.

Unfortunately, owing to the land settlement mentioned above, few campsites exist along the lake. There is supposed to be one near Cranberry Cove, but we failed to find it. Away from established campsites, finding a place to set up a tent is difficult; the land is rocky and full of hillocks and depressions.

Sysladobsis to Pocumcus Lake and Elsemore Landing

Near the south end of Dobsy, Big Island stretches almost two miles in length on a northwest-southeast axis. As you paddle southeast on the lake, keep to the left of the island (unless you have time to explore around it), passing two points of land with cottages on them. Stick to the shoreline and you will reach the lake outlet at Dobsis Dam and Dennison Portage about three-quarters of a mile from the second point. There is a campsite here (fire permit required) but no outhouses or picnic tables. Accessible by road, this campsite was heavily used and filled with trash when we camped here. The nicest site is by an old chimney.

From the campsite, Pocumcus Lake is an easy carry around the dam. Launch your boat into the stream on the left side of the dam (west). From here, it is about a five-mile paddle back to the campsite at Elsemore Landing. The section through Pocumcus Narrows is particularly nice; the south side is marshy with cattails and stumps of long dead trees.

Getting There

From Calais, take Route 1 north through Princeton. After passing Lewy Lake on the left, watch for a left-hand turn toward Grand Lake Stream. (If you are coming south on Route 1 from Topsfield, this turn [to the right] is 13.8 miles from the junction of Routes 1 and 6.) In 10.1 miles cross Grand Lake Stream (set your trip odometer here to help with the following directions). Stay on the main road, continuing straight where smaller roads turn off. The road quickly turns to gravel. Bear right at 0.5 mile, following the sign to Elsemore Landing. At 6.6 miles, turn right at another sign for Elsemore Landing, and at 7.4 miles bear right toward the water at the state campground. The campground host usually lives in a trailer parked to the right.

Black Flies and Mosquitoes
Scourges of the North

Anyone who has spent any time at all paddling or hiking in Maine's north woods knows these insects all too well. They can detract from outdoor fun throughout the summer and can make most of June virtually off-limits to outdoor recreation in northern parts of the state. So what are these little beasts that hover in clouds around your head, reducing you to a swollen, scratching, cursing basket case as you portage your canoe or attempt to tie a fly on your line? Though it will not take away any of the pain or itch, understanding these small insects may help you accept them as part of the ecosystem you so enjoy.

Black Flies: Black flies belong to the family Simuldiidae ("little snub-nosed beings"), and most of the species of concern to us are in the genus *Simulium.*

More than 1,500 species of black flies have been identified worldwide, 300 in North America. Only ten percent to fifteen percent of black-fly species cause all the problems: sucking blood from humans or domestic animals.

In parts of northern North America, black flies cause considerable losses to livestock—mostly weight loss because cattle do not eat well when tormented by the flies, but they actually kill cattle in some areas. In parts of Alberta, Canada, mortality rates from black flies range from one percent to four percent. Researchers have collected as many as 10,000 feeding black flies from a single cow! Black-fly problems in North America, however, pale compared to problems in Africa, where the aptly named species *Simulium damnosum* has infected an estimated twenty million people with onchocerciasis, or river blindness.

Black flies begin their life cycle in streams and rivers. Adult females deposit eggs in the water, and the emerging larvae attach themselves to rocks, plants, and other surfaces in the current. Two tiny, fanlike structures sweep food particles into their mouths. In some streams the black-fly larvae become so dense they form a slippery, mosslike mat. A several-hundred-foot stretch of a narrow stream can support more than a million larvae. In a river the population can be in the multibillions per mile.

After a period of days or weeks (depending on the species and available food), each larva builds a pupal case in which it metamorphoses into an adult black fly. When ready to emerge, it splits the pupal case open and rides to the water's surface in a bubble of oxygen that had collected in the case.

Adult black flies have one goal: to make more black flies. The trouble begins when female black flies seek the nourishing meal of blood they need to lay eggs. Only females bite (actually more of a puncture-and-suck routine than a true bite); males lead a pacifist life, sipping nectar from flowers and searching for the "right" partner. Black

flies rely heavily on eyesight to find prey, so they are active almost exclusively during the daylight. Some black flies fly more than fifty miles in search of blood meals.

No black-fly species sucks blood exclusively from humans. We are too new on the evolutionary chain to be a specific host to black flies, which arose during the Jurassic period 180 million years ago. An estimated thirty to forty-five black-fly species in North America feed on humans. There is one species (*Simulium euryadminiculum*) whose females feed only on loons.

Mosquitoes: Our other major insect nemesis of the Maine woods is the ubiquitous mosquito. Mosquitoes, members of the Culicidae family, number more than 3,400 species worldwide, including 170 in North America. Three-quarters of the mosquito species in the U.S. and Canada belong to three genera: *Aedes* (78 species), *Culex* (29 species), and *Anopheles* (16 species).

As with black flies, mosquito larvae live an aquatic life. Unlike black flies, though, most mosquitoes have adapted to still water. You can look in almost any stagnant bog or muskeg in Maine during the spring and summer months and see mosquito larvae wriggling about. They eat algae and other organic matter they filter out of the water with brushlike appendages. Larvae go through a number of different molts as they grow and develop into pupae. Both larvae and pupae breathe through air tubes at the surface of the water.

Adult mosquitoes have short life spans. Most females live about a month, while males live only about a week. The high-pitched buzz of mosquitoes comes from beating their wings at about 1,000 beats per second. Females generate a higher-pitched whine than males, which helps the males locate mates. Males have much bushier antennae than females.

Both male and female mosquitoes feed on plant juices and nectars as their primary energy source, but females of most species also require a blood meal to fuel egg production. The habit of female mosquitoes to feed on blood—and especially *our* blood—has given this insect its deservedly nasty reputation.

As with black flies, a mosquito does not really bite. Rather, she stabs through the victim's skin with six sharp stylets that form the center of the proboscis. Saliva flows into the puncture to keep the blood from coagulating while she sips it through her proboscis. The reaction most people have to mosquito bites—

itching and swelling—is an allergic reaction to the saliva. Upon repeated exposure to mosquito bites, one gradually builds up resistance.

While mosquitoes are really just a nuisance in New England, they cause death and destruction in the tropics. Disease-carrying mosquitoes cause more human deaths than any other animal. They carry more than 100 different diseases, including malaria, yellow fever, encephalitis, filariasis, and dengue. The most destructive of these, malaria, kills about one million people a year, mostly children, and worldwide as many as 200 million people carry the disease.

While there is far greater mosquito-species diversity in southern latitudes (as many as 150 different species can be found in a square mile in some parts of the tropics), numbers of individual mosquitoes generally increase farther north. In the Arctic, there are fewer than a dozen species, but adults can be so thick they literally blacken the skies. In one experiment, several rugged (and we suspect, intellectually challenged) Canadian researchers bared their torsos, arms, and legs to Arctic mosquitoes and reported as many as 9,000 bites per minute! At this rate of onslaught, an unprotected person could lose half of his or her blood in two hours.

So, you see, it is really not so bad in Maine. Our mosquitoes do not carry deadly disease, and even in Maine's northern bogs, we have found that it is rare to get more than a thousand bites a minute....

Black-Fly and Mosquito Control

Many different control strategies have been tried for black flies and mosquitoes. For mosquito control, we drained thousands of square miles of salt marsh during the 1930s and 1940s by building long, straight drainage ditches—many of which are still visible. (As much as half of the wetland area in the U.S. has been lost during the last 200 years—partly for mosquito control and partly for development and agriculture.)

Along with eliminating habitat, we have used thousands of tons of pesticides in the battle against these insects—mostly against mosquitoes. DDT was the chemical of choice for decades because of its supposed safety to humans and the environment—a claim that proved tragically untrue. Since DDT and other deadly chlorinated-hydrocarbon pesticides were banned in 1973, ospreys, bald eagles, peregrine falcons, and other important bird species have begun making a comeback.

Today, most attention focuses on biological control of these insects. Biological control relies on natural enemies of the pest: viruses, protozoa, bacteria, fungi, and parasites. The most successful control found has been a bacterium discovered in 1977 from samples of sand collected in the Negev Desert. This is *Bacillus thuringiensis* variety *israelensis,* generally known as Bti. Gardeners use another variety of this bacterium for controlling cabbage loopers, corn borers, and other garden pests, and foresters use it for gypsy-moth control. Bti bacteria produce protein crystals that react with other chemicals in the insects' stomachs, producing a poison that kills the larvae. While Bti currently enjoys high success rates, some researchers are concerned that there will be hidden problems with this solution, just as there were with DDT.

Protecting Yourself from Biting Insects: One option is to stay out of the woods—buy a good book on paddling and read about it. While a bit extreme, this is not a bad solution during June, when clouds of black flies and mosquitoes may stick in your mind as the most memorable part of an outing. Largely because of biting insects, in fact, our favorite times for canoeing are in the autumn and in May—during that narrow window between ice-out and the black-fly hatch.

During all but the height of the black-fly season in June, however, these is no reason to let insects spoil your trip. In fact, because you are out on the water where there is often a breeze, bugs are much less a problem for paddlers than hikers. Proper clothing forms the most important line of defense against both black flies and mosquitoes. During black-fly season, wear long-sleeved, tight-knit shirts with elastic cuffs. Turtlenecks work well as long as the material is thick enough and the weave tight enough that the flies cannot reach your skin through it. Wear long pants with elastic cuffs, or tuck your pants legs into oversized socks. Black flies land on your clothing and search for openings—wrists, ankles, and necks are prime targets. If you have good protection at your neck, a mosquito-cloth head net works well, but with a collared shirt, black flies will usually find a route in. Cotton gloves can be a big help, too.

Mosquitoes can penetrate soft clothing better than black flies, so a more rugged material such as canvas works well for shirts and pants. Tight cuffs are not as important because mosquitoes usually fly directly to their dining table. With mosquito-cloth head nets, the key is to keep the mosquito cloth away from your skin—buy one with a metal band from which the cloth hangs. Make sure it has a drawstring or elastic; otherwise, mosquitoes inevitably find their way in.

Insect repellents are generally more effective with mosquitoes than with black flies. The chemical of choice in Maine's north woods is DEET (N,N-diethyl-meta-toluamide). Fortunately, one of our coauthors is a chemist and able to pronounce this chemical. Unfortunately, he also knows enough about its chemical structure to be concerned about potential toxicity to humans. Most of the repellents Mainers swear by have DEET as the primary active ingredient; some are almost 100 percent DEET. Another problem with most DEET formulations is that the repellent is not effective for very long; you have to keep slathering it on. While we admit to keeping some high-test DEET around when the bugs get really bad, we recommend clothing as the primary defensive strategy.

A relatively new repellent for black flies that many claim to be highly effective is Avon Skin-So-Soft®. Applying a nontoxic skin softener instead of one of those toxic-sounding diethyl-type chemical concoctions sounds really great. We would be even more excited about it if it kept black flies away. Maybe it does have some effect, maybe it even provides ironclad protection for some people, but we aren't so sure. We found that up in northern Maine, at the height of black-fly season in mid-June, the repellent locals use is smoke. Lots of it. Called smudge pots, or just smokes, the idea is to build a fire in a bucket or large can, then stuff green leaves in so it spews forth thick smoke. And you stand in that smoke. It seems to work beautifully, but after seeing these smokes in use all over the place (and enjoying their protection a few times), we can only wonder if there is an elevated incidence of emphysema and other respiratory ills in northern Maine. Also, we find they do not work well in canoes.

Is There Anything Good about Black Flies and Mosquitoes? In reviewing all the problems with black flies and mosquitoes, one wonders what might possibly be good about the little beasts. The answer lies in the role they play in aquatic ecosystems, where they provide a vital food source for a wide variety of animals. Many of our choice game fish rely on black-fly and mosquito larvae for at least a part of their diets. One study found that black-fly larvae comprise up to 25 percent of the brook-trout diet. Even if black-fly and mosquito larvae do not provide a direct food source for our favorite game fish and waterfowl, chances are pretty good the larvae are a vital part of the food chain upon which these animals rely. If we appreciate angling for brook trout, listening to the evening song of the loon, or watching the stately great blue heron, we should recognize that these species might not be here without black flies and mosquitoes.

Not only that, but without these insect pests, every lake and pond in Maine might long ago have been sprinkled with vacation homes, and the solitude we so appreciate in the wilds of northern Maine might no longer exist. This is not to suggest, however, that we should not slap the little devils with a vengeance, occasionally slather on the DEET, and do everything in our power to prevent ourselves from serving as walking smorgasbords for them. But we should recognize that, yes, even black flies and mosquitoes have a place in the ecosystem.

Scraggly Lake (Southern) and Pleasant Lake

T5 R1 NBPP and T6 R1 NBPP

MAPS
> **Maine Atlas:** Maps 35 and 45
> **USGS Quadrangle:** Scraggly Lake

INFORMATION
> **Scraggly Lake area:** 2,758 acres; maximum depth: 42 feet
> **Prominent fish species:** smallmouth bass, white and yellow perch, and chain pickerel; also some salmon and lake trout
> **Pleasant Lake area:** 1,574 acres; maximum depth: 92 feet
> **Prominent fish species:** salmon, lake trout, and brook trout
> **Fire permits:** Maine Forest Service, St. Croix River District (207-738-2601) or Central Region Headquarters (207-827-6191)
> **Outfitting:** Maine Wilderness Camps, RR 1, Box 100, Springfield, ME 04487; 207-738-5052. Canoe-trip outfitting, transportation from Bangor airport, and year-round campground.

Scraggly Lake is one of our favorites. Called "southern" in this section to distinguish it from another Scraggly Lake farther north (see page 274), it is accessible either from Pocumcus and Junior lakes to the west and south, or from Pleasant Lake to the north and east (via a portage). The lake is only 3.5 miles long, but the highly varied shoreline extends nearly twenty miles along marshy coves and wild undeveloped islands. Wild and remote, this is the paddler's ideal lake: too shallow for most motorboaters and far enough from road access that you have to do some work to get here.

We paddled into Scraggly as part of a loop trip starting at Elsemore Landing on Pocumcus Lake and extending through Junior and Sysladobsis lakes (see previous section). On that trip, Scraggly makes a wonderful two- or three-day detour. More popular is a one-way trip starting at Maine Wilderness Camps on the northern shore on Pleasant Lake with a portage to the northeastern tip of Scraggly, then on through to Junior Lake and either Pocumcus or West Grand Lake. Maine Wilderness Camps is both a very nice campground and an outfitter that can set you up with gear and shuttle you to a starting or ending point.

Scraggly Lake is a wonderful place for wildlife. Paddling along the northern shore in the first light of morning, we surprised a magnif-

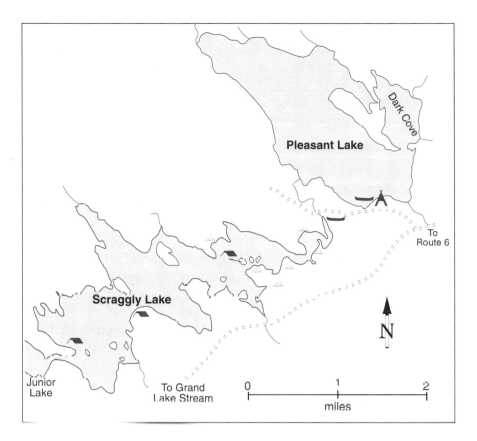

icent bald eagle that had been feeding at the water's edge. We saw a
number of eagles here, including an active nest in a large white pine
tree on an island in Junior Lake. Wood ducks, loons, ring-necked
ducks, deer, and a huge snapping turtle were among our other observations here. During a morning paddle from Scraggly up into Pleasant
Lake, we watched a playful family of otters in the glass-smooth water.
Though we did not happen to see moose while here, it appears to be
superb moose habitat. You may also see common terns here; we suspect they nest on large boulders protruding from the lake that are visible from the Scraggly Island campsite.

A number of designated campsites dot Scraggly Island. The
nicest site is a permitted site, meaning that you do not need to obtain
a fire permit to use it. The other two sites shown are permit sites. The
island's camping areas have fire rings, picnic tables, and lots of space
for tents. Unlike most sites in the area, you'll also find outhouses
here. During a visit at the end of June we found surprisingly few
mosquitoes on Scraggly Island, though some of the surrounding

marshy areas were quite buggy. From this island, a particularly interesting area to explore is the marshy area east and south of the island. If the water isn't too low, you can find a passage around the large marsh, though by midsummer passage would almost certainly be blocked by low water.

A Side Trip to Pleasant Lake

If you want to go from Scraggly Lake up into Pleasant Lake, paddle to the eastern tip and take your boat out at a steep gravel ramp (too steep for trailers). Carry up to the road (about fifty feet) then to the right (east). You can carry all the way to the state campground, where there is a launch onto Pleasant Lake (about a half-mile), or you can cut over to Pleasant Lake on a portage trail. We had a two-wheeled portage cart so we stuck to the road. The trail seemed to be poorly marked and hard to follow due to logging activity in recent years.

The state campground on Pleasant Lake is a stark contrast to the relaxing feel of Scraggly Lake; when we visited, it was crowded with thirty or forty small trailers and badly littered. Used by a heavy-drinking, hook-and-bullet crowd, the campground is known locally as "Rowdyville." When we launched here at around 7:00 A.M. most of the camp was still sleeping it off. Apparently, the state may begin clamping down on long-ignored regulations that limit the length of stay here (common practice today is to park a trailer here for the summer and use the lake as a weekend retreat). There is no charge to camp here, and if vehicles were somehow kept out this would be a great spot.

The best area of Pleasant Lake to explore by canoe is Dark Cove. Hundreds of boulders sticking out of the water and hiding just beneath the surface near the mouth of the cove effectively keep motorboats out. The water is very clear, and you will see thousands of fresh-water mussels sticking out of the sand on the bottom. White cedar is the dominant tree here, along with balsam fir, spruce, and white pine. Alders, bog laurel, sweet gale, and other northern species grow in profusion along the shore. We found a very pleasant campsite (unmarked on maps) near the north end, nestled beneath a grove of red pines.

At the north end of the main lake is Maine Wilderness Camps, which seems to be a good private campground with tenting and trailer sites as well as cabins. Owner Terry McGrath also provides canoe outfitting and shuttling service to area lakes and rivers. Those wishing to enjoy some wilderness canoeing but not a lot of driving, can even arrange for shuttling from the bus station or airport in Bangor.

Getting There

As mentioned, there are several options for getting to Scraggly Lake. You can launch your canoes at Elsemore Landing on Pocumcus Lake (for access directions, see page 159) and paddle north through Junior Lake into Scraggly. Plan at least a day to get to Scraggly; in windy conditions it may take longer. Be very careful paddling on Pocumcus and Junior lakes in windy conditions. These are big lakes with potentially dangerous conditions.

Alternatively, you can drive to Pleasant Lake and begin your trip there. If you are coming from Pleasant Lake, you might be more comfortable leaving a vehicle at Maine Wilderness Camps (there may be a small fee) than at the state campground. If you choose to leave your car at the campground, you can drive to the eastern tip of Scraggly, unload your gear, then drive back to the campground to park. A high-ground-clearance four-wheel-drive vehicle is recommended if you want to drive in; we have not tried it.

To reach Maine Wilderness Camps by car, take I-95 through Bangor to Exit 55 (Lincoln). Follow Route 6 east for approximately 34 miles through Carroll and across the Washington County line. Continue on Route 6 for 4.5 miles past the county line, and turn right at the sign for Maine Wilderness Camps. Follow the private road for 3.5 miles to the campground and shores of Pleasant Lake.

Pocomoonshine, Mud, and Crawford Lakes

Princeton, Alexander, and Crawford

MAPS
> **Maine Atlas:** Map 36
> **USGS Quadrangles:** Princeton and Crawford Lake

INFORMATION
> **Crawford Lake area:** 1,677 acres; maximum depth: 27 feet
> **Pocomoonshine Lake area:** 2,464 acres; maximum depth: 40 feet
> **Prominent fish species:** smallmouth bass, white perch, and chain pickerel; largemouth bass in the river; eel at the outlet dam on Crawford Lake. These two lakes are considered among the best smallmouth bass lakes in Maine.
> **Fire permits:** Maine Forest Service, St. Croix River District (207-738-2601) or Central Region Headquarters (207-827-6191)
> **Outfitting:** Sunrise County Canoe Expeditions, Cathance Lake, Grove Post Office, Maine 04638; 207-454-7708

We paddled Pocomoonshine twice, once in July and once in August. The southeastern boat access on Pocomoonshine Lake marks the start of the East Machias River trip. One can start here and paddle down the Maine River, through Upper and Lower Mud lakes, Crawford Lake, and into the East Machias River. You can take out on Crawford or Round lakes; you can continue on Rocky Lake Stream, taking out in Rocky Lake; or you can continue down the East Machias River through Second Lake, taking out at Hadley Lake or in East Machias. During July of a dry year, we opted for the middle-distance trip, taking out at Rocky Lake.

We recommend that you not try this entire trip in the late summer or anytime when water is low. Below Crawford Lake, we had to walk our boats for about three miles through boulder-laden riffles, seriously scratching our shins and boats to about the same degree. In the spring during higher water, you supposedly can sail right through this stretch. According to the AMC River Guide, the modest rapids are suitable for people with limited whitewater experience.

If you have questions about the water conditions, contact Martin Brown at Sunrise County Canoe Expeditions on nearby Cathance

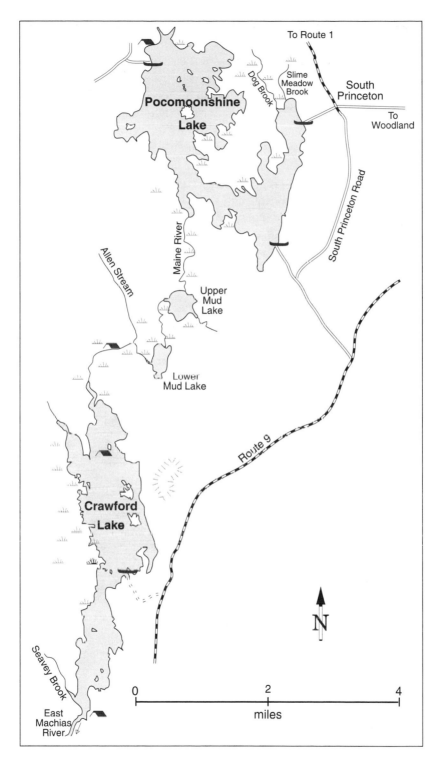

To Route 1

Slime
Meadow
Brook

South
Princeton

To
Woodland

Dog Brook

**Pocomoonshine
Lake**

South Princeton Road

Maine River

Allen Stream

Upper
Mud
Lake

Lower
Mud Lake

Route 9

**Crawford
Lake**

N

Seavey Brook

East
Machias
River

0   2   4

miles

Lake (see information below). They will arrange a ferrying service if you wish to leave your car at the take-out.

From the boat access on the southeast arm of Pocomoonshine Lake, paddle across to the far southwestern cove. Head south down this cove, staying to the left. The forested shoreline of Pocomoonshine Lake gives way to the slowly meandering channel of the Maine River. After a mile or so of travel through marshes with typical bog and floating-plant vegetation, the stream widens out, twice in quick succession, into Upper and Lower Mud lakes. It is hard to follow the channel here in these weed-choked waterways. We just stayed to the right and battled our way through the rushes and pickerelweed until we found the west-leading outlets of each lake. In Lower Mud Lake, it is best to stay out in the more open water until you are well down the lake; then look for an obvious channel leading off to the right (west). Dabbling ducks love these shallow lakes, and we tried our best not to disturb their foraging.

As you head west out of Lower Mud Lake, after a couple hundred yards you come to Allen Stream entering from the right. We paddled back up it for about a half-mile before returning to the river. Right where Allen Stream flows in, but on the left, is campsite 79. As

Joanne Hayes paddles a sea kayak down the Maine River between Pocomoonshine and Crawford lakes. While designed for ocean paddling, sea kayaks offer speed and ease of handling for the solo paddler.

you enter Crawford Lake, there is another campsite (78) on one of the northernmost islands, just off a peninsula jutting out from the left shore. The best take-out is a sloping granite boulder off the southwestern shore.

Because Crawford Lake is five miles long and narrow, it funnels wind and churns up swells and whitecaps whenever the wind is generally out of the north or the south. When we paddled down to the southern end of Crawford Lake, we doubled back up the meandering, marshy Seavey Brook. You can paddle way back in here, and it looks to be a true wild place, perfect for moose watching.

At the end of Crawford Lake, you have come more than eleven miles, and if there is any wind, it is unlikely you will be able to paddle this round trip in just one day. It is an ideal two-day trip, allowing time for side-channel exploration. Campsite 77 is located at the south end of Crawford Lake.

If the wind is out of the north and you are not doing the East Machias River trip, it might be best to explore the northern arms of Pocomoonshine Lake. From the South Princeton access, it is a beautiful paddle up Dog Brook, a meandering, wide, slow-flowing inlet of Pocomoonshine Lake. The shoreline, dominated by conifers, is quite far from the channel. White pine, tamarack, spruce, and hemlock grow in profusion. Dwarfed red maples grow out from the shore, and grasses and low-growing bog vegetation lead down to the stream channel, which is covered with bullhead lily, fragrant water lily, pickerelweed, and other aquatic vegetation.

After about a mile the channel narrows down, and it gets quite rocky. If you pick your way back through the rocks for another quarter-mile, a series of serious beaver dams appear. We did not portage above these dams, leaving it to you for further exploration.

While you are paddling on the northeast arm, check out Slime Meadow Brook. The beavers have opened a narrow channel, allowing you to paddle quite a way back in. Of course, when you try to turn your boat around, that's when you get slimed.

If you put in at the carry-in access on the northwest arm of Pocomoonshine Lake, you will be faced with a relatively large open expanse of lake, dotted with a few islands. The seemingly never-ending series of marshy coves, starting directly across from the boat access and extending south down the large peninsula separating the northern arms, provide the most interesting area to explore.

Getting There

There are three access points for Pocomoonshine Lake. The East Machias River trip starts at the boat access on the southeast arm. If you are not doing the river trip, choose any of the three access points. If the wind is out of the south, it would be best to circle around to the west and head down to the two Mud lakes and the north end of Crawford Lake. If the wind is out of the north, it would be best to use one of the two northern access points: either South Princeton on the northeast arm or the carry-in access on the far northwestern end of the lake.

To get to the southeast access from Calais, take Route 1 north (actually west). When Route 9 goes left, take Route 9. In about eight miles, watch for the Skyline Motel and signs for Pocomoonshine Lake Cottages. Turn right onto the access road, which goes straight down hill to the lake.

To get to the South Princeton access, turn right off Route 9 as above. When the road forks in 1.1 miles, take the right fork (South Princeton Road). Go 4.4 more miles down this road, and the access point is down a 0.3-mile-long dirt road on the left. There is a nice dock there, maintained by the town of South Princeton. Alternatively, there is a road off Route 1 going due west out of Woodland for about five miles that dead ends at this boat access in South Princeton.

To get to the far northwest carry-in access, go north from the junction of the South Princeton access road and South Princeton Road for about 3.4 miles (you can see Route 1 off in the distance), and turn left onto a well-traveled gravel road. Go for about 3.6 miles down this road, watching for a turn to the left leading to the boat access and a campsite. This access can also be reached off Route 1, about two miles east of Princeton—see the *Maine Atlas.*

Bearce Lake

Baring PLT

MAPS

  Maine Atlas: Map 36
  USGS Quadrangle: Meddybemps Lake East

INFORMATION

  Moosehorn National Wildlife Refuge, P.O. Box 1077, Calais, ME
  04619; 207 454 7161

Bearce Lake is a long way from anywhere, unless you happen to live in Calais on the New Brunswick border. But Bearce Lake provides a great place to paddle for a variety of reasons, and it is worth a trip if you have some time. First, it lies within the Moosehorn National Wildlife Refuge, operated by the U.S. Fish and Wildlife Service. The part of the refuge containing Bearce Lake, 4,680 acres in all, has been designated a Wilderness Area by act of Congress. In practical terms, this means no motors, no roads, and no human development.

The refuge was set aside to provide unspoiled habitat for the American woodcock, a strange-looking bird (but perhaps not to other

A porcupine munches balsam fir bark at the Moosehorn National Wildlife Refuge visitor center near Bearce Lake.

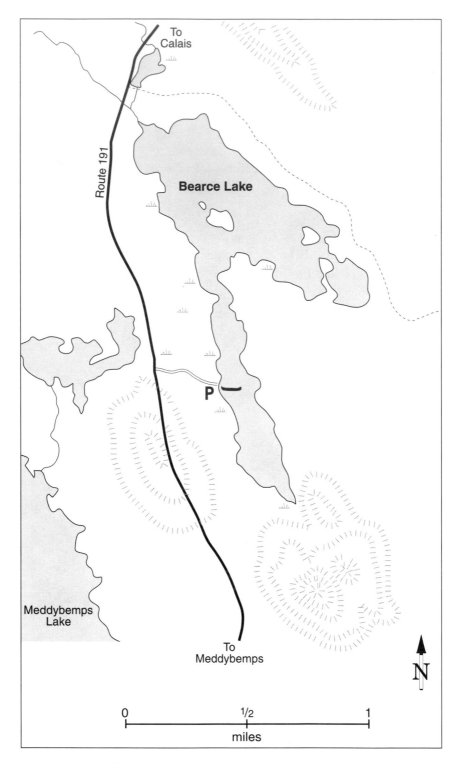

woodcock) with an inordinately long bill, which it uses to probe the mud of alder swamps and other wetlands for whatever wiggles. What are perhaps more interesting to most visitors, however, are the nesting bald eagles. As many as three pairs have nested at a time on the refuge. When we visited in the summer of 1993, a pair was nesting on a small platform within a couple hundred feet of the main highway, a few miles from Bearce Lake, apparently oblivious to the steady stream of cars.

Many different types of trees border this beautiful lake. With only casual observation, we noted the presence of paper birch, spruce, white pine, eastern white cedar, tamarack, hemlock, red maple, and gray birch. A well-developed understory and several marshy areas contribute to the high plant-species diversity. Look here for beaver, moose, wood ducks, and black ducks. When we visited, a huge flock of bank swallows darted continually over the water, trying its best to reduce the flying-insect population, which was also huge.

In the marshy areas, look for carnivorous pitcher plants. They are low growing, generally reddish in color, with leaves modified in the shape of pitchers. Unwary insects that enter the pitcher find themselves in a tube with stiff downward-pointing hairs. Because most insects cannot climb against these hairs or cannot fly back out the narrow tubes, the trapped insects eventually tire and fall into rainwater

The branches of a paper birch drape over the placid waters of Bearce Lake in the Moosehorn National Wildlife Refuge.

collected in the bottom of the pitcher. This rainwater is lethal, though, because the plant has secreted digestive enzymes into the water. The insects serve as a nitrogen source in the nutrient-poor bog environment. Carnivory has evolved separately in several plant families, but with one thing in common: almost all carnivorous plants are found in nutrient-poor soils, usually where a continual flow of water has leached out most soil nutrients.

Granite boulders lining the shore and poking up from the water add another dimension to Bearce Lake. Be careful paddling here, because this added dimension includes many barely submerged boulders. And these are not just typical boulders; most contain jagged, protruding quartz and feldspar crystals, the kind that produce deep gouges in pristine hulls.

Getting There

From Machias, take Route 191 north. After passing through Meddybemps, start marking mileage from the junction of Routes 191 and 214. Proceed north on Route 191 for 3.0 miles. Turn right onto a gravel road that leads to Bearce Lake and the boat access in another 0.3 mile.

From Calais, take Route 1 north (actually southwest here) through Baring to Route 191 south. Drive 4.0 miles and watch for the lake entrance on the left.

To get to the visitor center at refuge headquarters, proceed north on Route 191 for 4.0 miles from Bearce Lake to Route 1. Turn right onto Route 1, and go 2.3 miles. Turn right onto a paved road, and proceed 1.8 miles to the turnoff to refuge headquarters on the right. We watched a porcupine wandering about the headquarters grounds in the middle of the day.

# Central Region

Umbagog Lake
Magalloway PLT and Upton, New Hampshire

MAPS

Maine Atlas: Maps 17 and 18 (also New Hampshire)

USGS Quadrangles: Umbagog Lake South and Umbagog Lake North

INFORMATION

Area: 7,850 acres; maximum depth: 48 feet

Prominent fish species: smallmouth bass, brook trout, brown trout, pickerel, yellow perch, lake chub, and smelt

Lake Umbagog National Wildlife Refuge, P.O. Box 280, Errol, NH 03579; 603-482-3415

Camping: Umbagog Lake Campground, P.O. Box 181, Errol, NH 03579; 603-482-7795. Their backcountry sites are not cheap (eighteen dollars a night for two adults in 1994), but the sites are well maintained. The campground also has rental canoes available. When you contact the campground, ask for a map showing the campsite locations. If you will be paddling to the site with young children, be sure to note the scale of miles when you select a site. Even the closest sites are about two miles from put-in locations, and access from the southern end requires paddling across a sizable stretch of open water (on the north end, you can reserve a site near the mouth of the Androscoggin or Magalloway river to minimize paddling over open water).

With the tremendous variety of wildlife and the number of ducks nesting here, it is not surprising that Umbagog Lake has become one of our newest national wildlife refuges. The Lake Umbagog National Wildlife Refuge was established in November 1992 with the purchase by the federal government of the first tracts of land for the refuge. The

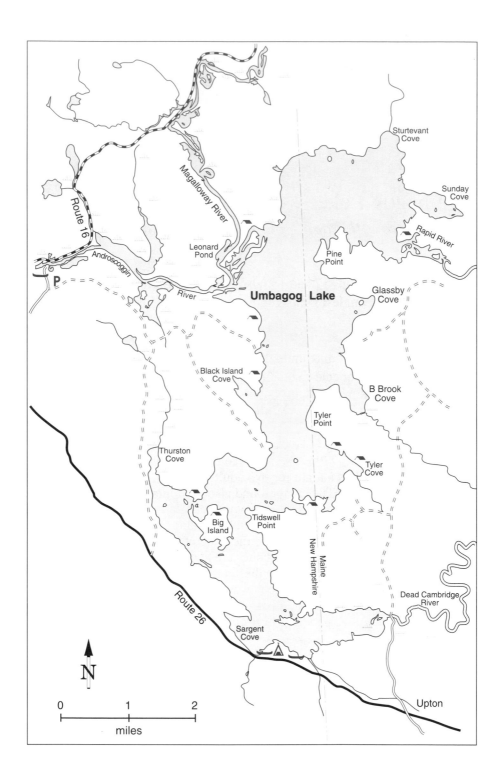

Sturtevant
Cove

Sunday
Cove

Rapid River

Magalloway River

Route 16

Pine
Point

Glassby
Cove

Leonard
Pond

Androscoggin

P

River

Umbagog Lake

B Brook
Cove

Black Island
Cove

Tyler
Point

Thurston
Cove

Tyler
Cove

Route 26

Big
Island

Tidswell
Point

Maine
New Hampshire

Dead Cambridge
River

Sargent
Cove

Upton

0   1   2

miles

N

actual refuge is still very small (just a few hundred acres), but the U.S. Fish and Wildlife Service is negotiating with several paper companies for title or conservation easements that would increase the refuge to nearly 10,000 acres.

Umbagog Lake straddles the Maine–New Hampshire border, covering more than twelve square miles. The lake, pronounced "um-BAY-gog," is oriented generally north-south, with a highly varied shoreline that extends more than forty miles, plus dozens of islands. Most of the lake is quite wild, yet readily accessible to the backcountry canoe-camper, with thirty wilderness sites around the lake managed by Umbagog Lake Campground. There are a few private cottages and camps on parts of the lake, and motorboat traffic has increased in recent years, but it is hoped there will be little if any future development. It might even be possible to petition the states of New Hampshire and Maine to restrict motorboat use.

Umbagog Lake is so large and its shoreline so varied that one hardly knows where to begin in describing it. It is a very shallow lake—the name means "shallow water"—with average depths of only about fifteen feet. There are many marshy areas that provide ideal nesting habitats for such duck species as ring-necked, black, mallard, wood, hooded merganser, and common merganser. Between 75 and 100 nesting boxes around the lake are used by wood ducks and hooded mergansers (our two common cavity nesters).

The largest marshy area, near the northwestern corner of the lake, is called Leonard Pond. It is an extensive thick, grassy marsh that has been in recent years the site of New Hampshire's only nesting bald eagles. In late summer 1993, though, the immature eagles destroyed the nest. The adult pair then abandoned the site and rebuilt a nest across the lake on the Maine side. They returned to the Maine site in the spring of 1994 and were nesting successfully when the male disappeared (and presumably died). The female then abandoned the eggs, but found a new mate. In the summer of 1994 the pair rebuilt the nest back on the New Hampshire side where the original nest had been.

Osprey, meanwhile, are having a better time of it. In 1994 there were approximately twenty-five nesting pairs in the vicinity of Umbagog Lake, and they successfully reared thirty-five chicks. Loons have had mixed success. There are a lot of loons summering on the lake—an estimated fifty to sixty—but relatively few chicks reared. In 1994 there were twenty-two territorial pairs and thirteen pairs that actually nested, fledging a total of eleven chicks. During May, June, and July, be particularly careful about nesting loons. Even a quiet paddler inadvertently getting too close to a nest can result in the adults abandoning it, and loons always nest very close to the water (see page 278).

Our favorite places on the lake include Leonard Pond, the coves along the inlet of the Rapid River on the northeastern end of the lake, and some of the small coves and islands along the shoreline east of Tidswell Point. In the early morning light, in a cove just east of Tidswell Point, we watched three moose grazing by the water's edge, and each little cove along here seemed to have its own family of wood ducks, mergansers, or black ducks. Big Island, which was purchased by the Society for the Protection of New Hampshire Forests in the 1980s, is also very nice and includes six campsites. For camping with kids, those sites on the north shore of Tyler Cove (21, 22, and 23) are particularly good because there is a protected sandy swimming beach at the end of the cove. Even the inlet of the Dead Cambridge River at the far southeastern end—the most developed part of the lake—is pleasant. In fact, we got our closest look at a moose not 200 yards from a cottage near the mouth of the river (which is not canoeable, at least in the summer). Except for the far northern shore of the lake, most of the houses and camps on the lake are along the southern section, below and to the east of Big Island.

The vegetation around Umbagog Lake is quite varied. In some areas conifers predominate: balsam fir, spruce, northern white cedar, hemlock, and white pine; other areas have a lot more deciduous trees, including yellow and paper birch, red maple, and an occasional red oak. We also saw a few relatively rare jack pines on the lake.

As you plan a trip at Umbagog Lake, be aware that it is a very large lake. Potentially dangerous winds and waves can come up very quickly, making open-boat paddling hazardous. Be ready to change your plans—or (horrors!) get ferried out to your campsite by the campground owners (for a fee). Paddling around the lake during a two-day period in August, we got into heavy winds both afternoons, even though the water had been calm as glass on each of those mornings. Wind blowing from the north across several miles of water can build up sizable waves—believe us!

There are lots of fish in Umbagog Lake—as evidenced by the large osprey population—but relatively few prime sport fish. In mid-August, we caught yellow perch, smallmouth bass, and lots of lake chub (a whitefish with large scales and a deeply forked tail), one of which was several pounds. In the deeper holes near the north end you may hook a salmon, brook trout, or brown trout. With the right bait, lures, or flies, one should not have too much trouble pulling a few tasty meals out of the lake.

Getting There

There are several ways to get onto the lake with your canoe, all of them in New Hampshire. The only public boat-launch area on the lake itself is at the southern end, off Route 26. Users of the backcountry camping sites can also park and put in at the Umbagog Lake Campground, just east of the public boat launch. Closer to the north end, paddlers can put in on the Androscoggin or Magalloway rivers. For those planning to leave their cars, the Androscoggin access is a better choice. From the south in Maine, take Route 2 to Newry (west of Rumford), and turn onto Route 26 north. After crossing the New Hampshire state line, the access to Umbagog Lake Campground is in about two miles on the right. The public boat access is another three-quarters of a mile past the campground, also on the right.

To reach the access on the Androscoggin River, continue north on 26 to Errol. Just before crossing the bridge over the Androscoggin as you are coming into Errol, turn right onto a dirt road (there is a sign, Access to Public Water, here). Follow the road about a mile and park at the end. From here, the main lake is about three miles up the Androscoggin—though you will be paddling against the current, it is an easy paddle along the slow-flowing, meandering river. Paddling toward Umbagog, a number of marshy ponds both to the right and left await your exploration. Keep an eye out for otter and mink here!

You can also put in on the Magalloway River north of Errol on Route 16. There are a number of places where a canoe can be launched along Route 16 (you will find one 4.7 miles north of the Routes 16 and 26 intersection in Errol). The Magalloway provides a great starting point for paddlers who are being dropped off, but we did not find good places to park a car overnight along Route 16. The Magalloway is even more serpentine in its path than the Androscoggin, with numerous oxbow ponds and marshes where the wide loops of river eventually get cut off by shortcut channels. You are quite likely to see moose along here.

Richardson Lake (Upper and Lower)

Richardsontown and Twp. C

MAPS

Maine Atlas: Map 18

USGS Quadrangles: Richardson Pond, Middle Dam, Metallak
  Mountain, Andover, and Oquossoc

INFORMATION

Upper Richardson area: 4,200 acres

Lower Richardson area: 2,900 acres

Prominent fish species: salmon, lake trout, and brook trout

Bureau of Public Lands, Maine Department of Conservation, State
  House Station 22, Augusta, ME 04333; 207-289-3061

Camping: South Arm Campground, Box 310, Andover, ME 04216;
  207-364-5155

Upper and Lower Richardson, once distinct lakes, merged at the Narrows
when the twenty-two-foot Middle Dam was built on the western side of
Lower Richardson in the early 1900s. The combined lake covers more
than eleven square miles and extends roughly fifteen miles in an S-curv-
ing north-south direction. The lake ranges in width from a few hundred
yards at the Narrows to about a mile and a half at the widest section of
Lower Richardson. Most of the lake is a little less than a mile across.

The size and orientation of the Richardson lakes make them potentially quite dangerous in bad weather. In some places, wind-driven waves
can build up over more than five miles of open water. Be ready to alter
your plans in threatening weather. If you must paddle on the lake in bad
conditions (returning from one of the boat-access campsites, for example), wear life vests, use extreme caution, and stay close to shore.

The shorelines of both Upper and Lower Richardson lakes are
rocky, with a generally sandy bottom. The clear water in these deep
lakes supports an excellent cold-water trout and salmon fishery (lake
trout, brook trout, salmon). Such softwoods as spruce, fir, cedar, and
white pine predominate, but much of the forest is fairly young, owing
to extensive cutting prior to state acquisition.

Seventeen primitive campsites dot the shores of Richardson Lake
and its islands. Managed by the South Arm Campground at the south
tip of the lake, the main campground there has an additional sixty-five
campsites, plus typical campground amenities. The primitive campsites
range from one-quarter mile to fifteen miles from the campground.

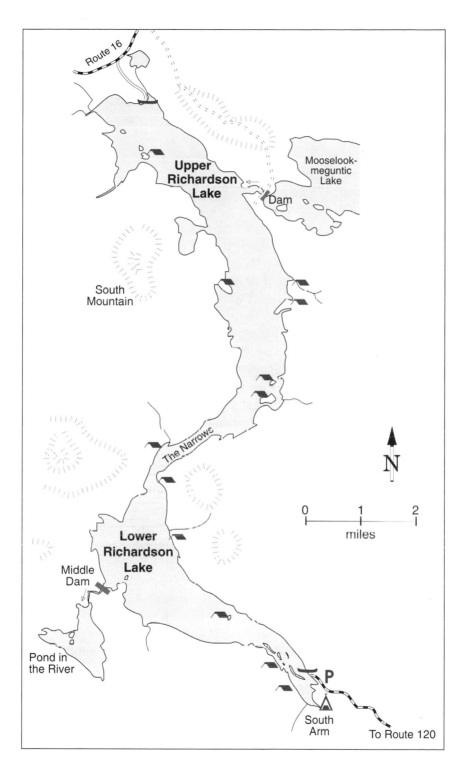

Route 16

Upper
Richardson
Lake

Mooselook-
meguntic
Lake

Dam

South
Mountain

The Narrows

N

0   1   2
miles

Lower
Richardson
Lake

Middle
Dam

Pond in
the River

P

South
Arm

To Route 120

Nearly all of the eastern shore of Upper Richardson Lake consists of public reserve land owned and managed by the state of Maine. The state acquired 80 percent of this 22,800-acre tract of land in 1984 from the Pingree heirs (Seven Islands Land Company) and James River Corporation, and the other 20 percent in 1978 from the Brown Company. As with other public reserve lands, the state manages the Richardson Unit for recreation, wildlife habitat, and timber. In parts of the unit within sight of the lake, the first two uses generally take precedence over the last. The Appalachian Trail passes a few miles east of the Richardson lakes.

Some of the nicer campsites you will pass paddling north from the South Arm Campground include Spirit Island, Sand Banks (which has a great sandy beach area), Portland Point at the Narrows with a protected sandy cove, Pine Island and Metallak Island in Upper Richardson (Pine Island used to have a bald eagle nest), Half Moon Cove on the western shore with two campsites, and Big Beaver Island.

If you paddle in the northern end of Upper Richardson, also check out Cranberry Cove, the most remote and most protected part of either lake. The entrance to the cove is rocky; at low water level—as was the case when we paddled here in late summer of a dry year—you have to pick your way carefully between the rocks. The shoreline of Cranberry Cove harbors a typical northern fen ecosystem, with tamarack, leather leaf, bog rosemary, pitcher plant, and sphagnum moss.

Getting There

You can launch a boat at either the north or south end of the Richardson lakes. To reach the boat access at the south end, drive north on Route 5 from Route 2, west of Rumford. Follow Route 5 to Andover, and turn right onto Route 120. You very quickly cross a bridge over the Ellis River (less than a half-mile from Route 5). After crossing the river, watch for a left turn at a sign to the South Arm Campground. Follow this road for 9.1 miles to the boat access on the left. The boat access is 0.4 mile past the entrance to the campground. There is plenty of parking space here.

To get to the northern boat access, take Routes 4 and 16 west from the town of Rangeley. Note your mileage where Routes 4 and 16 split at the northwestern tip of Rangeley Lake. Stay on 16 west for another 13.8 miles, then turn left onto a gravel road at the Public Boat Access sign. The boat access is 1.0 mile down this road. There is plenty of parking space here and an outhouse.

Gilman Pond

New Portland and Lexington Twp.

MAPS
  Maine Atlas: Map 30
  USGS Quadrangle: New Portland

INFORMATION
  Information on area, depth, and prominent fish species not available.

Gilman Pond is a delightful little out-of-the way pond in the Rangeley Lakes region. Nestled into a valley surrounded by forested hills, this picturesque pond offers the opportunity for several hours of quiet paddling, especially if you paddle all the way down to Route 16, a round-trip distance of about five miles.

Although we found the outlet to be most interesting, the north end of the pond, choked with sedges, equisetum, buttonbush, and other aquatic vegetation, is well worth exploring. Note Sandy Stream flowing down through the scattered silver maples on the northern peninsula. The fact that it has a good flow of water but is choked with impenetrable sedges indicates that boats do not ply these waters in great numbers. The cove on the northeast side of the peninsula is quieter and more marshy than the one on the other side. The shoreline sports a wide variety of tree species, but particularly noticeable on the north end are cedar, paper birch, spruce, hemlock, and balsam fir.

As you travel down the eastern shore (there is a small amount of development along the western shore) to the outlet, note the large number of tall red oaks. Paper and yellow birch, aspen, and maple show up in good numbers as well. When we paddled here, loons called from the center of the pond, kingfishers darted down the lake in front of us, and an osprey fished near the outlet. The presence of these three fish-eating birds together indicates that the pond must support a reasonable population of fish. Local fishermen told us fishing is pretty good for chain pickerel and an occasional lunker brown trout.

Paddling down the outlet, note the very tall tamaracks on the right-hand shore. On the left-hand side is an extensive marshy area. After passing it you can take a left turn and paddle back up into it. In mid-July when we visited, the water was still quite high, covering the roots of many shoreline trees, especially red maples. Their leaves were

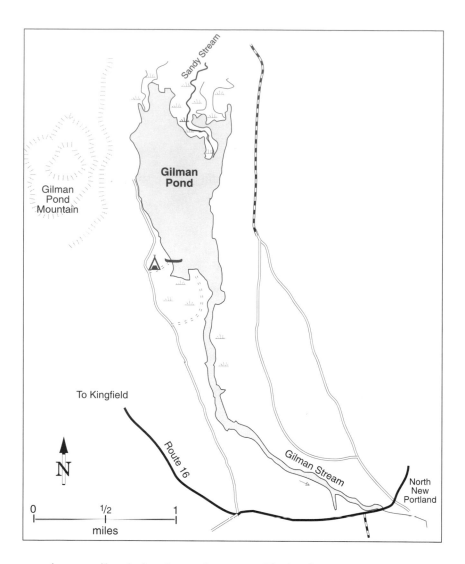

starting to wilt, obviously not because of lack of water. Instead, standing water impeded gas exchange between the air and their roots.

Many beautiful wild swamp roses were in bloom up and down the outlet, and there was evidence of extensive recent dogwood and viburnum blooms. Islands of buttonbush, with its terminal Osage orange–like green balls that later turn into large, round, puffy white flowers, occurred in large clumps out in the water. Side channels were filled with rushes. Sweet gale, with aromatic leaves that give off a wonderful scent when crushed, dot the shoreline in marshy areas. Because of this large diversity of plants and the opportunity to see many flowers in bloom, this is a great scenic place to paddle.

Getting There

The boat access for Gilman Pond is at the Gilman Pond Campground, run by a pleasant fellow who used to run the adjacent farm. Instead of bolting to Florida or Arizona upon retirement, he decided to stay and set up a modest campground on the pond. This would be a great out-of-the-way place to camp; the sites are well separated and well wooded, and there are few amenities other than picnic tables and fire grates that would draw rowdy crowds. He charged us two dollars to launch our boat.

Traveling west on Route 16 (coming from the vicinity of Skowhegan or Waterville), the road takes a sharp left in the town of North New Portland. In 0.1 mile cross the bridge over the Gilman Stream. Continue west out of town for 1.0 mile, watching for the sign to Gilman Pond Campground. Turn right off Route 16 onto the gravel road leading to Gilman Pond. Go straight down this road for 1.9 miles. Look for several white trailers on the right-hand side and a hard-to-see sign that says Gilman Pond Campground Office.

Branns Mill Pond

Dover-Foxcroft

MAPS
 Maine Atlas: Map 32
 USGS Quadrangle: Garland
INFORMATION
 Area: 271 acres; maximum depth: 15 feet
 Prominent fish species: white perch and chain pickerel

Branns Mill Pond is a real gem, full of wildlife and a joy to explore, especially in the early morning or late afternoon. On a windy day when other lakes in the area bristle with whitecaps, this pond remains much quieter and more suitable for paddling.

From the boat access on Notch Road, paddle southeast through the narrow section of the pond and into the inlet brook. The lazy channel winds for about a mile through biologically rich and highly diverse marsh habitat. Floating aquatic plants, especially bullhead lily, crowd the channel by early summer. In places, dense stands of cattail occur, but elsewhere, sedges, rushes, alder, sphagnum moss, and heaths dominate the marsh. Part of the creek is within the Penobscot-Piscataquis Wildlife Management Area.

tamarack

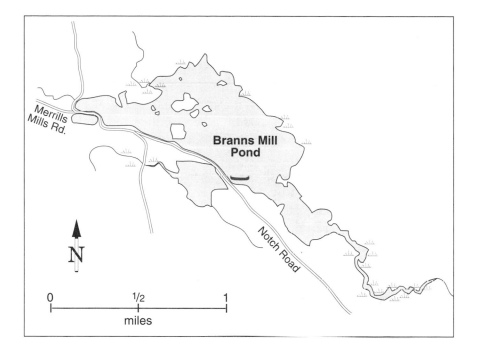

As we paddled quietly along here, we suddenly heard a very distinct munching sound. Muskrat? Beaver? It sounded more like an overzealous twelve-year-old just back from a Halloween foray, trying to consume as much candy as possible as quickly as possible. Then, fifteen feet away the bushes rustled, and out swam an otter. From the sounds of a feeding river otter, one can only conclude they enjoy eating as much as they seem to enjoy everything else. As dusk approached, we also saw a muskrat swimming along the creek and several beavers, who loudly announced our passage with slapping tails.

As you paddle up the creek, the channel narrows gradually and the current becomes more noticeable. After poling over the remains of an old beaver dam, the sound of running water meant we were nearing the end of our upstream explorations. At the end of the canoeable channel we came to a large stone wall and the ruins of a structure—probably Branns Mill, but we have not been able to learn anything of the history.

Notice that the trees growing on the banks get progressively shorter closer to the stream, evidence that the channel is gradually closing in. Aquatic plants and sphagnum moss gradually expand out over the surface of the water. Then shrubs such as leather leaf and alder take hold. As a root mat builds up, tamarack and cedar become established. You can see this succession clearly as you look from the water's edge to the forest on higher ground.

An interesting geology underlies this area. Unlike the granite covering most of central and northern Maine, the rock here is sedimentary. In places, the layered rock tilted up before the stream channel eroded it, so you'll pass jagged rocks extending out of the water like tombstones. Use caution paddling here; unlike rounded granite boulders, these jagged shales are sharp enough to puncture some canoes.

While we would choose the inlet channel first for exploration, we enjoyed much of the rest of the pond as well. The narrow section between the boat access and the inlet creek as well as the far western tip by the dam suffer from development, but most of the pond is fairly natural. The northern shore of the main pond has extensive marshy areas and is as rich with wildlife as the inlet creek. We saw at least one pair of loons on the pond and suspect they are nesting on one of the many islands, where their nests will be relatively safe from predators. Open areas on a few of these islands would make nice picnic spots, but we do not suggest overnight camping.

Getting There

Coming from the south, get off I-95 at Exit 39 (Newport). Follow Routes 11 and 7 north through Corinna, then continue north on Route 7. Turn right off Route 7 onto Merrills Mills Road 6.6 miles from Dexter, where Route 23 north turns off to the left (the turn onto Merrills Mills Road is a total of 20.9 miles from the interstate). From the Bangor area, you can reach Merrills Mills Road by driving north on Route 15 to Dover-Foxcroft, then turning left (south) on Route 7 and driving for 5.6 miles; Merrills Mills Road is on the left.

Follow Merrills Mills Road, which is gravel, to the east. Bear to the right after 1.4 miles, as you reach the western tip of the pond, and follow the road along the edge of the pond. In another 0.8 mile you will pass quite close to the pond on the left and a smaller pond on the right. The boat access and pull-over area are just past here on the left. There is room for four or five cars to park off the road; others could park along the edge of the road, which is fairly wide.

The Playful River Otter

If you paddle the more remote northern lakes in Maine, and if you get out on the water early in the morning or remain out as dusk approaches, sooner or later you are sure to see a river otter—or perhaps a family of these adorable mammals. Their playful antics, friendly facial expressions, and masterful swimming make them one of our favorite species.

The river otter, *Lutra canadensis,* once lived on virtually every watercourse in America, from the sun-warmed southwestern rivers to the icy far-northern lakes and streams. Today, because of trapping over the last 200 years, pollution of our waterways, and encroaching development, otter sightings remain uncommon over their extensive range. Because they eat at the top of the food chain, otters are susceptible to pollution and toxic chemicals in the environment, such as heavy metals, DDT derivatives, dioxin, and PCBs.

River otters grow quite large. Adults can reach four and a half feet in length and weigh up to thirty pounds. They have long thin bodies and a relatively thick, sharply tapered tail. Their dense fur, long prized by trappers, nearly led to their demise. The dark-brown fur above gives way to lighter colors on the belly and throat. Their long, distinct facial whiskers probably aid in finding food underwater.

Well adapted for their environment, otters' noses and ears close when under water, and their webbed toes aid in swimming. Otters swim fast enough to catch trout in open water, though they usually opt for slower-moving suckers, minnows, and crayfish. When hunting, otters come up for air every thirty seconds or so, though they can remain underwater for up to two minutes. When they come up to the surface, their heads generally pop up way above the surface and they look around—quite different from beavers and muskrats, which rise barely above the water's surface.

Though primarily adapted for water, otters do pretty well on land as well. Clocked at up to 18 miles per hour on land, they will travel as much as 100 miles overland in search of new territory. An otter's den is generally at the water's edge, with an underwater entrance. Natural cavities under tree roots or an abandoned beaver lodge may be used.

Otters eat smaller fish and crayfish at the surface of the water, while they take larger prey to shore or to a rock protruding from the water. In shallow water, you may see just an otter's tail sticking out of the water as it roots around in the mud for food. Ingenious hunters, otters have been known to herd fish into shallows where their prey are easily caught. They may even punch a hole in a beaver dam—allowing the water to escape—then wade in and feast on fish flopping in the shallow water. Because they are such successful hunters, they have plenty of time to play—a trait for which otters are famous.

The young of many mammal species play. Animal behaviorists believe such play provides practice for future hunting or courtship. But otters do not stop playing when they reach adulthood. They will roll in the water chasing one another, or climb repeatedly up on a snowbank and slide down into the water (though otter slides are not quite as common as children's books seem to imply). Animal behaviorists have not yet found reasons for otters' play other than just to have fun.

Otters mate in the late winter or early spring, but often birth does not follow until almost a year later. Like many members of the weasel family, implantation of embryos is delayed in otters, and development stops until the following fall or winter. Otters give birth to two to four cubs in a well-protected den any time between November and April (usually February to April). The cubs are born fully furred, but with eyes closed and no teeth. They will not venture outside of their den for about three months and remain completely dependent on their mother for at least six months. Though the mother provides all the care for the young cubs, the father may rejoin the family and help with care and teaching after they get to be about six months old. The young reach sexual maturity after two years.

Though otters are curious animals and relatively bold, keep your distance when observing them. Interference from humans may cause them to move away and search for more remote streams or ponds.

Pierce Pond and Upper Pierce Pond

Pierce Pond Twp.

MAPS
Maine Atlas: Map 30
USGS Quadrangles: East Carry Pond and Pierce Pond

INFORMATION
Pierce Pond and Upper Pierce Pond area: 1,650 acres; Pierce Pond maximum depth: 185 feet; Upper Pierce Pond maximum depth: 66 feet

Prominent fish species: salmon and brook trout. Fishing is with artificial lures only, with a twelve-inch minimum length on trout.

Harrison's Pierce Pond Sporting Camps, P.O. Box 315, Bingham, ME 04920; 207-672-3625 (radio phone). Winter: 603-279-8424. Nine guest cabins, American Plan.

Fire permits: Maine Forest Service, Arnold Trail District (207-474-3200) or Southern Region Headquarters (207-287-2275)

Pierce Pond is very deep, with a cold, well-oxygenated substratum, making this an excellent cold-water fishery and bringing a fair number of fishermen to its shores. But because it is out of the way and has more than 2.5 square miles of surface area, you can paddle in relative solitude here.

Beautiful forested hillsides surround both ponds, with conifers dominating the eastern shore and mixed conifers and deciduous trees sharing the western shore. Heavily forested islands lend a scenic quality, especially to the northern section of Pierce Pond and to Upper Pierce Pond. The islands break up the view of open water, making the ponds seem deceptively small. Lots of beautiful boulders poke up everywhere, especially guarding channels going up the right side of the middle and northern sections of Pierce Pond and in Upper Pierce Pond. The huge number of these rocks, some barely submerged, belie the depths under the open water.

There seems to be a camping spot on the Thoroughfare that connects the two ponds, as well as sites in the upper bay of Pierce Pond, one on the eastern shore and one on the western side of the two islands out in the middle. If you camp here, you will have to share the island shore with a monster beaver lodge and its inhabitants. On Upper Pierce Pond are a couple of camping spots, one on the south

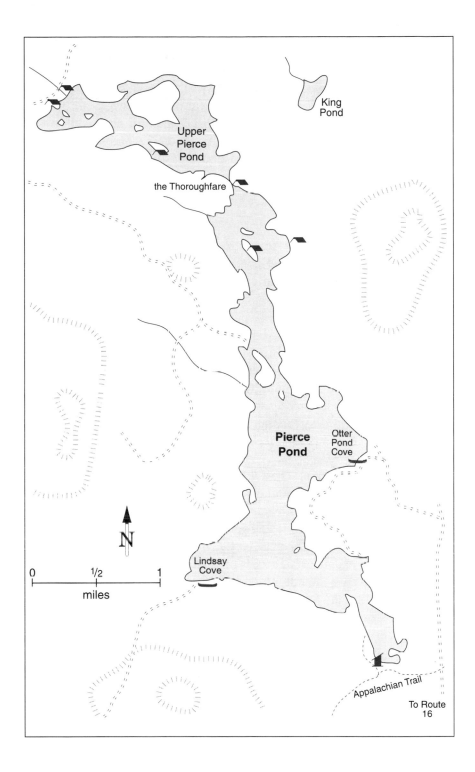

King
Pond

Upper
Pierce
Pond

the Thoroughfare

**Pierce
Pond**

Otter
Pond
Cove

N

0   1/2   1
miles

Lindsay
Cove

Appalachian Trail

To Route
16

end of an island to the left. Passing between the ponds requires a portage over some slippery boards, dodging the beaver cuttings. The depth here is deceptive because of the very clear water.

Lots of loons plied the clear waters of the ponds as we paddled this wild place nearly alone on a beautiful late July weekend. Purple damsel flies, with their backswept wings, landed on our paddles and arms. Northern white cedar, paper birch, white pine, and red pine covered the islands and hillsides. One could easily spend several days exploring this wonderful spot.

Getting There

From Bingham take Route 16 south. Take an immediate right onto a paved road after crossing the Kennebec River. Follow this progressively deteriorating road for about 22 miles as follows: at 4.2 miles, turn right, following the signs to Harrison's Pierce Pond Sporting Camps. Pavement ends at 4.4 miles. A public picnic area on Lake Wyman appears at 9.5 miles. The road deteriorates further at 12.0 miles. Take the right fork up the hill at 15.2 miles; watch out for rocks sticking up in the middle of the road. Reach Harrison's Pierce Pond Sporting Camps on the left at 19.0 miles; a few feet away, just after the bridge, the Appalachian Trail crosses the road. Continue on up the hill, turning left onto the access road at 20.2 miles. Take the left fork at 21.5 miles. The boat access at Otter Pond Cove on Pierce Pond is at 21.9 miles.

A word of caution: The Otter Pond Cove access road is nearly impassable because of large rocks jutting up in the middle of the road. If you do not have a high-clearance vehicle, it would be best to try one of the other access points. If you get stuck on this road, there is a resident caretaker at Otter Pond Cove.

Someone maintains an access on Lindsay Cove, and you can pay to launch there. We did not investigate this access, but we were told by residents and by the Department of Inland Fisheries and Wildlife that this access exists. Follow the directions as above, but instead of turning right up the hill at 15.2 miles, turn left instead. Follow this road, turning right after coming down a hill at about 6 or 7 miles. It would be wise to follow the *Maine Atlas* here.

Alternatively, one could stay overnight with the very nice people at Harrison's Sporting Camps, giving you very easy access to the pond.

Bald Mountain Pond

Bald Mountain Twp.

MAPS
   Maine Atlas: Map 31
   USGS Quadrangle: Bald Mountain Pond
INFORMATION
   Area: 1,152 acres; maximum depth: 62 feet
   Prominent fish species: brook trout
   Fire permits: Maine Forest Service, Arnold Trail District (207-
      474-3200) or Southern Region Headquarters (207-287-2275)

The north end of Bald Mountain Pond is part of the Maine Public
Reserve Land system, and the Appalachian Trail skirts the northern
shore. This is a wild place in a beautiful setting, with aptly named
Bald Mountain dominating the western skyline. Unfortunately, it
draws large crowds on summer weekends—although fewer people
camp here than at nearby Austin Pond. A visit here would be more sat-
isfying during the week or after Labor Day.

   When we paddled out on the last Sunday in July at 6:30 A.M., the
resident loons and we made the only ripples on the placid surface for
the first hour and a half after sunrise, while the weekend partiers slept
in. The only noise, other than an occasional loon call, came from the
large population of white-throated sparrows, with their "Old Sam
Peabody, Peabody, Peabody" call. We saw lots of wildlife, but the
highlight was a cow moose in the northeast cove, submerged to her
nostrils, trying to escape a huge cloud of biting flies. Several of these
tenacious flies broke off from the pack and annoyed us for about a
half-hour after our encounter with the moose.

   Beautiful, heavily forested islands enhance the picturesque nature
of Bald Mountain Pond. The surface in places is dimpled with hundreds
of granite boulders; unfortunately for boat hulls, many of these rocks are
barely submerged. Go cautiously when paddling near shore and when
exploring the many inlets. There is a nice campsite on the northern shore
of one inlet on the east side of the pond and another island site at the
north end of the pond. The boulder-strewn northern inlet comprises one
of the most scenic areas, making paddling up there well worthwhile.

   White and red pine, cedar, balsam fir, and spruce grow right
down to the water, and a fair number of yellow birch, maples, and
paper birch appear in and among the conifers. Fragrant water lilies

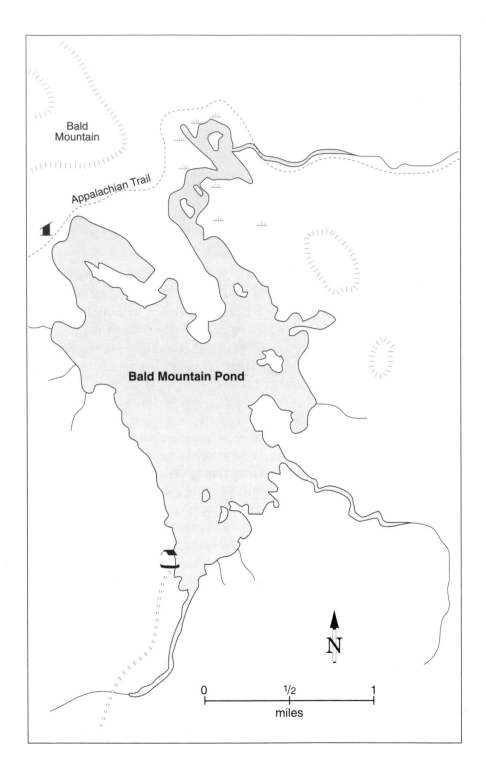

Bald Mountain

Appalachian Trail

1

Bald Mountain Pond

N

0   1/2   1
miles

A cow moose seeks relief from a buzzing horde of biting flies at the north end of Bald Mountain Pond.

abound in the coves and shallower parts. Bird species include ring-billed gulls, red-breasted mergansers, loons, black ducks, belted kingfishers, and double-crested cormorants.

Because of the many coves and inlets dotting the shoreline, it will take several hours to explore fully this wonderful place. Paddle out early to maximize wildlife viewing, and come during the week if you can to avoid the weekend camping parties.

Getting There

From Bingham at the junction of Routes 201 and 16, take Route 16 east for 5.4 miles. Turn left onto a gravel road about 150 feet before the white Mayfield Township sign. A sign at the start of this gravel road says the area is owned by the Scott Paper Company (sign may change to Sappi Co., which recently purchased Scott Paper). Start marking mileage at the beginning of this road.

At 2.8 miles, go over a bridge, take a sharp right turn, and join a larger road. At 2.9 miles, take the left fork. At 5.0 miles, take the right fork. At 6.9 miles, take a diagonal right. Cross a bridge at 10.3 miles, and come to the first campsite on Austin Pond at 10.5 miles. The boat access on Austin Pond is at 10.6 miles. Continue on around Austin Pond, taking the left fork at 11.5 miles. Stay straight at 12.3 miles; the left turn leads to Little Austin Pond. Stay left at 13.8 miles, and the boat access on Bald Mountain Pond is at the end of the road at 14.4 miles.

Spencer Lake and Fish Pond
Hobbstown Twp.

MAPS
Maine Atlas: Map 39
USGS Quadrangles: King and Bartlett Lake and Spencer Lake

INFORMATION
Spencer Lake area: 1,819 acres; maximum depth: 135 feet
Prominent fish species: lake trout, brook trout, salmon, and yellow perch

Hardscrabble Wilderness Camps and Lodge, P.O. Box 1899, Bangor, ME 04402; 207-990-4534. Five guest cabins, American Plan.

Fire permits: Maine Forest Service, Arnold Trail District (207-474-3200) or Southern Region Headquarters (207-287-2275)

The drive to these bodies of water is breathtaking, with dramatic views of the surrounding mountains—Number 5, Three Slide, Hardwood, and Hardscrabble. At the boat access of Fish Pond, we were greeted by several families of Canada geese grazing on flat grasslands and marsh across the pond. As we watched the low afternoon sun turn the billowing clouds hovering over Spencer Mountain to shades of gold and red, we knew we had come to a wild place. Other than the few people who come to fish for trout and salmon, you are likely to paddle here pretty much alone.

Nestled between two parallel ridges and ringed with peaks rising 1,300 feet above the water level, Spencer Lake fills a deep gorge, giving it depth not found in other lakes in this area. This depth keeps the lower layers, down to 135 feet, quite cold, much to the liking of the lake trout, brook trout, and salmon population.

When we paddled here, ravens croaked out their hoarse cries, and loons filled the air with plaintive songs, adding to the already incredible feeling of wilderness. Ospreys, great blue herons, and kingfishers, each in its own way, fished the surface waters. Spotted sandpipers bobbed their tails along the shore, and warblers hunted for insects in the trees hanging out over the water.

As we paddled through the access stream between Fish Pond and Spencer Lake, we encountered submerged stumps, a sand beach, and shallow water, which could be a problem when water levels are down.

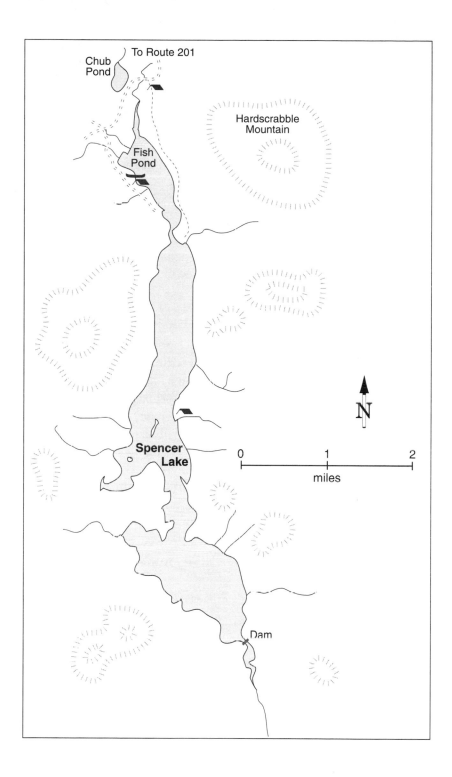

Chub
Pond

To Route 201

Hardscrabble
Mountain

Fish
Pond

N

Spencer
Lake

0   1   2
miles

Dam

The expected conifers—white and red pine, spruce, balsam fir, and northern white cedar—dominate the shoreline, intermingling with paper birch, red maple, and alder. Conifers and hardwoods share the western hillsides about equally, but deciduous trees dominate the eastern hillsides. Past logging practices may have altered the species composition here in this area of the northern spruce, pine, and fir forest.

As you paddle south into Spencer Lake, there is a lodge with several cabins over on the left, and farther down the lake, after passing a series of islands and a large peninsula on the right, another cluster of cabins appears on the left. A fair amount of marshland surrounds the large peninsula, while the rest of the lake is contained within a rocky shoreline. There are several campsites on Fish Pond and Spencer Lake. For those looking for cabin accommodations and meals, there is Hardscrabble Wilderness Camps and Lodge on Spencer Lake.

Getting There

From Bingham, drive north on Route 201. Note your mileage at The Forks and continue for another 13.9 miles. Just after the boat access on Parlin Pond, turn left onto a gravel road; a sign at the junction says Hardscrabble Lodge 15 Miles. The road into Fish Pond and Spencer Lake affords breathtaking views of forested mountainsides. The beginning part of this road is fairly straight, but after about 12 miles, the road narrows, there is a series of S-curves, and a narrow bridge. At 13.1 miles, make a hard left at a four-way intersection. Drive slowly down a potholed narrow road lined with balsam fir and red and striped maples, arriving at the boat access on Fish Pond at 13.5 miles.

There are three or four campsites right at the boat access.

Attean Pond and Holeb Pond
Moose River Bow Trip

MAPS

Maine Atlas: Map 39

USGS Quadrangles: Attean Pond, Catheart Mountain, and Holeb

INFORMATION

Attean Pond area: 2,745 acres; maximum depth: 55 feet

Holeb Pond area: 1,055 acres; maximum depth: 52 feet

Prominent fish species: salmon and brook trout. Fishing is said to be excellent.

Fire permits: Maine Forest Service, Arnold Trail District (207-474-3200) or Southern Region Headquarters (207-287-2275)

We cover Attean and Holeb ponds together because they form part of the popular Moose River Bow trip. We paddled this scenic thirty-four-mile loop in August over a three-day weekend. To maximize wildlife viewing and allow thorough exploration of the two ponds and some side channels on the river, four days would be better. To avoid crowded campsites on the river, try to start your trip on a Thursday or earlier in the week.

Holeb Pond and the neighboring part of the Moose River are protected by the Maine Public Land Reserve system. Bogs, fens, and marshes cover the landscape, supporting a large moose population. We saw two moose on our trip, and friends who made the same trip a year earlier saw five. In the evening, beaver swam before us, eventually slapping the water with their tails before diving out of sight as we ventured too near.

The Moose River Bow loop totally encloses Number 5 Bog, a National Natural Landmark. Inaccessible except by foot down an old logging road taking off north from Spencer Rips, this unique, pristine fen of more than 1,500 acres may be the most remote of the Northeast's large peatlands. Formed 10,000 years ago as glaciers retreated and now protected from logging and other development, Number 5 Bog sports large stands of jack pine, tamarack, and white cedar. Its sphagnum-covered open areas provide habitat for many plant species, including several rare orchids. The area is wetter than most other peatlands in Maine, such as the Great Heath just northeast of Cherryfield, and even boasts a substantial ninety-acre pond, Bog Pond.

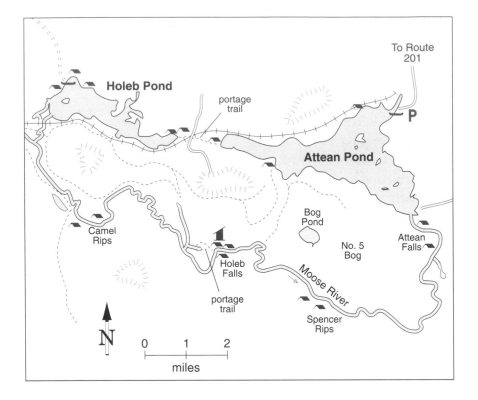

Other natural wonders abound in this area, starting with Attean Pond. With nearly sixty islands scattered over four square miles of water and with forested mountains all around, the pond is extraordinarily scenic. As you approach Jackman on Route 201, stop at the turnout overlooking the pond for a bird's-eye view of this often-photographed wonder. Although Holeb Pond is smaller and has many fewer islands, it too is set in beautiful surroundings with mountains off in the distance. The large granite boulders at the put-in enhance the scenic quality. There is generally less traffic on Holeb Pond because of more difficult access, much to the liking of the mature bald eagle we watched as it perched in a large white pine.

The trip starts at the boat access on Attean Pond. After paddling to the right for 4 miles across Attean Pond, portage for 1.2 miles into Holeb Pond on a well-marked trail with boardwalks across the swampy areas. When you get to the wide logging road after 1.0 mile, turn right, cross the railroad track, watch for a small sign, and take an immediate left for the last little segment down to Holeb Pond. Paddle across Holeb Pond to its outlet, Holeb Stream. Holeb Stream joins the Moose River, which, in turn, flows back into Attean Pond.

A mature bald eagle surveys its domain from a large white pine on the shores of Holeb Pond. Nearly driven to extinction by pesticides, this majestic raptor now inhabits many lakes in Maine.

Note the tall steeplelike spires of the many large balsam firs along the river. Mixed in are some very large tamaracks, while the shoreline for miles and miles is covered with alders. Occasional marshy openings intrude on the alders, and these locations, along with entering streams and side channels, provide excellent moose viewing.

In most places, the Moose River moves along slowly, but because Holeb Pond is seventy-three feet higher than Attean Pond, you must portage around a few falls, but you can run some during high water. By August in most years, you must portage Camel Rips and Spencer Rips, along with Holeb Falls and Attean Falls. Mercifully, these relatively short portages, some just a few feet, do not compare with the long portage into Holeb Pond. Campsites occur adjacent to these portages.

Finding the portage at Holeb Falls can be quite a challenge. As it shows on the map, take a left into the side channel and then an immediate right (to the left is an excellent place to look for moose). Go over two short drops on this, the left channel of the Moose River. You need to take a sharp left down a very narrow side channel after about a half-mile. It is easy to miss and just wide enough for one boat; the take-out is about 150 feet down this channel.

Calm water at dawn reflects surrounding hills from the boat access at the end of the portage into Holeb Pond.

Holeb Falls, just past the midpoint of the trip, is back out on the main river. To see it, after the portage, cross the river to the campsite at the base of the riffle. From there a hiking trail takes you up to the falls.

Between Holeb and Attean falls, the river can seem a little monotonous. Eventually, you will hope never to see alders again, and you will wholeheartedly root for the beavers in their attempts to gorge on alder bark. To break the monotony, take the time to explore the streams, side channels, and marshy areas along the banks. This area between the falls is the marshiest and is the best area to look for moose. Just as the river turns north toward Attean Pond, Catheart and other tall mountains appear off to the east and should help take your mind off the endless alders.

Two short portages confront you at Attean Falls. Both are marked; the first is on the left; the second is on the right. You paddle a few hundred feet between them.

When you return to Attean Pond, it will look as though the pond has shrunk. Most of the islands cluster between the Moose River inlet and the take-out point, blocking your view of the rest of the lake. These islands effectively damp wind-driven swells that might be a problem on more open water. Navigating through them can be some-what of a challenge, especially if you don't use your compass. A hint:

A great horned owl perches on a broken-off yellow birch that hangs out over the Moose River.

three narrow valleys, with no hills, lead down to the water. You have just left one, the Moose River. The one to the left is the portage to Holeb Pond. Head for the one to the right to get to the boat access by paddling north-northwest for about two miles and then northeast.

Getting There

From the railroad crossing in Jackman on Route 201, drive south 0.6 mile to Attean Pond Road (signpost). Routes 6 and 15 go left here where you will turn right. Follow this road to the end at the boat access on Attean Pond.

Cold Stream

Passadumkeag

MAPS
Maine Atlas: Map 33
USGS Quadrangle: Passadumkeag

INFORMATION—GENERIC

Cold Stream drains a huge bog in the towns of Passadumkeag and Lowell, about twenty miles north of Old Town. The stream itself, with all of its meanderings, is only about five miles long. Together with its tributary, Little Cold Stream, Cold Stream flows into the Passadumkeag River, which immediately empties into the Penobscot River.

From the boat access on the Passadumkeag, paddle right, upstream, for a very short way, then take a left into the mouth of Cold Stream. At the confluence of the two rivers, you will find dwarf willow and alder. These give way to typical low-growing bog vegetation along the border of the forty-foot-wide channel. Sweet gale and several members of the heath family grow right to the water's edge. At one point the channel wanders nearer high ground, where you will find a thick grove of silver maples.

beaver

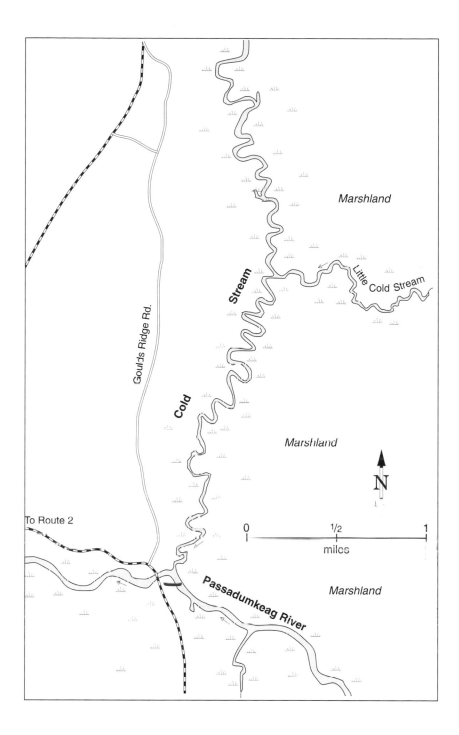

Marshland

Little Cold Stream

Stream

Cold

Gould's Ridge Rd.

Marshland

N

To Route 2

0   1/2   1
miles

Passadumkeag River

Marshland

This is wild country that—except for an occasional fisherman—sees few visitors. It is a great place to look for moose. Although we did not see any, we saw much evidence of their presence. We watched an osprey hover overhead, seemingly oblivious to us, waiting to dive on an unsuspecting fish. We also watched a northern harrier glide over the marsh, skimming the tops of the vegetation, waiting to pounce on any rodents foolhardy enough to be out in the middle of the morning. Formerly called marsh hawk, the harrier is distinguished by its white rump patch and its habit of buoyantly gliding over fields and marshes, tipping its upraised wings from side to side. Because the bird we saw was gray instead of brown, it was a male.

As we rounded one of the never-ending bends in the channel, we surprised a beaver. In typical fashion, it dove, resurfaced, and slapped its tail on the water. This one was so close that it splashed us as it dove again. Wherever you see patches of alder, look for beaver and beaver activity. We saw numerous cuttings, lodges, side channels dug out to provide access to lusher vegetation, and mud banks where they had collected mud to plaster on their lodges and dams. If you paddle here in the evening, you should see several of these industrious little engineers.

You can also paddle up Little Cold Stream quite a way, at least during high water, and these two streams are a great place to paddle on windy days when nearby lakes and the Penobscot River are too rough to enjoy.

Getting There

Take I-95 to Exit 54 at Howland and West Enfield, then turn onto Routes 155 and 6 east. At the junction with Route 2, turn right (south) on Route 2. After 4.4 miles turn left onto a paved road; stay on the paved road until passing over the Passadumkeag River bridge in 2.0 miles. The boat access on the Passadumkeag River is just over the bridge on the left.

Folsom, Crooked, and Upper Ponds
Lincoln

MAPS
  Maine Atlas: Maps 34 and 44
  USGS Quadrangle: Lincoln East
INFORMATION
  Information on area, depth, and prominent fish species not available.
  Fire permits: Maine Forest Service, St. Croix River District (207-738-2601) or Central Region Headquarters (207-827-6191)

These are gorgeous ponds, with very little development. However, at the hand-carry boat access on Folsom Pond there is a large sign that advertises twenty-seven lots for sale by Weber Timberlands. About one-third of the lots do not have water frontage. Not a pretty picture. Does every lake in Maine have to be for sale? Do we have to develop every pond, no matter how small or picturesque?

Folsom and Crooked ponds lie in a gorgeous setting, with rolling hills in the background. Their three sections, separated by narrow channels, are shallow, with water lilies and pickerelweed dominating many areas. There are a few small islands, and the land is thickly vegetated down to the water's edge. There is high tree-species diversity, with white cedar, white pine, lots of hemlocks, paper birch, and red maple in evidence.

We saw at least ten loons, and many ducks fed in the shallows. There is one cabin on the point to the right just as you enter Crooked Pond; development of Folsom Pond is pretty much limited to the southern shore, just down from the boat access, with none on the pond's west arm. With the extensive marshy areas in the farther reaches of the undeveloped arms, this is an excellent place for wildlife. It is best to paddle here early in the morning or in the evening, when wildlife viewing is at its peak.

Speaking of wildlife, they say that after about 500 mosquito bites in a season, you become immune, no longer swelling at the site of each attack. Anyone who paddles a lot in the spring in Maine should come to Folsom Pond in June. Spend about ten minutes out there, and you will not have to worry about mosquitoes for the rest of the season. Driving in to the boat access, we had to go slowly because of the hun-

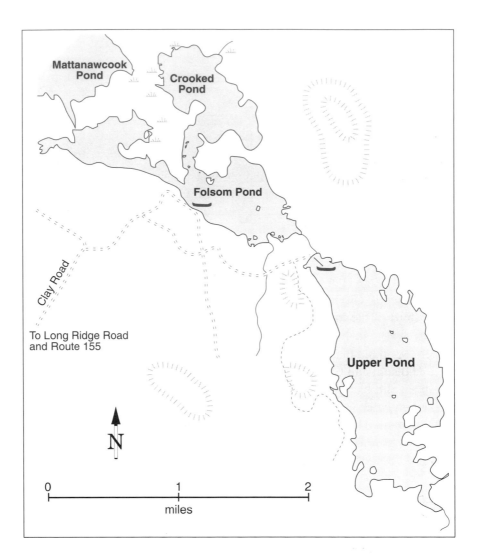

Mattanawcook
Pond

Crooked
Pond

Folsom Pond

Clay Road

To Long Ridge Road
and Route 155

Upper Pond

N

0   1   2
miles

dreds and hundreds of patrolling dragonflies. Clearly, they were not doing their job of controlling the mosquito population.

Upper Pond is separated from Folsom and Crooked ponds by a small stream, and you have to drive to the Upper Pond boat access. There is one cabin right at the boat access on Upper Pond, and the pond is much larger than the other two. The only marshy area is on the south shore, but aquatic vegetation appears regularly along the shoreline. Tree species lining the banks are similar to those of Folsom and Crooked ponds, and we saw just as many loons here—at least ten—as on the other ponds.

Four loons cavort on Folsom Pond in the calm waters of early morning.

Getting There

To reach Folsom and Crooked ponds, take Route 155 south from the junction of Routes 155 south, 2, and 6 in Lincoln. Go 1.1 miles, and turn left onto Long Ridge Road (unmarked) just before the Penobscot Valley Hospital. After about 2.5 miles, watch for a crossroads sign and turn left just after the sign. Note your mileage here. Bear left onto Clay Road after 0.6 mile; at 1.1 miles the road turns to gravel. At 1.6 miles, take the right fork and go downhill. At 2.2 miles, take the right fork again. At 2.8 miles, reach a crossroads, and turn left onto a rutty dirt road. At 3.2 miles, reach the hand-carry access on the right. There is room for several cars.

To reach Upper Pond, head away from the boat access on Folsom Pond, back to the crossroads where you turned left to come down to Folsom Pond. Turn left at the crossroads, and go 0.9 mile to the boat access on Upper Pond.

Seboeis Lake
T4R9 NWP

MAPS
   Maine Atlas: Map 43
   USGS Quadrangles: Endless Lake, Ragged Mountain, and
      Seboeis Lake
INFORMATION
   Area: 4,201 acres; maximum depth: 69 feet
   Prominent fish species: salmon, brook trout (streams only), small-
      mouth bass, white perch, and chain pickerel
   Bureau of Public Lands, Maine Department of Conservation, State
      House Station 22, Augusta, ME 04333; 207-289-3061. Seboeis
      Unit, 12,901 acres.
   Fire permits: Maine Forest Service, Moosehead District (207-695-
      3721) or Central Region Headquarters (207-827-6191)

We paddled Seboeis Lake twice, once in July and once in August, entering from different access points. In July, we entered from the boat access indicated on the map on the northern end, while in August we entered from the end of the small arm that juts out to the east, halfway down the lake (see directions below). Most of the lake is part of public reserve lands system and is managed by the state of Maine.

Seboeis Lake gets relatively heavy traffic from fishermen in small boats. At times there can be upwards of a dozen boat trailers parked at the access point. Fortunately, this is a large lake with plenty of room on its 6.5-square-mile surface. When we paddled here one August morning, we were alone until the first boat appeared at 8:30 A.M.

Several campsites exist, including a few right at the boat access. Several more appear on the two peninsulas that separate The Inlet from the main lake, three on the left going down the channel and two more on the spit jutting out from the end of the right peninsula. There is one on Dollar Island and one on the north end of Hammer Island. By evening on a July weekend, each one of these campsites will probably have an occupant. On both trips here, however, we saw at least one open campsite at the boat-launch area. If you want to camp on weekends, arrive early. All sites require fire permits.

The only word to describe Seboeis Lake is spectacular. From the main lake you can see Mount Katahdin in Baxter State Park to the north. There are beautiful tree-covered islands in many places, includ-

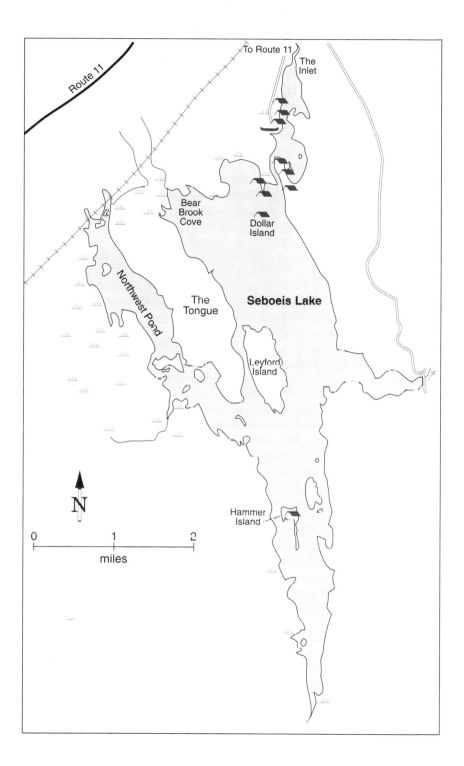

Route 11

To Route 11

The Inlet

Bear Brook Cove

Dollar Island

Northwest Pond

The Tongue

Seboeis Lake

Leyford Island

N

0   1   2

miles

Hammer Island

ing the entrance to Bear Brook Cove, Northwest Pond, down in the southern arm, and up in The Inlet. Large boulders line much of the shore, and if you paddle back into the outlet on the eastern shore halfway down the lake, you will see an extraordinary number of boulders both sticking up out of the water and submerged. A number of fairly large northern white cedars appear along the shore in this cove, which is lined with cattails and other marsh vegetation.

Shallow Pond and The Inlet are worth exploring, particularly the marshy islands of Shallow Pond. Be wary of barely submerged stumps when you paddle in this area. Going down the channel that separates The Inlet from the main lake, you will see large white and red pines lining the eastern shore. Indeed, pines and other conifers dominate the shoreline most everywhere.

Leyford Island, at 237 acres the largest island in the Bureau of Public Lands eastern holdings, is a special-protection resource, with only camping and hiking allowed. Moose and deer frequent the marshy coves, particularly those along the northwest shore and in Northwest Pond. Although we did not see any, we were told that bald eagles have built a nest in Bear Brook Cove.

Tall pines line the shores of the large islands in lower Seboeis Lake. The thin soil of these rocky islands supports few large deciduous trees.

Morning mists shroud the shore of Seboeis Lake. In late summer the lake's warm surface waters evaporate in the early morning chill, then recondense into a thick fog. As the rising sun burns off the fog, majestic Mount Katahdin appears to the north.

One can expect to see osprey, belted kingfisher, dozens of loons, and a colony of common terns, all using different methods to catch fish in these fertile waters. Fishermen come here to angle for landlocked salmon, brook trout, bass, perch, and pickerel.

Bangor Hydro-Electric Company maintains a dam on the outlet stream that can cause significant fluctuations in water level, adversely affecting both the fishing and the scenery. In dry years, we would avoid Seboeis Lake late in the summer.

Getting There

From Millinocket, go south on Route 11 for about 13 miles. Watch for a triangular road sign indicating a left turn and a green sign saying West Sebocis. Turn left here onto a paved road. The pavement ends in a half-mile, just before you cross the railroad tracks on your left at 0.6 mile. At 1.1 miles is a junction; if you go straight, you will end up at the boat access at 2.9 miles.

The left fork leads to the bridge over the outlet stream. If you follow this, cross the outlet stream bridge and turn right. You could put in here, but there is barely any room to park. Do not block access to the cottage or to the Bangor Hydro-Electric Company dam.

Prong Pond
Beaver Cove and Greenville

MAPS
   Maine Atlas: Map 41
   USGS Quadrangle: Lily Bay

INFORMATION
   Area: 427 acres; maximum depth: 27 feet
   Prominent fish species: smallmouth bass, white perch, and yellow perch
   State-park camping: Lily Bay State Park (207-695-2700)
   Fire permits: Maine Forest Service, Moosehead District (207-695-3721) or Central Region Headquarters (207-827-6191)

Prong Pond, a little-noticed pond on the southeast side of giant Moosehead Lake, is just the right size for a pleasant day of canoeing. Though it looks small, the pond offers nine miles of perimeter to explore, extending in several long, narrow arms, or prongs. Cedar, white pine, spruce, paper birch, and hemlock line the rocky shoreline of the main pond. Along some sections stately groves of tall red pine rise from the shore; a nice campsite lies under some of these pines on a point of land along the eastern shore of the pond. (Ownership of this land is unknown, but there were no restrictions posted when we visited in 1994.) We saw one pair of loons during our visit.

The narrow arms extending to the east and west provide a great opportunity to observe northern bog flora. Pitcher plants are common; in midsummer you will see their nodding flowers extending above the grasses, sedges, sweet gale, leather leaf, swamp rose, cranberry, and other low vegetation. At ground level, amid the sphagnum moss, look for the diminutive red leaves of sundew. Both pitcher plants and sundews obtain some of their nourishment from insects (for more on Maine's carnivorous plants, see page 117).

Though they are by no means as common as pitcher plants and sundews, keep an eye out for two of Maine's most beautiful orchids: rose pogonia and calopogon, or grass pink. We saw several good-sized patches of the rose pogonia (*Pogonia ophioglossoides*), which has one or two flowers on the stem and a small lanceolate leaf. We saw only two examples of the calopogon orchid (*Calopogon pulchellus*), whose flower stalk has three or more flowers and whose leaves

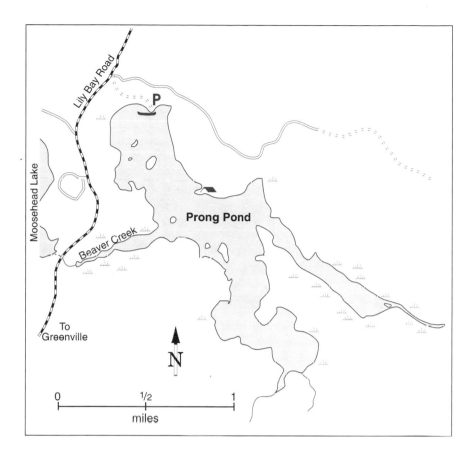

are long and grasslike. We watched a fascinating and beautiful crab spider on the calopogon flower, waiting for an insect to come along. The camouflaged spider was smooth and all white, except for a band of pink on either side of its globelike body. It sat there motionless with four long legs outstretched and fangs no doubt ready to impart a fatal dose of venom to a visiting pollinator. This spider has a unique ability to adapt its coloration to that of different plants.

The long shallow arm to the east has an extremely mucky bottom. Even if your paddle does not sink into the muck, the agitation will stir up the sediment and release bubbles of swamp gas (mostly methane). In some places the water seemed to boil behind us as we paddled along. At the far eastern tip of the prong you will reach a beaver dam and lodge.

The boglike arm extending to the west (Beaver Creek) has the same plants as the eastern arm. We also noticed more tamarack, the

Watch out for rocks in Beaver Creek at the western tip of Prong Pond.

larger ones farther back from the water marking the encroachment of land into the quiet stream. The many dead trees along here—sun-whitened snags and stumps—provide nesting habitat for tree swallows. We watched a sharp-shinned hawk dart between these snags as it tried to elude some blackbirds.

The wider section of the pond to the south is also nice, especially the marshy area at the tip, but we were disappointed to see some of the land being cleared, probably in preparation for construction of cabins. Supposedly, paper companies own some of the shoreline, temporarily keeping it from development, but the western shore of this southern arm does not have even that (modest) protection from shoreline development.

Along with the possibility of camping on the pond, Lily Bay State Park also offers camping a few miles away. Located on the prettiest areas of mammoth Moosehead Lake, the bay is protected from wind by dozens of islands. Note that park campsites are typically filled up throughout most of the summer, and reservations are recommended. Camping rates in 1994 were $11.50 for Maine residents and $15.00 for nonresidents (plus tax).

Getting There

Prong Pond is on the southeast side of Moosehead Lake, just north of Greenville. From the center of Greenville where Routes 6 and 15 turn left, continue straight on Lily Bay Road, following signs for Lily Bay State Park. Drive 6.8 miles north, and turn right onto an unmarked gravel road. Almost immediately, turn right again onto a rougher dirt road that takes you to the boat access in 0.2 mile. This last road was passable by car when we visited, but a high-ground-clearance vehicle is recommended, and conditions might be quite poor in the spring. There is space for six to ten cars, and the access is only suitable for hand-launched boats.

To reach Lily Bay State Park, turn right on Lily Bay Road after leaving Prong Pond, and drive 1.7 miles north to the state-park entrance.

Indian Pond

Indian Stream Twp. and Sapling Twp.

MAPS

> **Maine Atlas:** Map 40
> **USGS Quadrangles:** Indian Pond North and Indian Pond South

INFORMATION

> **Area:** 3,746 acres; maximum depth: 118 feet
> **Prominent fish species:** lake trout, brook trout, and salmon
> Indian Pond Campground, HCR 63, Box 52, The Forks, ME 04985;
> 800-371-7774. Owned by Central Maine Power, it is open mid-
> April through mid-October. There are twenty-seven sites; rate for
> two adults was $14/site in 1994.
> **Fire permits:** Maine Forest Service, Arnold Trail District (207-
> 474-3200) or Southern Region Headquarters (207-287-2275).
> Permits not required at Indian Pond Campground.

Indian Pond is large and very scenic. It truly is the country of the pointed firs. Little development intrudes on the shoreline, and the few boats plying the water have thirty-five miles of shoreline and nearly six square miles of surface area to share. This wildlife paradise sports healthy populations of deer, moose, bear, coyote, fox, beaver, osprey, eagle, loon, and fish. Because it is a big lake, one must be wary of winds from any direction, but it still represents a great opportunity for a two-to-four-day family trip.

There are many ways to get into Indian Pond, but only one of them is easy. You can drive to the south end of the lake on a paved road followed by a wide, high-speed gravel road. Or you can do something more exciting, such as paddling down the whitewater of the Kennebec River East Outlet as it leaves Moosehead Lake. Somewhere between these two options is paddling down the meandering West Outlet, putting in along the road just after the railroad bridge several miles downstream from Moosehead Lake. Although we did not try it, we believe you can also paddle back up this section; we watched an outfitter with five canoes disappear back up this stream after having paddled down the East Outlet a few days earlier.

By vehicle, the adventurous should try one of the three northern access roads. We finally made it down one of them, the one that ends at the campsite on the northwest arm. We would not try this without a

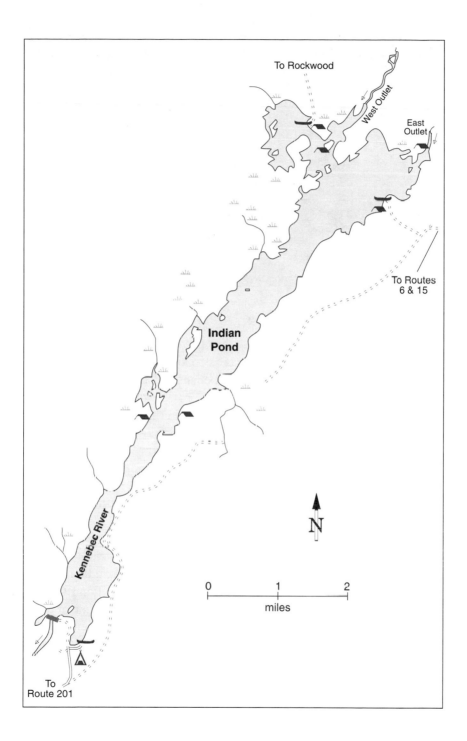

To Rockwood

West Outlet

East Outlet

To Routes
6 & 15

**Indian
Pond**

Kennebec River

N

0   1   2
miles

To
Route 201

A long telephoto lens gives a close-up view of the northern diver, the common loon.

high-clearance vehicle. The two access roads on the other side of the lake were impassable to mortal cars because of deep ruts, mud, and washed-out culverts.

Now, why would anyone want to come in the north end of Indian Lake? The answer is simple: The north end is more interesting, more scenic, and has far fewer people and motorboats. Most of the marshy areas occur from the midpoint up to the northern end, and there are far more islands in the north. This is the heart of moose country; we saw five moose along the road while driving from Greenville to Rockwood late one evening. The best chance for seeing moose on Indian Pond is in the shallow, marshy northern end.

If your car's clearance relegates you to the southern end, or if you plan to spend a few days on Indian Pond, by all means paddle up from the southern end. You can camp overnight at the Indian Pond Campground (reservations advised). There is a tremendous amount of congestion on the roads and at the access gate at the southern end of the pond, but almost all of it results from rafters and kayakers testing their ability to float after getting dumped on the Class IV and Class V rapids of the Kennebec River Gorge below Indian Pond. When we paddled here, as we gazed out from the boat access over the picturesque southern end of Indian Pond, we could see only one other boat.

Be sure to explore the two large, marshy coves about halfway up the left side. Both of those contain plenty of moose habitat. Also, there are two campsites here, one on either side of the lake.

White and red pine, balsam fir, tamarack, cedar, and spruce blanket the shores and islands on the north end of the lake. Occasional red maple and paper birch occur here and there, and on the shoreline there is a well-developed understory. Lots of drowned stumps are in the northwest arm, a legacy of the forty-year-old Harris Dam at the south end of the lake.

We saw many species of birds here in addition to ospreys and loons, including song sparrows, spotted sandpipers, hermit thrushes, ring-billed gulls, and cedar waxwings.

Getting There

From the north, try any of the three access roads. These are directions to the West Outlet stream and the northwest-cove access road. From Rockwood, drive south on Route 6. Just after leaving town, watch for the steel bridge in the distance. Turn right 0.2 mile before the bridge onto a wide gravel road. At 4.3 miles down the gravel road, pass under a railroad bridge; just past the bridge on the left is an access to the West Outlet. A better put-in is just down the road at the bridge over Churchill Stream. At 4.8 miles turn left onto the access road; cross a bridge over Churchill Stream at 5.0 miles (possible put-in). To get to the lake, continue on for 2.6 miles of narrow, high-center road (must have high clearance for this section).

From the south, take Route 201 north out of Bingham. Turn right onto a paved road at The Forks, leading to Lake Moxie. You will reach Lake Moxie and the end of the paved road in 5.2 miles. Turn left onto a high-speed gravel road and cross two narrow bridges in quick succession. The entrance to Indian Pond Campground and the boat access is 7.9 miles up this road. The Indian Pond Campground boat-launch access costs $1 per person.

Third and Fourth Roach Ponds
Shawtown and T1R2 WELS

MAPS
 Maine Atlas: Map 42 (41 for access)
 USGS Quadrangles: Wadleigh Mountain and Farrar Mountain

INFORMATION
 Third Roach Pond area: 570 acres; maximum depth: 26 feet
 Fourth Roach Pond area: 266 acres; maximum depth: 38 feet
 Prominent fish species: brook trout
 Lodging: Medawisla Sporting Camp, Route 76, Box 592, Greenville, ME 04441; 207-695-2690 (radio phone). They have six housekeeping cabins, rental canoes, and guiding services available.
 Fire permits: Maine Forest Service, Moosehead District (207-695-3721) or Central Region Headquarters (207-827-6191)

Third and Fourth Roach ponds are a little difficult to get into, but are well worth the effort. These remote, exciting ponds abound in wildlife. If you camp at the southeast end of Third Roach Pond you will likely have the whole place to yourself—along with the moose, deer, otter, eagles, and other wildlife that abounds.

During two days on these ponds in late July, we saw four moose, including one very large bull, two somewhat smaller bulls, and a cow; a deer with two fawns; two otters; quite a few loons, including one pair with two chicks; a large family of common mergansers; and an eagle. In the amount and variety of wildlife we have seen, these ponds rank near the top.

The woodland extending away from the generally rocky shoreline around most of the two ponds is typical of northern Maine, consisting of spruce, balsam fir, white pine, cedar, and paper birch. On the long point of land extending south into Fourth Roach Pond, however, you will see a very different red-pine forest. Red pine produces open forest cover. You can get out and walk, picnic, or camp under a red-pine canopy very easily, unlike most other forest types in this area.

There are a few marshy areas at the ends of the various fingers. At the northeast end of Third Roach the water becomes very shallow and mucky, with bullhead lilies and other floating vegetation, while

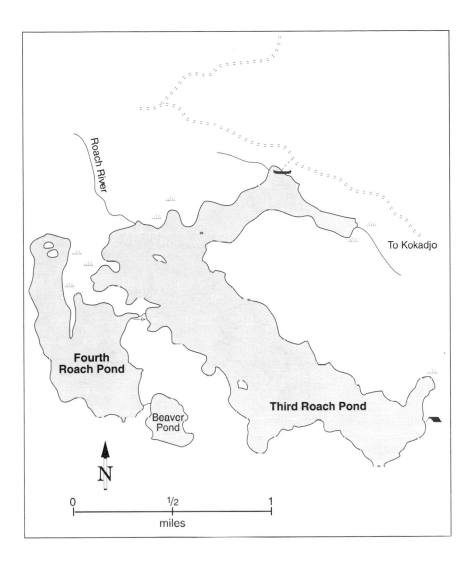

grasses and sedges grow along the perimeter. Right at the tip, we watched a bull moose neck-deep in the ooze grazing on this vegetation while protecting itself from biting flies. It is remarkable how they can extract themselves from such muck.

Third and Fourth Roach ponds connect via a small, rocky stream. In the spring, you can probably paddle between these ponds, but by midsummer you need to wade through the stream and pull your canoe. In a few places we had to pick up our canoe to negotiate rocks. Because the entire stream is only a few hundred feet long, though, you can quickly traverse its length.

A bull moose makes for the tree line at the northeastern cove on Third Roach Pond.

From these ponds, you get a clear view of the extensive clearcutting that has taken place on the surrounding hills. With binoculars we could see evidence of erosion on some of the newer cuts. The so-called "beauty strip" around the Roach Ponds—that ribbon of uncut woods that is left along the perimeter of most ponds—was almost paper thin. Looking into these woods as we paddled along, it was disconcerting to see bits of sky between the tree trunks. And driving along the paper-company roads to get here, we passed miles of barren, almost desolate, land where the sapling hardwoods—mostly birch—had been killed with herbicides to make room for more valuable conifers.

The campsite at the southeast end of Third Roach Pond is wonderful. Backed up against a hill rising 700 feet from the pond, the site offers a protected sandy beach for a relaxing swim after a day of exploration. If you want to build a fire here, you must obtain a fire permit from the Maine Forest Service.

Second Roach Pond is also nice, but has difficult public access. For those interested in more refined accommodations, there is a very nice sporting camp on Second Roach Pond about ten miles from Third and Fourth by road. Guests staying at Medawisla (a Native American name for loon) can easily put in on Second Roach Pond. Unlike most sporting camps, Medawisla emphasizes wildlife observation rather than hunting, and their location includes superb moose habitat. The loon recordings used in the movie *On Golden Pond* were made here.

Getting There

Drive north from Greenville to Kokadjo. After crossing the bridge in Kokadjo, continue another 1.9 miles, then turn right (note your mileage at this point). Stay on the main road along First Roach Pond. You will cross the outlet from Second Roach Pond at 5.4 miles. Bear to the right at the fork at 8.4 miles, after passing Trout Mountain on your left. Again stay on the main road, and at 10.4 miles continue generally straight where a road forks off to the right (there should be a sign for the Appalachian Trail pointing to the right here). At 13.4 miles bear right at the fork, and at 13.9 miles turn left at the T. From the T, drive another 1.3 miles and the boat access is on the left.

Watch for a chained-off driveway on the left. Just past the driveway is another road heading sharply back to the left. This road down to the pond is extremely rough, and there is no place to park by the pond. Park at the top, as far off the gravel road as possible, and carry your canoe and gear the 200 yards down to the pond. Except for the final carry down to the pond, the gravel access roads were in fairly good shape when we visited in late July, but early in the season they could be very rough and may not be passable with a passenger car. In 1994 we did not need to cross any gates or pay any fees to paddle or camp here.

Moose
The Genial Giant

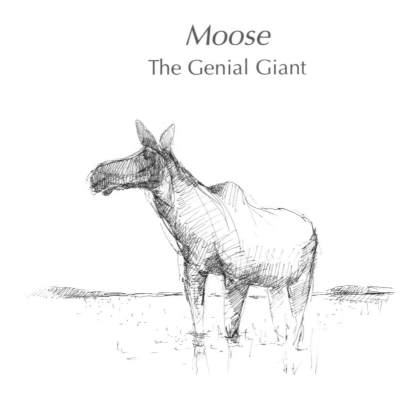

If you have yet to come across a moose in the wild, you are in for a treat. Coming across a huge bull moose as you round the bend of a marshy stream is truly awesome—and the high point of many trips into the Maine woods.

The moose, *Alces alces,* is the world's largest member of the deer family. Adult males can stand more than seven feet tall at the shoulders and weigh up to 1,400 pounds. Bull moose range in weight from 900 to 1,400 pounds; cow moose are typically three-quarters as large. To put this in perspective, a typical bull moose is three times as heavy as the second largest land mammal found in New England, the black bear. Among North American land mammals, only bison and Alaskan brown bear (a subspecies of the grizzly bear) commonly exceed the moose in weight; none approaches it in height.

The moose is well adapted to Maine's environment. Long legs allow moose to reach tree branches and wade into deep water. Wide hooves keep them from sinking too deep into bogs and snow. During the summer, one can often see moose in ponds, streams, and lakes, where they forage on aquatic plants. Moose sometimes stand neck-deep in water, trying to escape hordes of biting flies, and we have even seen moose totally submerged. By late August or early September, moose generally move into the deep woods, where you are less likely to see them. The territory of a typical moose is fairly small, a few square miles.

Adult moose vary in color from dark brown to almost black. Calves are much lighter in color than adults. Thick, dense fur helps protect them from biting flies. Around the neck and shoulders, the fur is often six inches long. Moose have a keen sense of hearing and smell, but poor vision. When frightened, they can run at speeds of up to thirty-five miles per hour for short distances. Their incredibly long legs help them run through bogs and muskegs. They swim slowly, but have been known to swim as far as twelve miles.

Moose derive most of their nourishment by browsing on trees and aquatic vegetation, but they may also graze on grasses, mosses, lichens, and low herbaceous plants. Because of their long legs and short necks, they often need to bend or spread their front legs, or they may actually drop to their knees to feed. They may rear up on their hind legs to feed on tree branches, and they some-times "ride down" saplings by straddling them and walking forward to bring upper branches into reach.

The rutting season for moose extends generally from the beginning of September through October, but may range into November and even early December. After an eight-month gestation period, cows bear one or two calves in May or June. Younger cows generally produce just one offspring. As one might expect, there appears to be a correlation between the incidence of twins and the availability of forage.

We see most moose during the early morning and early evening hours, though one can see them at any time of day. Moose often allow you to approach quite closely, but always use caution when doing so, as cows with young calves can be quite protective, and bull moose are unpredictable during the autumn rutting season.

The moose population has fluctuated considerably during the last two centuries in Maine. During colonial days they were common and an important food source for early settlers. But because they were so easily killed, populations plummeted, and by 1904 moose were found in only a few northern counties. In 1930, one estimate put Maine's moose population at about 2,000. The state prohibited moose hunting in 1935, and the population gradually recovered. Changes in logging practices also have affected moose populations. In recent decades, with widespread clearcutting in Maine resulting in the proliferation of low-growing browse, moose populations rebounded considerably. There are estimated to be 20,000 to 25,000 moose in Maine today.

A limited annual moose-hunting season was instituted in 1980, with 700 permits issued. The number of permits issued annually was increased to 1,000 in 1982 and to 1,200 in 1994. In 1996 the state is scheduled to offer 1,500 permits. The moose season is typically in early October.

We have paddled several thousand miles and visited hundreds and hundreds of lakes and ponds in the Northeast over the past five years. While there are countless wonderful paddling destinations in remote sections of Vermont's Green Mountains, the Adirondacks of New York, and the Berkshires of Massachusetts (to mention just a few), none approach Maine when it comes to moose. We never tire of that awe-inspiring, exhilarating feeling we get paddling into a marshy cove and coming suddenly upon an enormous bull moose or cow with calf. We have seen dozens and dozens of these majestic mammals in Maine, and we hope you see as many on your travels through the state's remote ponds and lakes.

Jo-Mary Lakes (Middle, Lower, and Turkey Tail)

T4 Indian Purchase and TA R10 WELS

MAPS

Maine Atlas: Map 42

USGS Quadrangles: Ragged Mountain, Pemadumcook Lake, and Nahmakanta Stream

INFORMATION

Middle Jo-Mary and Turkey Tail area: 1,152 acres; maximum depth: 18 feet

Lower Jo-Mary area: 1,912 acres; maximum depth: 64 feet

Prominent fish species: salmon, lake trout (Lower Jo-Mary only), brook trout, white perch, yellow perch, and chain pickerel

Public Relations Department, Bowater–Great Northern Paper, One Katahdin Ave., Millinocket, ME 04462; 207-723-5131. They should have information on whether a portage trail gets built between Lower Jo-Mary and Pemadumcook.

Fire permits: Maine Forest Service, St. Croix River District (207-738-2601) or Central Region Headquarters (207-827-6191)

Little known and rarely explored, this string of connected lakes—Turkey Tail, Middle Jo-Mary, and Lower Jo-Mary—are treasures. A few summer homes intrude on Turkey Tail and the south end of Middle Jo-Mary, but those are quickly left behind if you paddle north toward Lower Jo-Mary.

These lakes include about twenty-five miles of highly varied shoreline to explore, but the area we find most interesting is the winding channel of Cooper Brook between Middle and Lower Jo-Mary lakes. This slow-moving creek and the marshy Cooper Brook Deadwater it becomes provide superb marshy wildlife habitat. We saw two moose here, lots of beaver activity, ring-necked ducks, wood ducks, great blue herons, an American bittern, and songbirds galore.

If you paddle from Middle Jo-Mary to Lower Jo-Mary via this creek, you actually travel upstream initially, then downstream—though the current is hardly perceptible. Cooper Brook and Mud Brook enter from the west, and the current divides, with half flowing north into Lower Jo-Mary and half south into Middle Jo-Mary. Because of this, by midsummer in a dry year you might not be able to

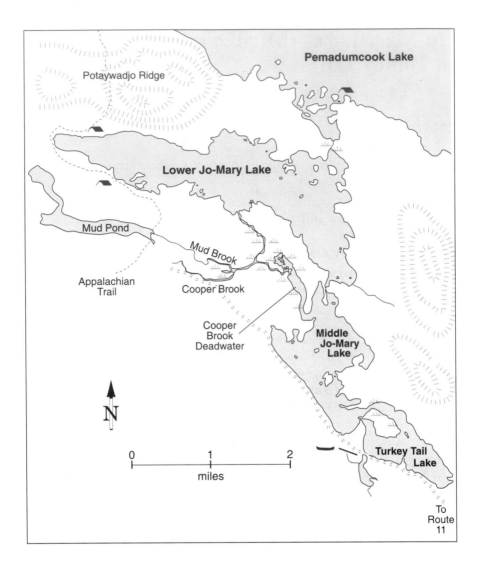

paddle through easily. We were here in mid-May (before the black flies and mosquitoes), when there was plenty of water.

From the Cooper Brook Deadwater, the brook is a little difficult to find, and it would be more difficult later in the summer with taller vegetation restricting your view. You simply have to explore the area, winding among the grassy islands and floating peat mats that form the shoreline here. Once you find the channel, it is quite distinct and easy to follow, generally lined with low alder and various heaths (blueberry, leather leaf, bog rosemary, and sheep laurel). About a half-mile from the Deadwater, you will reach a fork in the creek—actually this is the brook coming in from the left and dividing. To get to Lower Jo-Mary, bear to the right (northeast). But if you have some time, first explore to the left. We have not been farther up Cooper Brook, but from the USGS map it looks as if you could paddle a mile or so upstream on both Cooper Brook and Mud Brook, which flows into Cooper.

As you continue downstream toward Lower Jo-Mary Lake, you pass one rocky area that could be a problem at low water levels. We crossed a very small beaver dam with less than an eight-inch drop, and even in a fully loaded, somewhat tippy canoe, complete with golden retriever, we paddled right over the dam without incident. As you paddle out onto Lower Jo-Mary Lake, take a careful look at the several tall white pines so you can find the creek access if you return by the same route.

Lower Jo-Mary Lake

Lower Jo-Mary Lake is about four miles long, east to west. Rounded granite boulders extend above—and lurk just below—the water surface along the rocky south shore. Though you have to use care, it is worth exploring some of the coves along here. In a cove hidden by an island about a half-mile west of Cooper Brook, we watched a moose grazing on low cedar branches, and we saw a number of pairs of loons and watched two bald eagles soar by. Northern white cedar dominates the south shoreline. Thick, generally impenetrable shrubs line the banks.

You get a great view of Mount Katahdin across the lake as you paddle the south shore of Lower Jo-Mary. The farther west you paddle, the narrower the lake. About a mile from the western tip of the lake is a wonderful campsite on the Appalachian Trail. Nestled beneath a stand of tall red pines, it is one of the best-maintained campsites we have ever seen, thanks to the Maine Appalachian Trail Club.

The north shore of Lower Jo-Mary—especially on the western half of the lake—is very different from the southern shore. With full south exposure, the woods are drier and generally deciduous, and the banks are sandy. You will see trees more characteristic of southern New England, such as maple, beech, ash, and oak here, along with paper birch and aspen. Once the lake widens out farther east, though, and you leave the steep Potaywadjo Ridge, the shoreline returns to the wet, swampy, cedar-dominated vegetation you will see on the south shore and around most of the other lakes in this region.

We had hoped to find a portage path into Pemadumcook Lake from the northeastern tip of Lower Jo-Mary, but there was none in 1994. However, Great Northern Paper was putting in a new logging road and bridge through here, and it is possible that, when completed, it can serve as a portage path. As it is, there is a stretch of maybe fifty yards of whitewater under and below the bridge. In mid-May this water was fairly rough, but still readily canoeable by anyone skilled in whitewater paddling. Returning upstream, though, would be a real chore, as the woods are almost impenetrable, and the connecting stream too deep and too fast to wade.

If you want to run the section of whitewater, you could paddle the several miles across Pemadumcook to the northwest, and then portage into Third Debsconeag Lake. Thus, these lakes could provide a good one-way trip connecting with the route described in the section on the Debsconeag lakes.

While we were not fishing when we visited here, we saw many large trout or salmon at the section of stream connecting Lower Jo-Mary and Pemadumcook lakes. The several osprey we saw here provided further evidence of the superb fishing.

Several attractive islands dot the northeast corner of Lower Jo-Mary, but none has campsites that we could find. Paddling south from these islands into the southeastern tip of the lake, you will find another access into Middle Jo-Mary Lake. This inlet into Lower Jo-Mary, larger than the Cooper Brook access described above, also requires crossing a small dam, this one man-made. This dam might actually be a footbridge that fell into the connecting creek. Pull over to one side and drag your canoe over the six-inch dam. If you are out just for a day trip, you can make a nice loop by paddling into Lower Jo-Mary on Cooper Brook, then returning via this more southern connecting channel.

On Middle Jo-Mary, just below the connecting creek here, is a classic old private fishing camp: Buckhorn Camps. The small, rustic cabins seem to be out of a different age. The best camping site on these lakes is at the western end of Lower Jo-Mary Lake. The site on the Appalachian Trail does not require a permit for campfires; all other sites do require a fire permit. There is also supposed to be an island campsite on Pemadumcook Lake just north of the connecting stream. In general, at any undesignated campsite or site that requires a fire permit, it is best simply to use a gas stove or bring food that does not require cooking.

Getting There

The best access in 1994 was the logging road into Turkey Tail Lake. Coming from I-95, get off at Exit 56 and drive into Millinocket on Routes 11 and 157. At the school where Route 157 ends and you would turn right to go to Baxter State Park, turn left, staying on Route 11 south. From this point, drive 7.5 miles and turn right onto a gravel road at the southern tip of South Twin Lake, passing generally along the south shore for a few miles. The road turns from gravel to dirt about 4.0 miles from Route 11. Stay to the right at the fork here. You might notice a small sign in a tree saying Turkey Tail Road.

Continue on this dirt road. In 0.4 mile, it joins a larger logging road that was just put in (and thus does not appear on maps). Follow this new road generally west-northwest for 0.7 mile, then bear off to the left. There is a small sign in a tree here saying Continuation of Fire Lane 3. Stay on this main dirt road for another 1.6 miles (several smaller roads fork off of this) to a small bridge over Jo-Mary Stream and the access to Turkey Tail Road. There are several places to pull off the road here where a total of about ten or twelve cars could park. These roads were in good shape when we visited and did not require four-wheel drive.

Keep track of your mileage carefully and, if possible, use a dashboard compass to avoid getting mixed up on the many logging roads that crisscross this region. The new logging road, which runs for a short distance along the route of Turkey Tail Road, had us baffled for a while, but we finally found the lake by carefully keeping track of mileage and the direction we were heading.

Crooked Brook Flowage
Danforth

MAPS

Maine Atlas: Map 45

USGS Quadrangles: Brookton, Danforth, and Stetson Mountain

INFORMATION

Area: 1,645 acres; maximum depth: 20 feet

Prominent fish species: smallmouth bass, white perch, and chain pickerel

Fire permits: Maine Forest Service, St. Croix River District, (207-738-2601) or Central Region Headquarters (207-827-6191)

Paddling out from the boat access maintained by the town of Danforth, you will see numerous exposed stumps and rocks on the upper part of Crooked Brook Flowage. This section, which is long and narrow, also funnels wind. When the wind blows strongly out of the north or south, this area can have deep swells and whitecaps.

The western shore near the north end of the lake has several unobtrusive houses on the bluff above. They soon disappear from view, and there is hardly any more evidence of human presence until you get to the far end of the southeast arm. Deciduous trees predominate here, with occasional hemlocks and pines thrown in. Aspen, paper birch, red maple, and alder grow throughout.

The two southern arms are more interesting than the northern arm. You will find lots of coves to explore, many with inlet streams. The coves are shallow and thick with cattails and other marsh vegetation. The southeast arm is dotted with islands. Behind the large alder-covered island in Harding Cove is one huge marsh where we saw dozens of feeding ducks. You can paddle back up Baskahegan Stream about a hundred yards, until you round a bend and run into a series of riffles cascading down into the flowage. Note the beaver activity here; the clearcut alders make us wonder if the resident beavers are in training for paper-company careers.

Getting There

In the town of Danforth, turn off Route 1 onto Route 169, which goes downhill through town. After crossing the railroad track, the boat access is only 0.3 mile ahead on the left. Turn left off Route 169 onto

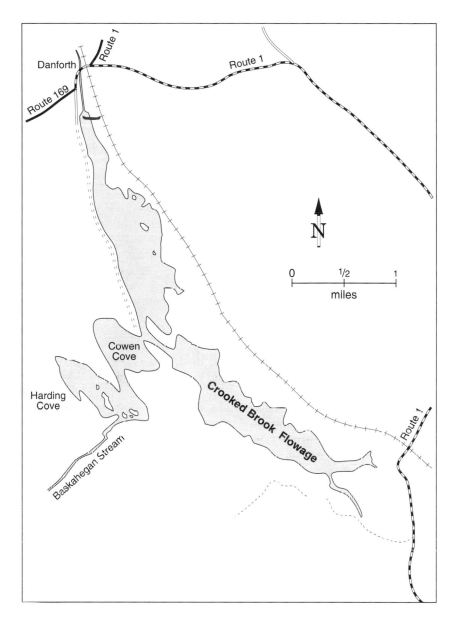

a paved road, and take another immediate left into the Danforth Town Park and boat access.

The *Maine Atlas* indicates a hand-launch access point at the end of the southeast arm. We found a road back to a small shack overlooking the water, but it looked private; it was on a bluff above the water, and the southeast end is choked by a cattail swamp. If you find a better access point, please let us know.

Northern Region

Lobster Lake
Lobster Twp.

MAPS

Maine Atlas: Map 49 (others for access)

USGS Quadrangles: Lobster Mountain, Penobscot Farm, and Big Spencer Mountain

INFORMATION

Area: 3,475 acres; maximum depth: 106 feet

Prominent fish species: salmon, lake trout, brook trout, white perch, and yellow perch

Maine Department of Conservation, Bureau of Parks and Recreation, State House Station 22, Augusta, ME 04333; 207-289-3821. Ask for information on Lobster Lake or the Penobscot River Corridor.

Public Relations Department, Bowater–Great Northern Paper, One Katahdin Ave., Millinocket, ME 04462; 207-723-5131 (for information about checkpoints and access-road conditions)

Lobster Lake is a gem, certainly one of the finest canoeing and camping lakes in Maine. To reach the lake, paddle up Lobster Stream from the boat access at the confluence of Lobster Stream and the West Branch of the Penobscot River. The paddle in is about two miles along the wide, deep stream, with barely perceptible current. In fact, the stream actually changes direction depending on the volume of water coming down the West Branch of the Penobscot. At high flow in the spring, Lobster Stream can reverse direction and serve as an inlet into Lobster Lake. The marshy shoreline, dense with alder, sweet gale, and other water-tolerant plants, is home to beaver and moose, though we missed both on our visit.

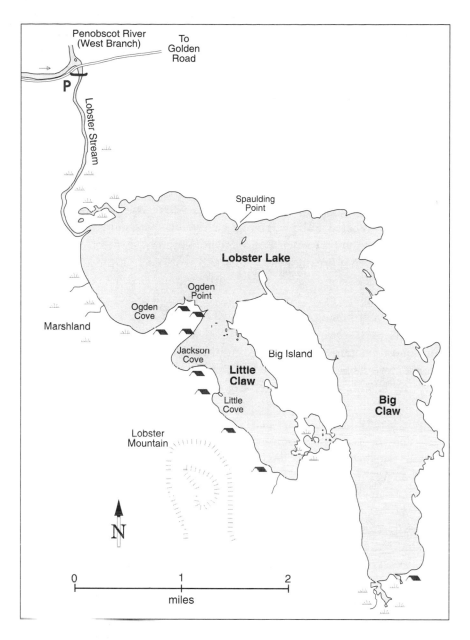

Penobscot River
(West Branch)

To
Golden
Road

P

Lobster Stream

Spaulding
Point

Lobster Lake

Ogden
Point

Ogden
Cove

Marshland

Jackson
Cove

Big Island

Little
Claw

Little
Cove

Big
Claw

Lobster
Mountain

N

0   1   2
miles

Lobster Lake is large (more than 3,000 acres) and shaped like the two parts of a lobster claw. The first section you reach when paddling up Lobster Stream is a large round cirque more than a mile across. This part of the lake is shallow, with a sandy bottom. Its perimeter is lined with alder swamp and sandy beaches—an odd combination because alders are more common in swampy areas with mucky soils.

After entering the lake, head left (north) where several coves extend into the marsh. We came upon a moose in the deepest of these, along with a family of common goldeneye ducks.

Across this northwestern end of the lake—in Ogden Cove—are several very nice, well-maintained campsites, complete with picnic tables, fire rings, sites for at least a half-dozen tents, and superb sandy beaches for swimming. This is a great spot if you are traveling with young children, because the shallow water extends quite a way out.

Around Ogden Point from Ogden Cove, you enter the portion of Lobster Lake known as Little Claw. In windy conditions—and wind is often a concern in northern Maine—this is where you will want to be. It is more protected and has the feel of a much smaller, more manageable lake. Rounding Ogden Point and looking down into Little Claw almost takes your breath away. Gulls and terns nest on the small, protruding, rocky islands, and jagged cliffs extend down into the clear blue water, interspersed here and there with sandy coves. Wind-sculpted cedars and pines perch precariously on the high overlooks, ferns and mosses festoon the rocks, and all this is nestled beneath picturesque mountains. In our paddling throughout Maine, we have not seen a more scenic spot.

Big Island, which separates Big Claw and Little Claw, is particularly attractive. The 2,000-acre island includes tall cliffs of dark, jagged granite, sandy beaches, and protected marshy coves. Thick groves of red pine and some huge hemlocks grow on the higher sections of the island. Northern white cedar, white pine, and the unusual jack pine grow along the shore. A rare tree in Maine, jack pine is found in profusion here, including some unusually large specimens. The needles are very short (3/4" to 1-1/2"), twisted at the base, and grow in bundles of two. The cones take two years to grow and, until mature, are oddly twisted. After maturing, they may stay on the tree for more than a dozen years. Fires help open the cones and disperse seeds.

On Ogden Point are three separate campsites (Ogden North, Ogden Point, and Ogden South), each with room for multiple tents. All of these sites have sandy swimming beaches and great views over the lake and across to Big Island. Farther south along the western shore of Little Claw are three other fine campsites: Jackson Cove, Little Cove, and Little Claw.

At the south end of Big Island you can paddle through a narrow channel into Big Claw. This marshy channel and the large cove it leads into are spectacular. Lined with sedges and thinly sprinkled with bullhead lily, fragrant water lily, and bur reed, the area provides rich

Cow and calf moose at the south tip of Lobster Lake.

habitat for moose and numerous bird species. Paddling here in late July, the sound of songbirds filled the air, and we saw several wood ducks in the protected cover of vegetation along the shore. Though we did not see moose here, we saw plenty of tracks in the mud where they had been foraging on the aquatic vegetation.

The Big Claw portion of Lobster Lake is less varied than Little Claw. At three and a half miles in length and as much as a mile across, Big Claw can also get pretty rough in windy conditions. At the southern tip of the lake, there is a wonderful marshy area well worth exploring. Rounding a point of land into this marshy cove during an evening paddle, we were greeted by three moose: a cow with calf and a yearling cow. Grasses, sedges, bulrushes, and the aromatic sweet flag (*Acorus calamus*) grow in profusion here. Though the marshy cove does not extend too far, one could easily spend an hour or two exploring it.

Just to the east of that cove at the south end of Big Claw is another campsite, complete with sandy beach. This and two other campsites on Lobster Lake are designated as group campsites; groups with more than a dozen people should select these sites. The thirteen campsites on Lobster Lake are extremely well maintained by the Maine Bureau of Parks and Recreation.

At the north end of Lobster Lake are a few private cottages; a private sporting camp at Spaulding Point comprised of a cluster of buildings; a ranger cabin; and one commercially operated sporting camp

(Lobster Lake Camps—whose future was uncertain in 1994). Primary access to these facilities (except the ranger cabin) is by boat.

In 1981, the state acquired from Great Northern Paper a permanent conservation easement to the shoreline of Lobster Lake, extending back 500 feet from the high-water line of the lake. The easement protects the shoreline from development and timber harvesting. At present, Big Island is privately owned and not protected from development, though it has been very well protected by the owners.

Register (and pay) to camp here when you enter one of the Bowater–Great Northern Paper checkpoints. Be sure to specify that you will be camping at Lobster Lake when you register, and bring your camping permit with you into Lobster Lake, because the resident ranger is likely to ask to see it. Camping is permitted only at the designated campsites, and all are permitted sites (i.e., you do not need to obtain a fire permit). Be aware that with the Bowater–Great Northern access fees and camping fees, costs can add up for a family.

Getting There

You can reach Lobster Lake through either Millinocket or Greenville. If coming via Millinocket, take I-95 to Exit 56 and drive west on Routes 157 and 11 into Millinocket. At the T where Route 157 ends and 11 turns to the left, turn right (there is a large brick school on the right). Drive one block and turn left, following signs to Baxter State Park. In Spencer Cove (Millinocket Lake on the right and Ambajejus Lake on the left), cut across to the parallel Golden Road and stop at the Millinocket Gate 1.0 mile from Spencer Cove. From the gate, stay on the Golden Road for 42.3 miles (it is paved for the first 24 miles, then is well-maintained gravel). Then turn left at the sign for Lobster Lake and Northeast Carry. In 3.3 miles you will reach a bridge across the West Branch of the Penobscot. Cross over the bridge and park in the lot just past it on the left.

If you are coming via Greenville, get off I-95 at Exit 39 in Newport, and drive north on Route 7 to Dexter. In Dexter, take Route 23 north to Guilford, then take Routes 6 and 15 through Monson to Greenville. Where Routes 6 and 15 turn left in Greenville, continue straight on Lily Bay Road north, staying on the main road to Kokadjo. Continue through Kokadjo to the Sias Hill Checkpoint of Bowater–Great Northern Paper. Continue on this road for 9.5 miles to the Golden Road and turn left. Stay on the Golden Road for 15.0 miles, then turn left on the road to Lobster Lake and Northeast Carry. The Lobster Stream access is in 3.3 miles.

Canada Falls Lake

Pittston Academy Grant and Soldiertown Twp.

MAPS
Maine Atlas: Map 48
USGS Quadrangles: Canada Falls Lake and Tomhegan Pond

INFORMATION
Area: 2,627 acres; maximum depth: 24 feet
Prominent fish species: brook trout
Fire permits: Maine Forest Service, Moosehead District (207-695-3721) or Central Region Headquarters (207-827-6191)
Bowater–Great Northern Paper, Public Relations, One Katahdin Ave., Millinocket, ME 04462; 207-723-5131

Don't be shocked when you arrive at the Canada Falls Lake boat access. The relatively large campground will be filled with campers, dogs, children, beer cans, and noise in the middle of the season. We could not wait to get out onto the much more peaceful lake. When we paddled here on a weekend at the end of July, with only light breezes rippling the surface, we saw one other boat on the water up close, and that one was trolling at idle speed down the long outlet channel. Fishermen seem to like Canada Falls Lake for the same reason that signs warn away the high-speed boating crowd. A gazillion submerged and not-so-submerged stumps provide plenty of hiding space for fish and make speedboating dangerous.

A jumble of roots, stumps, and downed timber covers the shore in many places, which detracts a bit from the dark-hued rows of pointed fir and spruce receding back into the many-layered hillsides. Entering the main lake, one is immediately taken with the beauty of three sawtoothed peaks off in the distance. You will find the enchanting calls of loons from one of the remote campsites as the sun sets over the distant peaks far preferable to the barking of dogs at the campground by the boat access.

We watched in solitude as an osprey wheeled about doing aerial acrobatics in search of a meal. It seemed as if some invisible hook held one wingtip fixed as it pivoted in the sky for a better look, eventually flying off to a quieter cove with improved visibility into the water below. Ring-billed gulls, white-throated sparrows, cormorants, black ducks, loons, great blue herons, and many other birds

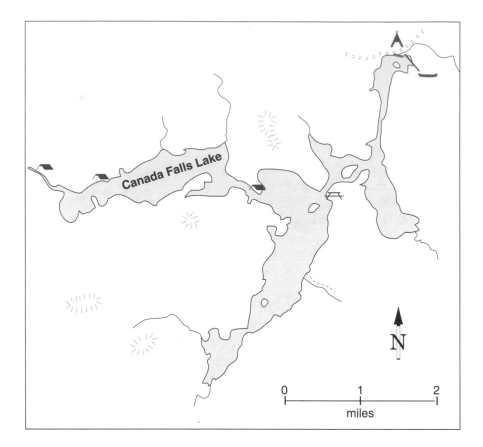

Canada Falls Lake

announced their presence. A female merganser with a raft of young in tow fled before us, ducking under the safety of some downed timber near shore.

The northern coniferous forest dominates the shoreline and hillsides surrounding Canada Falls Lake, but spruce, pine, and fir have not totally squeezed out the deciduous species, as we saw many small red maple and paper birch trees, along with some quite large yellow birch. In places, beaver had stripped some of the deciduous trees of their bark. As we came around through the marshy area behind the big island at the end of the outlet channel, we surprised a deer that had come down for a drink.

Although there are few marshy areas to explore, we very much enjoyed our paddle on Canada Falls Lake. The lake has several long arms and lots of nooks and crannies to explore; certainly one day is not enough to explore fully the extensive shoreline of this wonderful place.

osprey

Getting There

From Rockwood, heading west on Routes 6 and 15, turn right 0.1 mile after the Texaco station and cross Moose River, the outlet of Brassua Lake. Turn right at the T, and follow this good gravel road about 16.5 miles to the Bowater–Great Northern Paper 20 Mile Checkpoint (follow signs to Seboomook Wilderness Campground and Store on Beautiful Moosehead Lake). At the checkpoint, you will have to pay to continue. For Maine residents: $4/day or $24/season entrance fee for each car; $3/night for camping (1994 rates). For flatlanders, all fees are doubled.

Immediately after clearing the 20 Mile Checkpoint, do not follow the Seboomook signs; instead, go straight (left fork). Turn right at the yield sign. Turn left at the stop sign 3.5 miles from the checkpoint. Cross a bridge at 3.8 miles, with a Forest Service office at 3.9 miles. Turn left sharply back at 4.2 miles at the sign for Canada Falls Lake. The boat access is at 6.7 miles from the checkpoint.

Debsconeag Lakes

T2 R10 WELS

MAPS
Maine Atlas: 50 and 42
USGS Quadrangles: Abol Pond, Rainbow Lake East, and Nahmakanta Stream—also, for access from south, Pemadumcook Lake and Norcross

INFORMATION
First Debsconeag Lake area: 320 acres; maximum depth: 140 feet
Second Debsconeag Lake area: 189 acres; maximum depth: 28 feet
Third Debsconeag Lake area: 1,011 acres; maximum depth: 162 feet
Prominent fish species: lake trout, salmon (First Debsconeag), and brook trout
Bowater–Great Northern Paper, One Katahdin Ave., Millinocket, ME 04462; 207-723-5131

Outfitting
Penobscot River Outfitters, Katahdin Shadows Campground, P.O. Box H, Route 157, Medway, ME 04460; 207-746-9349
Allagash Wilderness Outfitters, Box 620, Star Route 76, Greenville, ME 04441; 207-695-2821 (summer), 207-723-6622 (winter)
See appendix for other outfitters and float-plane companies.
Fire permits: Maine Forest Service, St. Croix River District (207-738-2601) or Central Region Headquarters (207-827-6191)

The Debsconeag lakes are wild, remote, pristine, and magical: the essence of Maine's north woods. Paddling here on a quiet morning or listening to the wail of the ever-present loons from one of the rustic campsites, you can imagine what much of this country must once have been like.

Rushing brooks and portage paths connect several lakes; depending on your energy level and time, you can stay on just one lake or carry through to the others, spending a day or two at each. The more adventuresome can arrange a dropoff and paddle an extended one-way trip through these lakes and on to Pemadumcook and either Ambajejus or the Jo-Mary lakes.

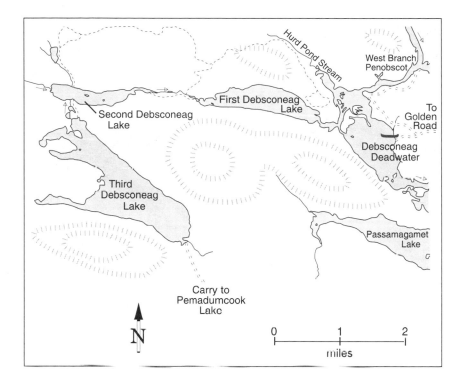

On the map: Hurd Pond Stream, West Branch Penobscot, First Debsconeag Lake, Second Debsconeag Lake, To Golden Road, Debsconeag Deadwater, Third Debsconeag Lake, Passamagamet Lake, Carry to Pemadumcook Lake, N, 0 1 2 miles

The boat access described below (we use the term "boat access" loosely, because it is not accessible by most vehicles) delivers you at Omaha Beach on the Debsconeag Deadwater. Loons may greet your arrival, as does Mount Katahdin to the north, which seems to stand guard over many lakes in this region. Along the shore you will see northern white cedar, jack pine (a relatively rare, very short needled pine with quite flexible branches and cones that may stay on the tree for ten years or more), red maple, paper birch, balsam fir, red spruce, and a few hemlock.

When we visited in mid-May (before the black flies and mosquitoes hatched!), the very heavy runoff from the mountains after a snowy winter had flooded the Deadwater. In fact, half of the beach on the western side was underwater, as were a number of the campsites near the inlet of the West Branch of the Penobscot River. It was a little disconcerting to paddle over fire rings!

The unusual swampy island area at the northern end of Debsconeag Deadwater provides nesting habitat for wood ducks, and it keeps the many resident beavers happy. In the spring you can actually

Omaha Beach at Debsconeag Deadwater with Mount Katahdin, still snow-covered in late May, in the background.

paddle between the maple trees, though as the water level subsides more solid ground appears.

The north end of Debsconeag Deadwater narrows to a swampy channel where Hurd Pond Stream enters. We saw a bald eagle searching for its next meal here. There are nice campsites on the Deadwater: at Omaha Beach, with its wonderful white-sand swimming beach; where the Penobscot flows in at the northeastern end; and at the inlet from First Debsconeag.

First Debsconeag Lake

Debsconeag Deadwater and First Debsconeag Lake connect through an open, readily canoeable channel. The fair current in the spring subsides later in the season. Stronger current flows along the narrows between the island and the southwest shore—where water from the Penobscot River circles around the island. Some great campsites are found on both sides of the channel here.

Paddling along the southern shore of First Debsconeag, you will get a spectacular view of Mount Katahdin the whole way—when it is not enshrouded in clouds. Because of the view, one could easily miss the granite boulders waiting to scrape canoe bottoms. Except for the boulders, the bottom is sandy, clean, and populated with fresh-water mussels. From the north shore, marked by a small sign, a trail leads to some ice caves, but we only found out about this later.

Oddly, our favorite thing about Debsconeag lakes is not the water at all, but the surrounding banks and woodland, with their carpets of mosses, club mosses, lichens, ferns, and wildflowers. Trailing arbutus, wintergreen, and creeping snowberry (all diminutive members of the heath family—relatives of rhododendron, laurel, and blueberry) grow thickly in some areas. Thick cushions of moss and polypody fern drape over many of the boulders here.

Second Debsconeag Lake

A great way to see the woods is to portage into Second Debsconeag. Even if you do not want to carry your canoe, walk the three-quarters-of-a-mile trail anyway. It is an easy walk, the first part running parallel to the connecting creek. Just up from the portage is a nice wooded bridge across the creek, where you can dangle your feet over the edge and watch the rushing cataract. Even with the thirty-foot rise in eleva-

A quiet cove on Second Debsconeag Lake. A passenger waits patiently.

tion between the two lakes, the portage remains generally flat and remarkably dry—even when some pockets of snow remain, as we found in mid-May. We got a good view of a ruffed grouse on the walk. With canoe or gear, the portage should take about twenty to twenty-five minutes.

Second Lake is much rockier than First, especially on the western end. Paddling close to shore (as we usually do), you are almost certain to scrape bottom once or twice, but the rounded granite boulders should not do more than leave a scratch or two. There are a couple of islands and a nice campsite on the western shore, roughly opposite the inlet brook. In the more boggy areas, look for the reddish leaves of pitcher plants.

Because you can get into Second Lake only by portaging or by float plane, you should not see any motorboats here.

Third Debsconeag Lake

You can portage from Second into Third Lake via a trail that starts about a hundred yards east of the inlet brook on the south shore. This trail is both harder to find and steeper in places than the trail connecting First and Second lakes, but it is only half the length. A side trail leads down to one of two small ponds the trail passes between the lakes. The portage should take ten to fifteen minutes one-way.

Third Debsconeag Lake seems just as wild as Second, but much larger. Pressed for time, we explored only the north end. Keep an eye out for common terns. We saw a few and believe they are nesting on the large granite boulders protruding from the water near the north end. In Minister Cove we saw lots of beaver activity as well as seemingly ever-present loons and common mergansers.

There is a drivable portage up into Third Debsconeag Lake from a sporting camp on Pemadumcook Lake, so motorboats can get here, but we doubt many motorboaters will risk the boulder-filled water at the north end and in Minister Cove.

Most campsites in this area require fire permits; a permit is not required for camp stoves.

Getting There

Caution: The access road to Omaha Beach is in very bad shape. Don't even think about taking it unless you have four-wheel drive and high ground clearance; even then, significant damage to your vehicle is very possible from protruding rocks. Check with the Bowater checkpoint to find out if the road has been improved by the time you read this.

Take Routes 157 and 11 west from Exit 56 of I-95 into Millinocket. At the T where 157 ends and 11 turns left (at a school), turn right, then in one block turn left, following signs to Baxter State Park. Take this road 8.2 miles to Spencer Cove (you will be on a paved public road that roughly parallels Golden Road, owned by Great Northern Paper Company). At Spencer Cove, where the two roads come almost together, switch over and get onto the Golden Road. In 1 mile you will get to the Millinocket Checkpoint of Bowater–Great Northern Paper.

You need to pay a day-use fee at the checkpoint and also a camping fee if you plan to camp. Day-use fees in 1994 were $4/day per vehicle for Maine residents and $8/day per vehicle for nonresidents (season passes, $24 and $48, respectively). Overnight camping is $3/night per vehicle for residents and $6/night per vehicle for nonresidents.

From the checkpoint, continue northwest on the paved road for 2.9 miles, then take a shallow left onto an unimproved road. Look carefully for Omaha Beach painted on a concrete post. (Be careful not to take the sharper left, which will take you on a logging road through a recently cut area; ask at the gate for more up-to-date instructions.) Follow this road for 2.9 miles, using extreme care. We just barely made it with a four-wheel-drive minivan, and we are sure the vehicle is a little worse for the wear.

An alternate access involves paddling on a larger lake that is prone to heavy wind and waves. You can launch a canoe in Spencer Cove onto Ambajejus Lake and paddle southwest into Pemadumcook Lake. Then paddle across Pemadumcook to the western end, where there is a portage up to the southern tip of Third Debsconeag (total distance from Spencer Cove is nine or ten miles). A modification to that access is to paddle up through Turkey Tail, Middle Jo-Mary, and Lower Jo-Mary lakes, then run a bit of whitewater into Pemadumcook. This puts you closer to the western end of Pemadumcook, but we could find no portage between Lower Jo-Mary and Pemadumcook (see section on Jo-Mary Lakes, page 235).

The Northern Forest
A Treasure Too Good to Lose

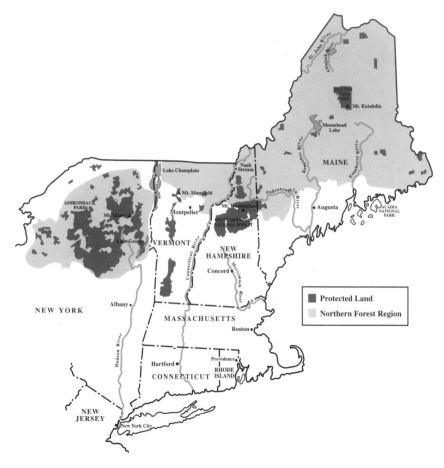

Whether scaling a mountain, paddling the marshy inlet of an out-of-the-way lake, or strolling along an abandoned logging road, one cannot help but be awed by the beauty of the Northern Forest. Stretching from New York's Adirondack Park to the farthest reaches of eastern and northern Maine, the Northern Forest encompasses some 26 million acres of deep, tree-covered woodland.

Words alone cannot define this part of New England. The Northern Forest is better understood by the experience of spotting a majestic bald eagle soaring overhead or a moose browsing along a slow meandering river. The forest is the vibrant greens of newly unfurled ferns along a clear bubbling stream, the seemingly endless sea of blue-gray mountain peaks fading into the twilight, the rhythmic dip of a paddle into the still water of a wilderness lake in the morning's first light.

All is not well, though, with the Northern Forest. Those of us fortunate enough to have spent time there watch with anxiety as the land is bought and sold in corporate takeovers, liquidated of its mantle of timber at an ever-quickening pace, and increasingly subdivided into vacation-home lots. Areas of the Northern Forest where once you could paddle for days in virtual solitude are now sprouting No Trespassing signs, and the call of the loon is being supplanted by the whine of the Jetski.

It used to be assumed that the large private land holdings in the Northern Forest would stay in the hands of forest-products corporations that allowed public access for recreation such as hiking and paddling. But that assumption ended in the late 1980s when a huge block— 90,000 acres—of scenic timberland in New Hampshire and Vermont was sold by Diamond International to a development consortium, Rancourt Associates. The owners refused offers from The Nature Conservancy and other organizations to buy the land and the move sent shock waves through the envi-ronmental community. Fortunately, after intense negotiations, most of the land was ultimately either purchased or protected with conservation easements using federal and state funds. However, the event was a wake-up call to those interested in preserving public access and multiple use for the land.

Around the same time, other factors began to affect the world of the Northern Forest. Economic recession led to cutbacks at paper mills and began a period of buying and selling of industrial forestlands that continues today, particularly in Maine. Since 1976, a total of more than 5 million acres of industrial timberland in Maine has changed hands. The largest single property in the state, Bowater–Great Northern's 2.1-million-acre-tract in north-central Maine, has been sold twice since 1990. Scott Paper's 900,000 acres in Maine were sold to a South African company, Sappi, in 1994.

While sales of large tracts of industrial forestland generated the most news, smaller private, nonindustrial landholdings were, and are, increasingly developed. Some 70 million people live within a day's drive of the Northern Forest, putting pressure for vacation homes on this rural landscape. In Maine's North Woods, the number of houses increased by 23 percent between 1980 and 1990. Vacation homes accounted for three-quarters of the new homes. Most troubling to paddlers, the majority were built around lakes and ponds.

Recognizing development pressures and the increasingly unstable forest-based economy, in 1988 the federal government laid the groundwork for a study of what could be done to protect both land and economic livelihood in the Northern Forest. The U.S. Forest Service was given funding to conduct a Northern Forest Lands Study. After extensive public meetings, the Northern Forest Lands Council issued its final report, "Finding Common Ground: Conserving the Northern Forest," in September 1994. The report includes recommended measures to foster stewardship of private land, protect exceptional resources, strengthen economies of rural communities, and promote more informed decisions. While some forms of protection involve the purchase of private land, many others—indeed the majority of strategies discussed—address not the purchase of land but the retention of large private land ownership with incentives to keep the land in sustainable timber and pulp production. Measures such as property-tax reductions, estate-tax reform (to reduce pressure on heirs to sell undeveloped land), help for nat-

ural-resource-based business, and liability and regulatory reform were all included in "Finding Common Ground."

From the beginning the Appalachian Mountain Club has played a leading role in addressing the Northern Forest issue. AMC chairs the Northern Forest Alliance, a coalition of more than twenty diverse organizations with a common goal of protecting the Northern Forest. Building on the council's recommendations and public comment, the coalition established three goals for future action:

- healthy, well-managed forest-lands;
- permanently protected wildland areas that assure ecological balance and natural beauty for the benefit of present and future generations;
- strong, diverse regional and local economies that will thrive over the long term.

As the future of the Northern Forest is debated, individuals like you will play the biggest role. We have an opportunity to protect for future generations this unique and irreplaceable natural resource and to enable survival of strong, locally based economies. Here's what you can do:

1. Get to know the Northern Forest. Spend some time in the 26 million acres of northern New York, Ver-

mont, New Hampshire, and Maine. This book and many others will help you enjoy the many recreational opportunities awaiting you.

2. Join one or more of the organizations promoting protection of the Northern Forest. The AMC and other organizations such as The Nature Conservancy, the Maine Natural Resources Council, and the Maine Audubon Society, play leading roles and deserve your support.

3. Write to your state and federal elected officials and express support for measures to protect the Northern Forest. The AMC maintains a special Northern Forest Activist Network to assist letter-writing and other activities. Contact the AMC for more details—the address is in the back of this book.

4. Host local gatherings to teach others about the Northern Forest and bring more people into the policy-making arena. The AMC's Activist Network can help you with this.

5. Support the Northern Forest economy by purchase of wood products from well-managed forests in the region. Information on these so-called certified forests may be obtained from Scientific Certification Systems in Oakland, California (510-832-1415).

6. Recycle paper and buy recycled paper. These efforts make our forest resources go farther and help reduce logging pressures in the Northern Forest.

Upper and Lower Togue Ponds and Abol Pond

T2 R9 WELS

MAPS
   Maine Atlas: Map 51
   USGS Quadrangles: Abol Mountain and Trout Mountain
INFORMATION
   Upper Togue Pond area: 294 acres; maximum depth: 34 feet
   Lower Togue Pond area: 384 acres; maximum depth: 53 feet
   Abol Pond area: 70 acres; maximum depth: 34 feet
   Prominent fish species:
      Upper Togue: chain pickerel
      Lower Togue: salmon, white and yellow perch, chain pickerel,
      and smelt
      Abol Pond: brook trout
   Baxter State Park, 64 Balsam Drive, Millinocket, ME 04462; 207-
      723-5140

It just does not get much prettier than the view of Mount Katahdin from the Togue ponds. Located just six miles to the north, Baxter Peak rises 4,670 feet from the level of the ponds. If you happen to paddle here in the spring (ice-out is typically in early May), you will think you are in the West, with the dramatic snow-capped peak dominating the landscape.

The Togue ponds are readily accessible by car—unlike some of the more remote lakes in the area, which require a high-ground-clearance, four-wheel-drive vehicle. There is a very nice picnic area between the ponds just before you get to the gate to Baxter State Park. You can park here and put in your canoe, without having to pay an entry fee to the park just to reach the pond.

Of the two ponds, Upper Togue (on the west side of the road) is a little more remote and the shoreline more varied, but both are nice. Red pine dominates here: You will notice the reddish bark, long needles in bundles of two, and small cones. You will also see white pine (five needles per bundle), jack pine (very short needles with two per bundle), some white cedar along the shore, a few red spruce and balsam fir, red maple, and paper birch. Most of the shoreline is thick with various low, bushy shrubs of the heath family: blueberry, sheep laurel,

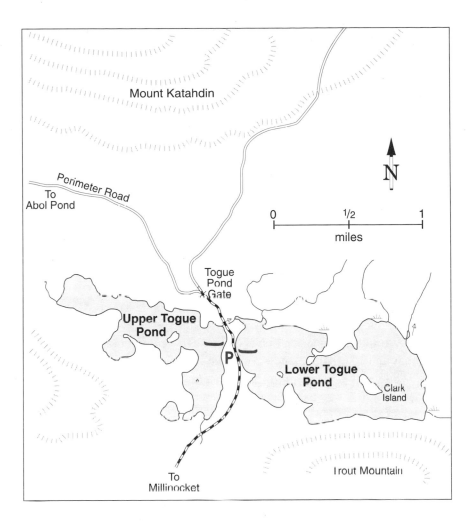

leather leaf, bog rosemary, and Labrador tea. Mixed in with these are bracken fern, alder, and a wide range of mosses and lichens. In some of the coves and along the northern shore of Lower Togue, you will see pitcher plants growing on the hummocks of sphagnum moss (see page 120 for more on pitcher plants).

The water is reddish brown from natural tannins, but very pure. If you look carefully in the sandy bottom, you may see some fresh-water mussels, which stick partway out of the sand and filter microscopic algae and other foods from the water. We saw several pairs of loons here, a broad-winged hawk, and lots of warblers (including yellow-rumped and yellowthroat) and other songbirds at the far western inlet on Upper Togue. We also saw a half-dozen painted turtles at the inlet.

Among mammals, beaver abound, as evidenced by several lodges and lots of stumps. When we visited there was a very active lodge on Upper Togue on the western shore of the cove extending farthest to the south—in fact we have never seen such a cut-over hillside as the one along here, with aspen and birch trees strewn as if part of a logging operation. In the boggy inlet into Lower Togue we watched a mink scurry along the shore looking for its next meal. Mink are very curious; if you catch a glimpse of one, wait around and chances are pretty good he or she will come out of hiding to take a another peak at you.

There are a few cottages along the shores of both ponds (the eastern shore of Upper Togue and the western shore of Lower Togue near the road) and on Clark Island in Lower Togue. A sizable scout camp, with several dozen canvas tent-cabins, lies on the southwestern cove of Lower Togue Pond, so during the summer camp season, this area may be a little more active than the rest of the ponds.

Boats are limited to ten horsepower in Togue ponds. There are picnic tables and outhouses at the picnic area, where you can launch a canoe into either Upper or Lower Togue. The camping area on Upper Togue is an old private campground that is no longer in use.

While in this area, you might also want to paddle on Abol Pond, a narrow pond that runs along the Perimeter Road several miles from

Lower Togue Pond provides spectacular views of Mount Katahdin throughout the paddling season.

mink

the Togue Pond gate. Abol Pond has a nice sand beach and picnic area, and it offers a pleasant few hours of paddling. The shallow pond is thick with vegetation: water lilies, bur reed, and lots of submerged plants. There are a few boggy areas where you can find pitcher plants, cranberry, sphagnum moss, tamarack, and other northern fen species. We saw a deer and a pair of loons with a chick while paddling here on an August afternoon.

Getting There

To reach Togue ponds, take Routes 157 and 11 west from Exit 56 on I-95 into Millinocket. Where 157 ends and Route 11 turns to the left (at a school), turn right. Drive one block and turn left, following signs for Baxter State Park. Continue on this paved road for 14.3 miles, and turn right onto a gravel road toward the Togue Pond gate. In 1.4 miles you will reach the Togue Pond picnic area, where you can park and launch your canoe.

If you want to paddle on Abol Pond, continue on the gravel road past the Togue ponds to the Togue Pond Gate. Drive northwest on the Perimeter Road for 2.9 miles, then turn left and drive another 0.4 mile to the parking area, where you can hand-launch a boat.

South Branch Ponds

T5 R9 WELS

MAPS
Maine Atlas: Map 51
USGS Quadrangle: Wassataquoik Lake

INFORMATION
Upper South Branch Pond area: 84 acres; maximum depth: 76 feet
Lower South Branch Pond area: 93 acres; maximum depth: 60 feet
Prominent fish species: brook trout
Baxter State Park, 64 Balsam Drive, Millinocket, ME 04462; 207-723-5140

Spectacular. Awesome. Superlatives have a hard time adequately conveying the beauty of these ponds and the surrounding mountains. The ponds are perched in an alpine valley at about a thousand feet above sea level. The surrounding mountain peaks rise another 2,500 feet, much of that rise in exposed rock faces.

The South Branch ponds themselves are very small—each less than a mile in length and among the smallest bodies of water included in this guide—and their shorelines are without much variation. The ponds are extremely oligotrophic: crystal clear and nearly devoid of life. If the light is right, you can see down more than twenty feet. Apparently, though, enough fish are here to support a pair of loons on Upper South Branch Pond, and there must be enough microscopic life to support the fresh-water mussels we saw here. Except for park boats used in emergency, motorboats are prohibited. Both canoes and rowboats are available for rent at very reasonable rates. (Canoe rentals are also available at a few of the hike-in ponds with camping areas, such as Russell Pond.)

From a paddling perspective, the other problem with the South Branch ponds is heavy usage. There is a very popular campground at the north end of Lower South Branch Pond with twenty-one tent sites, twelve lean-tos, and a bunkhouse. There is a picnic area at the boat access on Lower South Branch Pond, a ranger cabin occupied throughout the season, and trails that extend along the eastern shore of both ponds. So you should not expect to "get away from it all" here.

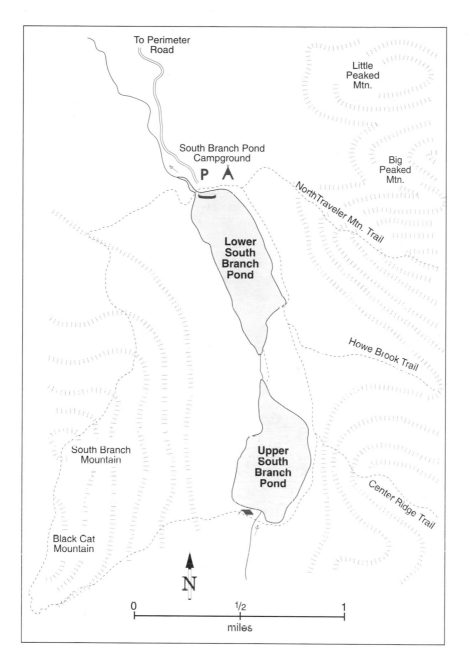

At the southern tip of Lower South Branch Pond (on the eastern shore) you will find a portage trail over to Upper South Branch Pond. The carry is several hundred yards, fairly flat, and very easy. Upper South Branch Pond is even more spectacular than Lower Pond. Jagged, sheer cliffs of Baxter's Katahdin granite extend down into the water. The ridges of Traveler Mountain to the east are steep and dramatic. The charcoal-gray rock on these ridges is rhyolite and very different geologically from the pinkish Katahdin granite. The granite cooled very slowly deep underground, so the crystals are fairly large. The rhyolite found on Traveler Mountain is the solidified lava from a volcanic eruption some 400 million years ago.

Another interesting geologic feature at the South Branch ponds is the fossiliferous rock you can find here. Look along the shoreline of these ponds for pieces of sandstone or shale embedded with fossils of small mollusks called brachiopods. These fossil-bearing rocks were carried here by glaciers. There are relatively few fossils in Maine, and this is one of the best places to find them.

The vegetation around the South Branch ponds is almost entirely hardwood: paper birch, red maple, sugar maple, and beech. A few white pine, red pine, spruce, and fir are scattered amid the hardwoods. In the understory you will see the large-leafed striped maple and beaked hazelnut (which produces an edible nut like the filbert). The area of Baxter State Park was logged beginning in the mid-1800s, first for white pine, then spruce, and finally pulpwood for paper making. The last logging in the park ended in 1965, when the remaining logging rights were exhausted, according to the terms of deeds negotiated by Percival Baxter when he acquired the land. Governor Baxter gave to the state of Maine 200,000 acres of land he acquired over a period of forty-five years—one of the most impressive private land-protection efforts ever. We can all be thankful to Governor Baxter for his farsighted vision in preserving the beauty of this area.

From the campground, enjoy some of the spectacular hikes in this part of Baxter. The North Traveler Mountain Trail provides dramatic views down into the South Branch ponds. The Howe Brook Trail leads to a spectacular cascading waterfall on the side of Traveler Mountain. You can also backpack from here south along the Notch Trail to Russell Pond and remote Wassataquoik Lake, which provides the most remote canoeing in the park. (There are several canoes available for rent on an honor system.)

Getting There

The best way to get to the South Branch ponds is to enter Baxter State Park at the northern entrance. Take I-95 to Exit 58. Turn left on Route 158, which turns into Route 11 north, and follow Route 11 north to Patten. In Patten, turn left on Route 159. Route 159 ends at Shin Pond and turns into Grand Lake Road. From Shin Pond, continue on the main road for 15.9 miles to the park gate. The road is paved for all but the last mile and a half. You will cross over the East Branch of the Penobscot River flowing out of Grand Lake Matagamon and then the boat access to the lake before reaching the park gate. From the park gate, continue on the Perimeter Road for 6.9 miles, then turn left at the sign for South Branch ponds. This road takes you to Lower South Branch Pond in 2.2 miles.

Be aware that Baxter State Park has very specific regulations on the size of campers in the park. Pets are prohibited. Reservations are strongly advised for camping, as campgrounds are full throughout much of the camping season. Camping is permitted in the park only in designated campsites. Reservations must be made in writing or in person at the park headquarters in Millinocket; they cannot be made by phone. Camping fees in 1994 were $12/night, plus $6/person (over six years of age) if there are more than two people per site. The Perimeter Road is narrow and slow-going. Nonresidents must pay a day-use fee ($8 in 1994) to use the park, though if staying in the park, the camping fee covers additional days. When we visited the area at the end of May in 1994, the park was still closed because of snow, though the typical season runs from May 15 to October 15.

Mattawamkeag Lake
Island Falls and T4R3 WELS

MAPS
>   **Maine Atlas:** Map 52
>   **USGS Quadrangles:** Mattawamkeag Lake and Oakfield

INFORMATION
>   **Area:** 3,330 acres; maximum depth: 47 feet
>   **Prominent fish species:** white perch, smallmouth bass, and pickerel
>   Darrell Whittaker Lodge on Mattawamkeag Lake, P.O. Box 521,
>   Island Falls, ME 04747; 207-532-0243
>   **Fire permits:** Maine Forest Service, East Branch District (207-
>   463-2331) or Northern Region Headquarters (207-463-2214)

In addition to paddling Mattawamkeag Lake, one can also paddle the very scenic, fairly wide Mattawamkeag River. Except for a few fishermen, the river sees little boat traffic. The river is an excellent choice whenever the wind is up on the lake itself. Because the river meanders, the wind has few lengthy straight sections to build up waves. When we paddled here one August afternoon and evening, three-foot swells greeted us out on the lake, while a few ripples were all that the river could dish up. The late-summer current was so lazy that the slightest breeze would blow you back upstream.

From the boat access on the Mattawamkeag River, you wind around in a generally eastward direction toward the lake. Occasional weedy fields interrupt the generally wooded shoreline. Boulders line the shore in places, and some protrude from the water out into the river. Although tree diversity is quite high, silver maples are most abundant. Hemlock, balsam fir, spruce, white pine, northern white cedar, sugar maple, yellow birch, and many other species grow along the fertile river bank. Several potential campsites lurk under the dense canopy of large hemlock and other conifers. At one point, a nice rope swing trails out over the water from a large yellow birch.

Major game trails lead down to the water's edge, a white-tailed buck snorted at us from the dense undergrowth, and numerous beaver slapped the water with their tails as we paddled back to the boat launch at sunset. In addition to flocks of cedar waxwings, several great blue herons, and a few osprey, we came very close to a mature bald eagle before it flew from its aerie. Rounding a bend, just past an

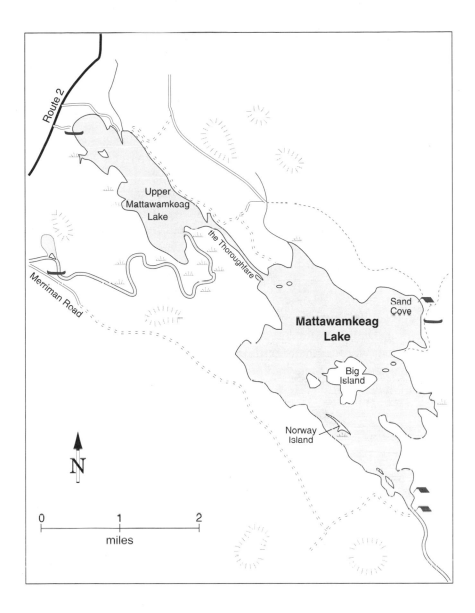

alder swamp, we surprised an American bittern standing in some grass, and it exploded into the air with a squawk.

As you paddle out onto Upper Mattawamkeag Lake, emerging from an extensive stand of rushes, note the tiered farm on the distant hillside. After clearing the river mouth, paddle around to the right about a mile down through the Thoroughfare to Mattawamkeag Lake. If you look carefully around the edges of the channel at what look to be cattails, you will see an occasional patch of sweet flag, with its three-inch-long dense flower spikes growing out of the center of the stem, rather than the tip as with cattails. The leaves are distinguished by an off-center midvein and a spicy aroma (the entire plant is aromatic). Horsetail, bullhead lily, pickerelweed, and other aquatic plants crowd the edges of this shallow channel.

As you clear the channel, the forested Bug Islands appear, with emergent rocks all around, making this end of the lake quite scenic. Paddling out into the middle and looking back, you can see Mount Katahdin off in the distance on a clear day. There is some development on the north end of the lake, but the south end has only a few cottages. Teddy Roosevelt used to stay at the cottages on Hook Point. The shoreline is heavily forested, mainly with deciduous trees, but farther back there are spruces, balsam fir, and other conifers.

There are lots of osprey on Mattawamkeag Lake, and when we paddled here there were four bald eagles—two adults and two immatures—in residence. They usually nest on Norway Island. The eagles and osprey like to perch on a bare pine branch just down the lake shore from Darrell Whittaker's Lodge, where we stayed. Because of the abundant wildlife, the beautiful surroundings, and the views of the mountains in Baxter State Park, the state is negotiating to protect the unincorporated T4 R3 eastern portion of the lake.

Getting There

Take I-95 to Exit 59, Island Falls. Take Route 159 east to the junction with Route 2. Take Route 2 west (road goes south here), and drive 0.6 mile, turning left onto Merriman Road (unmarked). Pavement ends in 0.7 mile, and the boat access is 1.6 miles from Route 2. The last section of dirt road is not very good. The boat launch is a hand-carry access, not the trailer access indicated on the *Maine Atlas*.

It is nearly impossible to get to the boat access at the end of Sand Cove, as depicted on the *Maine Atlas*. Because of a washed-out culvert and millions of rocks, we did not get within a mile and a half of the access. Instead, we stayed with very knowledgeable former Maine Guide Darrell Whittaker at his lodge on the northwest shore of the lake, right next to the Island Falls–T4 R3 boundary.

Sawtelle Deadwater

T6 R7 WELS

MAPS
> **Maine Atlas:** Maps 51 and 57
> **USGS Quadrangle:** Hay Lake

INFORMATION
> **Area:** 218 acres; maximum depth: 30 feet
> **Prominent fish species:** yellow perch
> Maine Department of Inland Fisheries and Wildlife, 284 State
> Street, Station 41, Augusta, ME 04333. Ask for information on
> the Francis Dunn Wildlife Management Area.
> **Fire permits:** Maine Forest Service, East Branch District (207-
> 463-2331) or Northern Region Headquarters (207-463-2214)

The Sawtelle Deadwater was created when a dam was built years ago to power a sawmill. In 1955, when the mill was moved, wildlife biologist Francis D. Dunn of the Department of Inland Fisheries and Wildlife urged the state to buy and manage the area as waterfowl habitat. The purchase was finally completed thirty years later, and in 1985 the Wildlife Management Unit was dedicated to Dunn. You will see nesting boxes for wood ducks and hooded mergansers, and you may find some wild rice that was planted by the department.

The winding marshy channel of Sawtelle Deadwater is one of the best spots to see moose throughout the summer until late August. Paddling here in early August we counted six, some on shore, others wading in the water and muck. We are told that it is not unusual to see a dozen or more.

At almost the opposite end of the animal kingdom hierarchy from moose is another animal you may see here: an unusual invertebrate of the phylum Bryozoa. These colonial bryozoa, *Pectinatella*, are more common farther south—we have seen them in only a few lakes and ponds in Maine. Look underwater for globular masses attached to submerged sticks or rocks. The individual units (called zooids) appear as small bumps on the mass, and the entire colony looks a bit like a jellied pineapple. Each zooid has a rim of ciliated tentacles that filter microscopic food particles out of the water; these tentacles retract at lightning speed into the protective ectocyst. Colonies of this bryozoa can grow to the size of a watermelon by the end of the summer. *Pectinatella* is an excellent indicator of pure water, so you can be pretty sure that

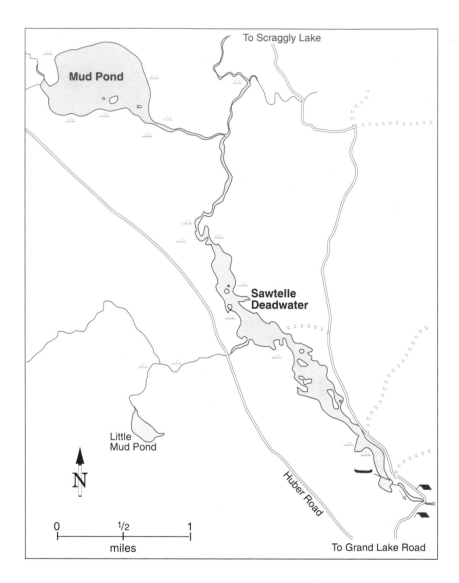

the Sawtelle Deadwater remains uncontaminated with pollutants. Look amid the rocks in the outlet just below the dam for the *Pectinatella* colonies; this area was thick with them when we visited, and we saw a smaller number farther up the deadwater on submerged sticks and logs.

Lush marsh vegetation grows along the shores of Sawtelle. Cattail, pickerelweed, bulrushes, arrowhead, sweet gale, bullhead lily, water shield, pond weed (*Potamogeton* genus), and bladderwort are among the many aquatic and littoral plant species you will see here. The submerged vegetation is thick throughout much of the deadwater, and watching the movement of these plants underwater is the only way to tell which way the current is flowing. Farther away from the water the common tree species include cedar, white pine, paper birch, big-tooth aspen, red maple, balsam fir, and red spruce. On the right side as you are paddling upstream, there is one sizable grove of red pine.

Everywhere along here are kingfishers. Look for them diving into the water after two- to three-inch fish, of which they consume many each day. Those kingfishers with a rust-colored band on the chest are females; those without are males or immature females. We also saw numerous great blue herons and several ospreys.

The southern section of Sawtelle Deadwater is fairly wide and strewn with grassy islands. Some of these you can paddle around; others are dead ends—at least by midsummer. As you paddle north, the deadwater narrows gradually to a channel twenty to thirty feet wide. Eventually you will reach the remains of an old bridge, and several hundred yards past that the channel divides. We are not sure how far you can paddle if you take the right fork. If you take the left fork, you can paddle about two-thirds of a mile up to Mud Pond.

Mud Pond

Mud Pond is appropriately named, though we might have chosen to call it Muck Pond. Your paddle can penetrate easily at least a foot or two into the organic ooze at the bottom of this wide, shallow pond. All is not soft, though; our canoe picked up a few scratches from hidden rocks during our exploration. We saw a moose cow and calf browsing along the western shore of Mud Pond, and I am sure if you spent any time at all here, you would also see deer enjoying the copious vegetation along the shore.

Getting There

From the south, take I-95 to Exit 58. Turn left on Route 158, which turns into Route 11 north, and follow Route 11 north to Patten. In Patten, turn left on Route 159. Route 159 ends at Shin Pond and turns into Grand Lake Road. Note your mileage when you cross the water at Shin Pond.

Continue on Grand Lake Road for 6.5 miles, and turn right (as you are going uphill) on a gravel road with a sign for Scraggly Lake Management Area. Stay on this road for 1.8 miles, and the boat access for Sawtelle Deadwater is on the left. There is room for a half-dozen cars to park here. There is a possible campsite right at the boat-launch area, but if others are paddling or fishing here you may not get much privacy. For camping, it makes more sense to continue on to Scraggly Lake (see the following section).

Scraggly Lake (Northern)
T7 R8 WELS

MAPS

    Maine Atlas: Map 57 (also 51 for access)

    USGS Quadrangles: Hay Lake and Trout Brook Mountain

INFORMATION

    Area: 842 acres; maximum depth: 70 feet (western arm: 39 feet)

    Prominent fish species: salmon, brook trout, lake trout, yellow perch, and smelt

    Bureau of Public Lands, Maine Department of Conservation, State House Station 22, Augusta, ME 04333; 207-289-3061

    Fire permits: Maine Forest Service, East Branch District (207-463-2331) or Northern Region Headquarters (207-463-2214)

Scraggly Lake lies just northeast of Baxter State Park in northern Maine, entirely within a 10,000-acre tract of land owned and managed by the Maine Bureau of Public Lands. Because of public ownership, the land is managed not only for timber, but also for wildlife, important plant communities including several tracts of old-growth forest, and recreational

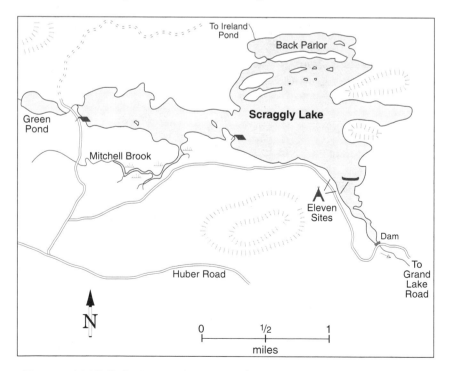

opportunities. About a dozen campsites are accessible by car; several others scattered around the lake are reachable only by canoe.

By almost any standards, Scraggly Lake is a treasure. The 842-acre lake is crystal clear, with a highly varied shoreline. In fact, the deep coves and the long, sinewy inlet to the southwest provide more than twelve miles of shoreline to explore, along with dozens of islands. In late spring and early summer, however, use care if exploring around the shoreline—and especially islands—because five loon nesting sites have been identified.

Mitchell Brook, which flows into the western arm of the lake from the southwest, is paddlable for about a mile, including both forks. This quiet, meandering channel flows through a northern bog ecosystem, replete with pitcher plants, sundews, sphagnum moss, leather leaf, cranberry, bog rosemary, and the feathery light-green tamarack—the first tree to take hold as a mat of sphagnum moss and bog vegetation extends into a body of water. There is no perceptible current here, and the bottom is a thick muck your paddle sinks into effortlessly. When we explored here just after sunrise in August, the first rays of sunlight filtering through the mist illuminated thousands of dew-covered spiderwebs on the low bog vegetation, giving the place a magical, jewellike appearance.

Daybreak on Scraggly Lake.

The morning sun's first rays illuminate spiderwebs in the southwest inlet to Scraggly Lake.

On the northern shore of the western arm of Scraggly, we watched a mink for several minutes as it peered out at us from the protective cover of a fallen tree. Keep an eye out for mink along the shoreline of ponds, where they hunt for food—fish, chipmunks, frogs, and such. If you catch a glimpse of one, stick around for a few minutes; curiosity is likely to get the better of it, and it will peek out from its hiding spot for another look at you.

Also along this section of shoreline, you will see a large rock pile, evidently an old rock slide. Some mammal had taken up residence here when we visited. We repeatedly heard a low guttural snorting and growling, and we tried unsuccessfully for about a half-hour to catch a glimpse of it. We suspect it was a raccoon or otter but never did find out.

The northern section of the main lake is particularly beautiful, with numerous rocky islands. At one point, you can walk several yards over a narrow spit of land into the long east-west arm of the lake at the northern end. Or, at the northeastern end of the lake, you can paddle into the deep cove. Note the lone, ancient, old-growth white pine on one of the points of land extending into the lake here. If you get out of your canoe, you will see that this last remnant of the stately white-pine forest that once dominated the land was almost cut down many decades ago—perhaps more than a century—and the wedge cut has gradually grown over. With a trunk more than three feet in diameter, the tree could be 500 years old.

We saw signs of moose around the lake, but did not happen to see any when we visited. We did see a number of white-tailed deer grazing along the shore and, in one case, chest-deep munching on pipewort—an aquatic plant that sends long narrow stems and buttonlike flowers above the water's surface. We also saw a great blue heron, black ducks, a wood duck, common mergansers, a pileated woodpecker, and quite a few loons.

The shoreline is mostly pebbly and the bottom sandy—except in boggy areas. We saw lots of fresh-water mussels. Most of the shoreline is wooded with white pine, hemlock, cedar, red spruce, balsam fir, white and yellow birch, white ash, and sugar maple. About a mile west of the lake in the Scraggly Lake Management Unit is an eighty-acre section of old-growth hemlock forest (the largest such remnant forest in the state), with trees up to 400 years old.

North of the lake, around Ireland Pond, there are two stands of significant mixed-age woodland comprising 137 acres. While some cutting has occurred here, so the stands are not true "old growth," we understand there are many large individual old-growth trees of various species, including red spruce, hemlock, balsam fir, white pine, sugar maple, and yellow birch. There is no vehicle access to Ireland Pond, but the adventurous could take a day trip hiking into this scenic thirty-five-acre pond. There is a campsite on Ireland Pond.

A sizable campground lies at the south end of the lake, along the western shore. There are about a dozen individual campsites here, some with access to the water. This is a popular spot for people fishing for the trout and landlocked salmon found here. As a result, the campground can be pretty crowded. More attractive for canoeists are several campsites located around the lake that are accessible only by boat.

Getting There

Take I-95 to Exit 58. Get on Route 158 west, which turns into Route 11 north, and follow Route 11 north to Patten. In Patten, turn left (west) on Route 159. Route 159 ends at Shin Pond and turns into Grand Lake Road. Note your mileage when you cross the water at Shin Pond. Continue on Grand Lake Road for 6.5 miles, and turn right (as you are going uphill) on a gravel road with a sign for Scraggly Lake Management Area. (This road is 0.7 mile past the bridge over the Seboeis River.) Stay on this gravel road for 4.7 miles (you will pass the boat access for Sawtelle Deadwater after 1.8 miles), and turn left at the junction. There was a sign here saying J. Huber Corp. Project Landshare when we visited. Stay on the main road, and you will reach the Scraggly Lake boat access and campground in another 5.3 miles.

The Loon
Voice of the Northern Wilderness

No animal better symbolizes wilderness than the loon, whose haunting cry resonates through the night air on most of Maine's larger lakes and ponds. The bird seems almost mystical, with its distinctive black-and-white plumage, daggerlike bill, and piercing red eyes. But like our remaining wilderness, the loon is threatened over much of its range. As recreational pressures on our lakes and ponds increase, the loon gets pushed farther away. We who share its waters bear the responsibility for protecting this wonderful bird.

Along with being a symbol of northern wilderness, the common loon, *Gavia immer,* is one of the most extraordinary birds you will ever encounter. A large diving bird that lives almost its entire life in the water, it visits land only to mate and lay eggs. Loons have a very difficult time on land because their legs, positioned quite far back on their bodies to aid in swimming, prevent them from walking.

Loons have adapted remarkably well to water. Unlike most birds, which have hollow bones, loons have solid bones, enabling them to dive to great depths. They also have internal air sacks, which they compress or expand to control how high they float in the water. By compressing these sacks, loons can submerge gradually (like a submarine) with barely a ripple, or swim along with just their heads above water.

Their heavy bodies and rearward legs make takeoff from the

water difficult. A loon may require a quarter-mile of open water to build up enough speed to lift off, and it may have to circle a small lake several times to build enough altitude to clear nearby hills or mountains. On occasion a migrating loon will mistake a highway for a body of water and crash-land, injuring its feet. Unable to take off again, it will die unless brought to a large enough body of water. When migrating, a loon flies fast—up to ninety miles per hour—but cannot soar.

Loons generally mate for life and can live for twenty to thirty years. The female lays two eggs in early May, and both male and female, which are indistinguishable by features and plumage, take turns incubating the oblong moss-green eggs. If the eggs are left unattended, the embryos can die in just half an hour. Because loons cannot walk on land, they always place their nests very close to shore— where a passing boat can scare the birds away and a motorboat wake can flood the nest with cold water. Loons often nest on islands, where raccoons and skunks will be less likely to find and devour the eggs. On some lakes and ponds, you will see floating nesting platforms, built by concerned individuals or organizations to improve the chances of nesting success. On reservoirs with varying water levels, these platforms take on special importance, because they rise and fall with the water level, reducing the likelihood of flooding or stranding a loon nest.

Loon chicks hatch fully covered in black down, and they usually enter the water a day after hatching. Young chicks may be seen riding on a parent's back, but they grow quickly on a diet of small fish and crustaceans. By two weeks of age, they have grown to half the size of the adult and can dive to relatively deep lake bottoms, covering more than thirty yards underwater. Loon chicks remain totally dependent on their parents, however, for about eight weeks, and they do not fly until ten to twelve weeks of age. After leaving the nest a day after hatching, loons do not return to land for three or four years, until they reach breeding age. The young mature on the sea, having followed their elders to saltwater wintering areas.

While loons are threatened or endangered in most states in the Northeast, they are plentiful in Maine. The last statewide aerial survey of loons by the Maine Audubon Society in 1990 found a total of 3,949 adults. More thorough surveys in the southern half of the state found the adult population to range from

1,649 to 2,251 between 1988 and 1993, and the number of chicks fledged ranged from 163 to 368. Loons have fared quite well throughout the state in recent years, but as development encroaches on our lakes—destroying loon nesting habitat—and as recreational use increases, loons become increasingly at risk.

Because loons react to disturbance when nesting, it is extremely important for paddlers to keep their distance and be aware of warning displays during the nesting season of early May through mid-July. (If a nest fails, the loons may try up to two other times, though the later the chicks hatch the lower their chances of survival.) If you see a loon flapping its wings and making a racket during the nesting season, it probably has a nest or young chicks nearby. Paddle away from shore.

Canoeists can be a serious threat to nesting loons, because both loons and paddlers prefer shallower protected coves and inlets. If you see a nesting site marked with buoys or warning signs, as is done on some lakes and ponds, always respect those signs and keep your distance.

Loons have lived in this area longer than any other bird—an estimated 60 million years. Let's make sure this wonderful species remains protected so future generations may listen to its enchanting music on a still, moonlit night. For more information on loons, contact the Maine Audubon Society, P.O. Box 6009, Falmouth, ME 04105; 207-781-2330. You might also want to pick up a copy of the excellent book *The Loon: Voice of the Wilderness* by Joan Dunning (Yankee Books, Dublin, New Hampshire, 1985).

Grand Lake Matagamon

Trout Brook Twp.

MAPS
> **Maine Atlas:** Maps 51 and 57
> **USGS Quadrangles:** Frost Pond and Trout Brook Mountain

INFORMATION
> **Area:** 4,165 acres; maximum depth: 95 feet
> **Prominent fish species:** salmon, lake trout, and yellow perch
> Matagamon Wilderness Campground, P.O. Box 220, Patten, ME 04765; 207-528-2448. Reservations recommended.
> Baxter State Park, Reservation Clerk, 64 Balsam Drive, Millinocket, ME 04462; 207-723-5140. Reservations by mail recommended. Campsites do not require fire permits.

About half of Grand Lake Matagamon lies within the boundaries of Baxter State Park. Although the park allows motors here and on Webster Lake, these bodies of water are protected from development. With 6.5 square miles of water, coupled with its remoteness, Grand Lake Matagamon provides a large measure of solitude and will take two or more days to explore fully. The park maintains five campsites on the lake, and camping is available at nearby Trout Brook Farm, 2.6 miles into the park, and at Matagamon Wilderness Campground on the East Branch of the Penobscot River outside the park, just down from the lake outlet.

From the boat access, distances to the five campsites are: Togue Ledge, 2.5 miles; Boody Brook, 4.7 miles; Second Lake, 4.9 miles; Pine Point, 6.1 miles; Northwest Cove, 7.1 miles. Register for these sites at the gate house. We advise that you arrive the evening before your trip, because these sites fill up every day. The campsite fee is $6/person per day, with a $12 per day minimum.

Grand Lake Matagamon has changed from the time Thoreau paddled it in the mid-1800s. Much of it remains wild, but the downed timber he had to negotiate drowned long ago with higher lake levels caused by a new concrete dam. An obstacle course of exposed and barely submerged stumps remains in shallower areas, but most of the lake is now easily accessible by boat.

When Thoreau stopped on Louse Island, he found all three species of pine, and those three species remain there today. Besides

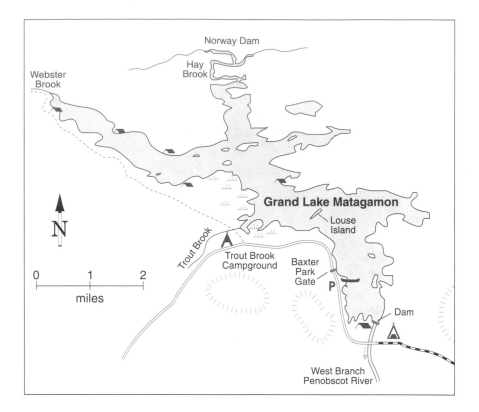

the widely distributed red and white pines, rare jack pines are found in fair numbers on Louse, as well as on other islands and in isolated pockets along the shore. Maine represents the southern extension of the range of jack pine, which grows almost to the Arctic Circle in Canada, the farthest north of any pine species. It can be distinguished from the other pines by its short, 1- to 1^1/$_2$-inch-long needles. Note the persistent thin, curved cones from 1 to 3 inches long, often with two cones growing on opposite sides of a branch. The seeds from these cones are important food for wildlife.

As you paddle out from the boat access, go left around the first island to get your first view of a thick stand of jack pine, along with paper birch and quaking aspen. Besides breaking up the view and making the lake very scenic, dozens of islands provide beautiful spots for picnics, swimming, or just lounging around—bugs permitting.

Continuing around to the left, a series of coves appears, one of them connecting to Trout Brook, which leads up to Trout Brook Farm Campground in Baxter Park. When the wind is up on the main lake, one could put in at the campground and paddle down Trout Brook to the lake, through an extensive marshy area. When we paddled here, a pair of osprey was nesting at the lake inlet. More marshlands, seldom visited by boaters, appear just south and north of the inlet. Because this is the largest expanse of marsh on the lake, look for moose here in the early morning and evening. Another good moose area is in the marsh and alder swamps on the sinewy north inlet called Norway Dam. Although we did not see moose on Grand Lake Matagamon, we saw more white-tailed deer along the shore than on almost any other lake. Many were out in the middle of the day.

Balsam firs, topped with pointed spires, occur with great frequency in the Trout Brook area. Note the beautiful dark-purple cones, two to four inches long, pointing upward from the branches. An important browse plant for moose and white-tailed deer, the dense balsam foliage provides refuge for spruce grouse and many smaller birds as well. We watched flocks of cedar waxwings darting from the alders and firs to catch insects out over Trout Brook, with its absolutely crystal-clear water.

Several flickers have chipped out holes in the dead trees of the marshland, inadvertently providing homes for numerous cavity-nesting birds, such as wood ducks, common and hooded mergansers, chickadees, nuthatches, wrens, tree swallows, bluebirds, kestrels, and

deer

screech owls. Matagamon offers hours—even days—of bird watching and wildlife viewing for the quiet-water paddler.

Besides Thoreau's writings, there are two other, possibly apocryphal, tales about Matagamon. First, Louse Island supposedly got its name from returning timbermen who would stop there, just before reaching the end of their many-day stay in the woods, to burn their clothes. Coupled with a bath, that would certainly effect louse removal. The second story concerns Native American braves, returning from long hunting forays, who would see the form of a beautiful sleeping maiden on the south shore of Second Lake (the western end of Matagamon). As they approached closer, the form would turn ugly as reality intruded on fantasy. We saw clearly what could be this sleeping form, but we leave the final judgment to you.

Grand Lake Matagamon is wild and beautiful, filled with forested islands and boulders appropriate for picnicking, swimming, and sunning. Wildlife abounds, and solitude awaits those who would explore the marshy coves and inlets. Combined with the extensive hiking-trail system of Baxter State Park, the lake offers the opportunity for an exciting and varied vacation.

Getting There

The boat access on Grand Lake Matagamon is on the northeastern edge of Baxter State Park. From the south, take I-95 to Exit 58, and follow Route 11 north to Patten. Take Route 159 west out of Patten, through Shin Pond, eventually ending at the Grand Lake Matagamon boat access and the adjoining Baxter State Park entrance. Parking exists for many cars. The boat access is thirty-five miles from Exit 58.

Loon Lake and Big Hurd Pond
T6 R15 WELS

MAPS
   Maine Atlas: Map 49 (others for access)
   USGS Quadrangles: Caucomgomoc East, Caucomgomoc West, and Ragmuff Stream

INFORMATION
   Data on Loon Lake unavailable.
   Big Hurd Pond area: 250 acres; maximum depth: 27 feet
   Prominent fish species: (Big Hurd Pond): brook trout, white perch, and yellow perch
   Bowater–Great Northern Paper, Public Relations, One Katahdin Ave., Millinocket, ME 04462; 207-723-5131 (for information about checkpoints and access-road conditions)
   Fire permits: Maine Forest Service, Moosehead District (207-695-3721) or Central Region Headquarters (207-827-6191)

We set out on Loon Lake on a calm July evening, with scarcely a ripple on the surface of the water. The only sound was the steady dip of paddles into water and the plaintive cry of loons on this aptly named lake. We left behind our thoughts of the long drive getting here—on bumpy logging roads through clearcuts and third- or fourth-generation spruce/fir regrowth. Few people visit Loon Lake; most pass by on their way to more famous canoeing destinations.

Loon Lake is a wonderful place. Unlike the nearby Allagash River and Allagash Lake, this is generally off the beaten path yet readily accessible by vehicle. Loon Lake offers about 10 miles of shoreline to explore, plus a paddlable section of the Loon Stream inlet. Big Hurd Pond provides another 3.5 miles, plus islands. We saw one cabin on Loon Lake, and—much to our disappointment—it appeared that one might be going up on Big Hurd.

Loon Lake and Big Hurd Pond have quite varied shorelines, with coves to explore, marshy areas providing great bird habitat, rock outcrops draped in moss and ferns, and majestic white pines overlooking the water in places. Though we did not see the nest, we saw an adult bald eagle and several immatures, so we suspect a nest is nearby. We lost count of osprey and loons.

Our favorite section of Loon Lake is the Loon Stream inlet. This shallow, marshy area, dotted with islands, has abundant wildlife. Float-

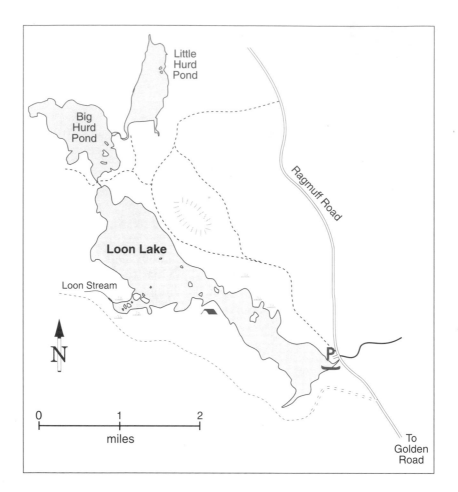

ing vegetation crowds the channel, and we saw nesting ring-necked ducks here. We suspect the eagle nest is in this area. You can paddle some distance up the inlet stream, at least if the water level is high.

There is a very nice campsite midway up the lake on the left (south). Because this is not a permitted site, you will need to obtain a permit from the Maine Forest Service if you want to make an open fire.

Big and Little Hurd Ponds

With a high water level—as was the case when we visited in mid-July—you can paddle easily from Loon Lake into Big Hurd Pond. We are told, though, that the level of Loon Lake can drop considerably, making access into Big Hurd more difficult. Even at high water, watch out for rocks in the connecting channel.

A young paddler takes a turn in the solo canoe on Loon Lake.

Big Hurd Pond is small compared with Loon Lake, and it has a protected feel to it. When we paddled in from Loon Lake as the sun was dipping down over the western hills, the place seemed magical. Near the access from Loon Lake, several islands crop up, along with a few more near the center of the pond. The islands are mostly solid rock, with huge boulders of granite reaching down into the water in places, thick carpets of moss and lichen, and copious blueberries in season.

To get from Big Hurd into Little Hurd Pond, paddle up a shallow stream, then carry your canoe for about a hundred feet over a rocky area and small ledge. When we explored Little Hurd Pond in the early morning we saw four deer (three were bucks) and a moose. In quite an unusual sight, two of the deer and the moose were browsing close together along the Little Hurd Pond outlet —they would have fit into one camera frame. Common terns skimmed the surface of the pond continually during our paddle here.

Though we saw lots of wildlife at Little Hurd, the pond is not enjoyable to paddle. Extremely shallow—few places are deeper than a foot—the lake also has a bottom of thick organic ooze. The water currents created by paddling agitate the bottom, leaving a trail of thousands of tiny bubbles of marsh gas. Even a family of common goldeneye ducks swimming along left a trail of bubbles. As a pond, Little Hurd probably does not have too many centuries of life left before it is fully filled in and taken over by the encroaching tamaracks and bog vegetation.

Getting There

Take I-95 to Exit 56, and drive west on Routes 157 and 11 into Millinocket. At the T where Route 157 ends and 11 turns to the left, turn right (there is a large brick school on the right). Drive one block and turn left, following signs to Baxter State Park. In Spencer Cove (Millinocket Lake on the right and Ambajejus Lake on the left), cut across to the parallel Golden Road, and stop at the Bowater Gate 1.0 mile from Spencer Cove. (You have to pay both day-use and camping fees.)

From the Bowater gate, stay on the Golden Road for 45.5 miles (it is paved for the first 24 miles, then is well-maintained gravel). After 45.5 miles (and just 1.7 miles after crossing the West Branch of the Penobscot River at Hannibal's Crossing), turn right on Ragmuff Road. Stay on the main road at several sharp turns, following signs to the Caucomgomoc checkpoint of North Maine Woods. At 17.6 miles after turning onto Ragmuff Road, cross a bridge over Loon Stream. Just past the bridge, turn left and drive to the dam and access. There is room for a half-dozen cars to park here.

Caucomgomoc Lake
Rowe, Round, Daggett, and Poland Ponds

T7 R15 WELS

MAPS

Maine Atlas: Map 55 (others for access)

USGS Quadrangles: Caucomgomoc Lake West, Caucomgomoc Lake East, and Allagash Lake

INFORMATION

Caucomgomoc Lake area: 5,081 acres; maximum depth: 79 feet

Round Pond area: 375 acres; maximum depth: 17 feet

Daggett Pond area: 461 acres; maximum depth: 20 feet

Poland Pond area: 490 acres; Maximum depth: 34 feet

Prominent fish species:

Caucomgomoc: salmon, lake trout, brook trout, and white perch

Ponds: brook trout, white perch, and yellow perch

North Maine Woods, Inc., P.O. Box 421, Ashland, ME 04732; 207-435-6213

Bowater–Great Northern Paper, Public Relations, One Katahdin Ave., Millinocket, ME 04462; 207-723-5131 (for information about Bowater checkpoint and access-road conditions)

Fire permits: Maine Forest Service, Moosehead District '(207-695-3721) or Central Region Headquarters (207-827-6191)

Cabin accommodations: Loon Lodge, P.O. Box 480, Millinocket, ME 04462; 207-695-2821 (radio contact)

These bodies of water lie in the heart of northern Maine canoe country. While more famous for river canoeing (especially the Allagash), this area also offers superb lake and pond canoeing. Caucomgomoc Lake provides a good starting point, but be aware that this large lake, with its northwest-southeast orientation, often suffers from strong winds and rough water; be ready to alter your plans or hold over for a day or two if you plan to paddle here.

For the quiet-water paddler, the nicest parts of Caucomgomoc are the western end—where the lake does not seem so large—and the eastern end, where one can travel up into Round, Daggett, and Poland ponds. The more adventuresome can reach Caucomgomoc by paddling or poling downstream (north) from Loon Lake or can use Caucomgomoc as an access into Allagash Lake (see sections on those

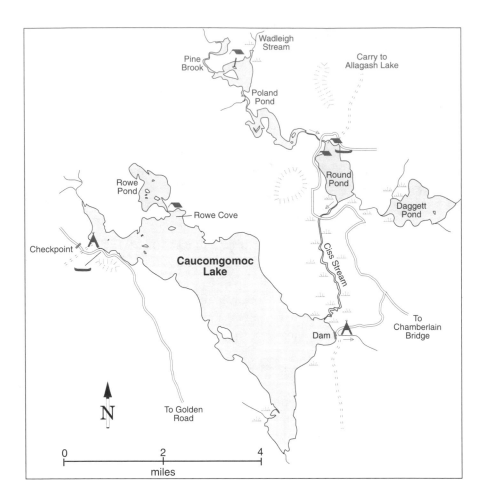

lakes). We put in at the camping area by the Caucomgomoc check-point of North Maine Woods and spent several wonderful days explor-ing this area. We started out paddling the northwestern inlet and the shoreline over to Rowe Pond, staying our first night at the Rowe Cove campsite at the entrance into Rowe Pond.

Caucomgomoc Lake has a wild and highly varied shoreline. In the narrow inlet channel at the northwestern tip, we spotted an otter, and we watched another for about a half-hour between Rowe Cove and Caucomgomoc Dam. We saw lots of loons, several bald eagles, ospreys, a moose, and a deer along here. Rowe Pond is dotted with gorgeous islands, including Henry's Island, which has a small camp-site on it. During an early morning paddle on Rowe Pond, we heard a group of coyotes howling not too far into the woods. The splendid

A family sized canoe, with lots of space for people and gear, offers a comfortable paddle on Caucomgomoc Lake.

campsite at Rowe Cove does not require a fire permit. At Caucomgomoc Dam you will find a nice picnic area and campsite—though the roar of the dam may make for a somewhat wakeful night.

Ciss Stream and Round Pond

Just northwest of Caucomgomoc Dam, Ciss Stream enters the lake. With adequate water level, Ciss Stream provides very enjoyable paddling up into Round, Daggett, and Poland ponds. The barely perceptible current will not impede your progress as the stream wends its way through a broad, flooded valley. Wide and strewn with sun-whitened stumps and fallen trees, the stream bears watching to avoid getting blocked by downed logs. Because Caucomgomoc Dam controls Ciss Stream, its level—and navigability—can drop appreciably when Great Northern Paper drops the level of Caucomgomoc Lake. In the past, drawdown of Caucomgomoc Lake often made Ciss Stream unnavigable by canoe, but apparently that has changed, at least to some extent, with new paper-company watershed-management practices.

We watched ospreys fish along here in their characteristic hovering manner, spooked a few ducks, and then watched a huge bull moose at close range just below the bridge, near the entrance into Round

Pond. Most of Ciss Stream is too boggy to get a good look at moose, but near the bridge solid ground comes closer to the stream channel.

The thickly wooded shoreline, without a great deal of variation, makes Round Pond attractive but not exceptional. Three campsites exist at the north end (two were permitted sites when we visited in 1994). The Round Pond Inlet Campsite, at the inlet from Poland Pond, seemed nicest. In choosing a campsite, however, also consider wind conditions—in bug season the normally annoying wind can be an ally. Also, both of the permitted sites receive quite heavy usage during peak vacation times.

Loon Lodge perches on the northeast shore of Round Pond. This very nice and relatively new sporting camp offers various levels of accommodations, as well as canoe-ferrying service partway into Allagash Lake (see section on Allagash Lake). Loon Lodge is the only sporting camp in this part of Maine, making it ideal for canoeists preferring more luxurious accommodations.

Daggett Pond

Round Pond provides access into two very nice ponds. At the southeast end of Round Pond you can paddle Little Ciss Stream east into Daggett Pond. Watch quietly for moose, deer, and otters as you round the many bends of this gentle stream. Daggett Pond, 1.5 miles long, offers about 5 miles of shoreline to explore. The pond is beautiful, highly varied, and rich with wildlife. We watched three moose along the marshy shore at the northwest end of the pond.

Firm ground comes right down to the water on the more wooded eastern half of the pond. On the point of land extending into the pond along the northeastern shore is Fort Daggett—not a fort at all, but an elegant summer camp built by a corporation back in the early 1900s and rarely used today.

Poland Pond

Poland Pond, to the north and west of Round Pond, differs markedly from Daggett Pond but also provides for a great day trip from Round Pond. You have to do a bit of upstream poling or pulling your canoe to get there—through a few hundred yards of quickwater. If wading and lining your canoe upstream, be sure to wear water shoes or a pair of old sneakers, as the bottom is rocky and slippery. At the remains of an old dam you have to carry your canoe about thirty feet up over a small rise to get into the pond. Going back downstream, if the water is high enough, you should be able to paddle the modest rapids below the carry.

Because an old dam failed, dropping the water level, a band of younger vegetation grows along the shore of Poland Pond, providing superb deer forage. We counted six deer—including two large bucks—as we paddled on the pond one mid-July day. Some sections of the pond are boggy, with tamarack and other northern fen species present.

Poland Pond is long, narrow, highly convoluted, and divided by a narrow channel at its midpoint. Pine Brook, which flows into Poland Pond at the northwest tip, is blocked by downed logs, but with a little work you might be able to get through and explore farther to the north. At the northeastern tip of the pond, you can explore the Wadleigh Stream inlet farther up. There is an outpost cabin of Loon Lodge available for rent up here (see address on page 289).

The smaller island at the northern end of Poland Pond also has a very nice campsite, from which you can walk over to a huge rock face and look out over the pond—often at deer or moose grazing on shoreline vegetation. There is a small beach at the campsite and several others at this end of Poland Pond. To build a campfire here, you must obtain a fire permit from the Maine Forest Service, but no permit is required if you use a camp stove.

Looking south into Poland Pond from Pine Brook at the north end.

Drift logs add a playful diversion to a day's paddle on Poland Pond.

Getting There

You can put in at the campsite by the Caucomgomoc gate of North Maine Woods by taking the Golden Road and Ragmuff Road from Millinocket. This route is about seventy miles from the Bowater gate (Great Northern Paper) and seventy-one miles from the last real gas station at Spencer Cove. We advise bringing extra gas and a good spare tire or two when driving out here in the sticks.

From I-95, get off at Exit 56, and drive west on Routes 157 and 11 into Millinocket. At the T where Route 157 ends and Route 11 turns left, turn right (there is a large brick school on the right). Drive one block and turn left, following signs to Baxter State Park. In Spencer Cove (Millinocket Lake on the right and Ambajejus Lake on the left), cut across to the parallel Golden Road, and stop at the Bowater Gate 1.0 mile from Spencer Cove. Begin checking your odometer at the gate. (Because you are just passing through the Bowater–Great Northern Paper land en route to North Maine Woods land, you should not have to pay a fee here.)

Stay on the Golden Road for 45.5 miles (it is paved for the first 24.0 miles, then is well-maintained gravel). After 45.5 miles (and just 1.7 miles after crossing the West Branch of the Penobscot River at Hannibal's Crossing), turn right on Ragmuff Road. Follow Ragmuff Road north for 25.1 miles to the North Maine Woods Caucomgomoc checkpoint, following signs where the road turns. Register at the checkpoint for your stay on North Maine Woods land, and put in at the camping area 0.2 mile from the gate (to reach the camping area, turn right just before the gate). You can drive in without going through the gate, but you still have to register for camping and day-use.

To drive all the way to Round Pond, go through the Caucomgomoc checkpoint and follow signs for Loon Lodge; it is about thirteen miles from the checkpoint. The road past the Caucomgomoc checkpoint is likely to be in somewhat worse shape than the road up to the checkpoint. To drive into Round Pond, you can also come in via the Telos Road, then left at Chamberlain Bridge (refer to the current edition of the *Maine Atlas* and ask about road conditions at checkpoints).

Allagash Lake and Johnson Pond

T8 R14 WELS

MAPS

Maine Atlas: Map 55 (others for access)

USGS Quadrangles: Allagash Lake and Tramway

INFORMATION

Area: 4,260 acres; maximum depth: 89 feet

Prominent fish species: brook trout and lake trout

Allagash Wilderness Waterway, Bureau of Parks and Recreation, State House Station 22, Augusta, ME 04333; 207-287-3821

North Maine Woods, Inc., P.O. Box 421, Ashland, ME 04732; 207-435-6213

Fire permits: Camping permitted only at authorized campsites, for which fire permits are not required.

Cabin accommodations: Loon Lodge, P.O. Box 480, Millinocket, ME 04462; 207-695-2821 (radio contact)

Outfitters: Katahdin Outfitters, P.O. Box 34, Millinocket, ME 04462; 207-723-5700

Allagash Lake is at the top of our list, one of our very favorite lakes in Maine. It is a large lake, subject to heavy winds, but the lake geometry prevents waves from building up as much as they do on some other large lakes in the region. And wind does not affect the large number of protected areas on the lake.

There are several reasons Allagash Lake is so great. It is beautiful, of course: nestled beneath Allagash and Poland mountains, lined with moss-covered rocks, marshy inlets, and—everywhere—deep, wild forest. But Allagash is also special because you will not hear the putt-putt of motors, you will not see or hear automobiles, you will not even see float planes landing here. Allagash Lake is the *only* body of water in Maine to exclude *all* motors (even electric motors).

Allagash Lake is part of the Allagash Wilderness Waterway, created by the state in 1966. Most of the waterway is far better known— Allagash River and the string of connected lakes—Chamberlain, Eagle, and Churchill—that some 10,000 canoeists travel each year. Far fewer paddlers visit Allagash Lake, a side trip off the main waterway, connected by Allagash Stream. Canoes may use up to ten-horsepower motors on most of the Allagash Wilderness Waterway, but not on Allagash Lake.

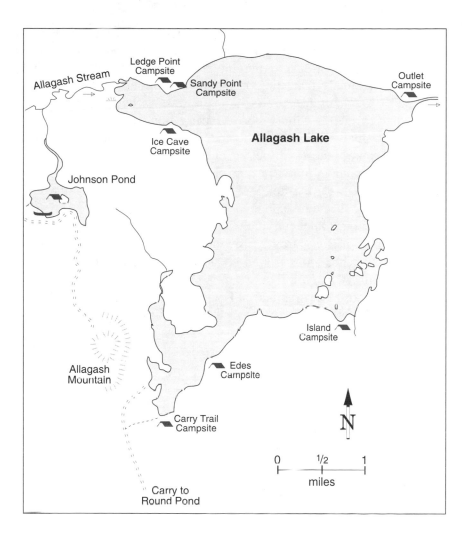

No direct access to Allagash Lake exists. You can drive over pretty rough roads to an upstream launch site on Allagash Stream or Johnson Pond. You can pole or line a canoe upstream from Chamberlain
Lake. Or you can portage your canoe in from Round Pond (see section
on Caucomgomoc Lake and connected ponds). However you do it, it
takes substantial effort to get into Allagash Lake, and that makes it all
the more special.

When we visited, we spent most of our time in the southern end,
protected from the wind, which seems to be almost ever-present in
northern Maine. Two permitted campsites are found at the south end:
the Carry Trail Campsite and Edes Campsite. Large groups traveling
through Allagash Lake from Round Pond and Caucomgomoc use the

Carry Trail Campsite pretty heavily. For small groups, Edes is nicer, with a sandy beach, nice fire ring, and several flat tenting sites.

The cove of the lake extending from the south end up to the northwest is simply fantastic. On an early morning paddle here we watched a couple of deer browse along a grassy section of shoreline, and we surprised a young moose eating pond vegetation as we entered the small pond at the north end of this cove. Along the way to that pond, take a close-up look at classic northern bog vegetation: tamarack, sphagnum moss, pitcher plant, sundew, cranberry, swamp rose, sheep laurel, leather leaf, sweet gale, and—perhaps our favorite—the delicate rose pogonia orchid. We watched several families of common goldeneye ducks along here, studied the graceful ternlike flight of Bonaparte's gulls, saw ospreys and a broad-winged hawk, and watched loons from a great-enough distance to avoid disturbing them.

Farther north, mosses and polypody cover the granite boulders separating sections of thickly wooded shoreline. The clean water and generally sandy bottom support numerous fresh-water mussels that filter microscopic food particles out of the water. The many little coves and inlets provide lots of opportunity to look for deer, moose, otter, mink, and other mammals that call this home.

Several species of gulls as well as common terns nest on a few rocky islands. We saw ring-billed gulls, herring gulls, and Bonaparte's gulls, the last an uncommon summer resident in New England.

As the shoreline curves to the west, you will reach the Ice Cave Campsite. A short hike up the hill from here takes you to several fascinating ice caves that can be quite refreshing on a hot, humid day. Bring a flashlight, and prepare to get a little muddy as you squeeze down into the cold granite caves, where ice lasts well into the summer.

Also explore the numerous islands with one campsite in the southeastern corner of Allagash Lake. Because this part of the lake is not on a route into or out of the lake, it gets less visitation. Campsites at the north end, near the inlet and outlet of the lake, receive the heaviest use. Quite a few groups come through Allagash Lake as part of extended trips north on the Allagash River. During three days here, we saw an Outward Bound group and a large group from a wilderness-experience camp.

Johnson Pond

If you have time and want to do some more-extended exploring, you can take a nice trip up Allagash Stream and a side stream to Johnson Pond. This fairly wide, deep section of Allagash Stream, entering at the northeastern tip, flows slowly enough that paddling is easy (there are just a few riffles in places). Watch for a narrow stream coming in from the left about a mile and a half from the lake. You can make your way up this tiny stream, though you have to pull your canoe up over several beaver dams and literally pull yourself through thick alder swamps in places.

After the last (and largest) barrier, the stream opens up gradually into Johnson Pond. Initially the pond is narrow and surrounded by grassy marsh, but it widens out into a simply gorgeous pond about two-thirds of a mile across with a large island in the center. A sizable campsite exists on the island with several separate camping sites. Several outfitters store canoes on the island in order to bring in clients by float plane and outfit them for a trip downstream. When we visited here in 1994, merlins were nesting in a tree on the island. These small, rare falcons (they look somewhat like small peregrine falcons) are more common in northern Canada.

Getting There

Of the several ways into Allagash Lake, none is particularly easy or convenient. Putting in at Johnson Pond or farther upstream on the Allagash Stream will avoid a lengthy portage, but the roads may be bad and you may have to deal with shallow water. The best way to drive into Johnson Pond or the Allagash Stream access is to take the Golden Road and Ragmuff Road (through Bowater–Great Northern Paper land) to the North Maine Woods Caucomgomoc checkpoint (see access description for Caucomgomoc Lake). Pass through the North Maine Woods checkpoint and stay on the main road for approximately 11 miles to a T (St. Francis Lake will be right in front of you). After the right turn, drive 5.5 miles, then turn right (the road crosses Allagash Stream here). Drive approximately 2.8 miles, then turn right on a smaller, less maintained road, and you will reach the Allagash Stream access in 4.0 miles (where the road passes close to the stream—there is room for a number of vehicles to park along the road here), or continue another 3.0 miles to Johnson Pond (bearing left at the one sizable fork). We recommend highly that you use a current edition of the

DeLorme *Maine Atlas* and ask about road conditions at the Caucom-gomoc checkpoint.

To carry in from Round Pond, either park at the camping area near the Caucomgomoc checkpoint and paddle to Round Pond (see section on Caucomgomoc Lake), or drive to the campsite at the north end of Round Pond and carry from there. Round Pond is accessible from the Caucomgomoc checkpoint or from Telos Road and Longley Stream Road. From the Caucomgomoc checkpoint, turn right in 4.5 miles, following signs for Loon Lodge. Follow this road for about 6 miles, and turn left, again following signs for Loon Lodge. After crossing a bridge between Poland and Round ponds, you will see a campsite on the right and the road up toward Allagash on the left. To drive in from Telos Road, follow the *Maine Atlas*. Either way, you should ask about road conditions at the relevant checkpoint.

Loon Lodge, a sporting camp on Round Pond (past the road up toward Allagash Lake), offers cabins and meals for those who want a night of relative luxury before or after a trip into Allagash. Loon Lodge offers canoe-ferrying service up to the gate a mile from Alla-gash Lake. The service was priced reasonably in 1994 and saves about two and a half miles of portage. If you carry the whole way, bear left at the one fork. About three-quarters of a mile past the gate, stay on the road rather than taking the Carry Trail. The road is in much better shape than the Carry Trail and leads to a ranger cabin where you can launch your canoe. If you stay off the Carry Trail, the whole portage is along a dirt road and works well with a portage cart. A cart will not work on the Carry Trail.

No matter which route you take in, you have to pay when you register at the North Maine Woods checkpoint. If you pass through Bowater–Great Northern Paper land getting to North Maine Woods land, you should not have to pay a fee there as well, since you are only passing through. Registration fees get pretty complex, with different rates for Maine residents and nonresidents, both day-use and camping fees, and different rates for camping on North Maine Woods land and state land. See Introduction (page xviii) for details.

Deboullie, Pushineer, Gardner, and Togue Ponds

T15 R9 WELS

MAPS
Maine Atlas: Map 63
USGS Quadrangles: Deboullie Pond and Gardner Pond

INFORMATION
Deboullie Pond area: 266 acres; maximum depth: 92 feet
Pushineer Pond area: 55 acres; maximum depth: 52 feet
Gardner Pond area: 288 acres
Togue Pond area: 388 acres; maximum depth: 85 feet
North Maine Woods, Inc., P.O. Box 421, Ashland, ME 04732; 207-435-6213 (access and camping charges)
Maine Department of Conservation, Bureau of Public Lands, State House Station 22, Augusta, ME 04333; 207-289-3061
Outfitting: Pelletier's Campground, RR 1, Box 9, St. Francis, ME 04774; 207-398-3208
Sporting lodge: Red River Camp, P.O. Box 16, Portage, ME 04768; 207-435-6000 (Winter: 207-528-2259)
Fire permits: Maine Forest Service, Allagash District (207-435-6644) or Northern Region Headquarters (207-463-2214)

Tucked away in the northern reaches of the Pine Tree State, this cluster of small but beautiful deep ponds provides opportunity for a wonderful *north* Maine woods experience. Be forewarned, though: Unless you live in the northern tip of the state or in New Brunswick, Canada, be prepared for some driving to get here.

Deboullie, Gardner, and Togue ponds, along with about a dozen smaller ponds, are located in a section of Maine public reserve lands southwest of Fort Kent. Thankfully, you will not see massive clearcuts here. Because of the steep mountainsides, there are some significant patches of old-growth forest—a rare occurrence. The land around these ponds is either permanently off-limits to all timber harvesting or designated for modified harvest only to improve wildlife habitat or provide recreation benefits. Although large areas of land under such protection surround Deboullie and Gardner ponds, the south side of Togue Pond has only a narrow band of protection.

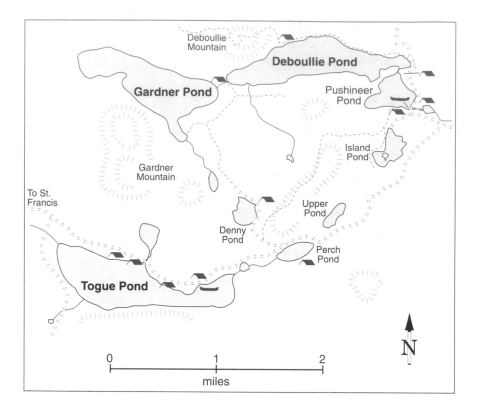

Like most public reserve land in Maine, the Deboullie Management Unit was acquired by the state primarily through land swaps
with private landowners. When Maine was divided into hundreds of
six-mile-square townships and auctioned off during the eighteenth and
nineteenth centuries, each township retained a small portion of land in
public ownership. Consequently, the public lands consisted of very
small, widely scattered units sprinkled throughout the state. Beginning
in the 1970s, the state consolidated many small parcels through land
swaps with paper companies and other private landowners. Out of
450,000 acres of public reserve lands, some 300,000 have now been
consolidated into twenty management units ranging in size from 3,000
to 30,000 acres.

Deboullie and Pushineer Ponds

To paddle on Deboullie, put in on Pushineer Pond at the eastern end.
A short section of stream connects Pushineer and Deboullie ponds,
with a slight elevation rise into Deboullie. We paddled right through

The top of Deboullie Mountain offers a superb view of Deboullie and Pushineer ponds (right), and Black Pond (left).

the two slight riffles from Pushineer, but we noted some new beaver work here, so be prepared to drag your canoe up over a beaver dam.

The French *deboullie* means "rock slide," and one can easily see how appropriate the name is as you scan the pond. A large talus slope creeps down along the north shore of the pond, and several exposed cliffs look out over the pond. The cliffs and talus slopes here provide habitat for a number of rare plant species.

Deep woods surround Deboullie and Pushineer ponds; the shorelines are thick with spruce, fir, birch, and red maple. Farther from shore yellow birch and sugar maple mix in with the conifers. Here and there along the shores you will see mountain ash (in the rose family), whose flower clusters provide a nice spot of white during June, and whose bright orange-red berries add variety to the early autumn colors. Along the shore is a band of dense alder, so disembarking just anywhere is out of the question. The shore itself is rocky with sharp chunks of granite. Use care paddling here; these rocks can put rather deep scratches in your canoe.

There is a wonderful (though steep) hike from Deboullie Pond up to the top of Deboullie Mountain and a fire lookout tower. You reach the trail about two-thirds of the way up the lake on the northern shore—keep an eye out for a campsite and small stream that enters the pond here (the campsite is quite wet until midsummer). The trail to

Deboullie Mountain climbs about 800 feet in 0.6 mile. It should take about a half-hour—less if you are in good shape—and reward you with a gorgeous view of the area ponds and forestland. You can also get onto this trail from the campsite area at the eastern end of Deboullie Pond.

Deboullie, Pushineer, and Gardner ponds have populations of the threatened blueback trout (more correctly a char, in the same genus as brook trout and lake trout). Blueback char (*Salvelinus alpinus oquassa*), found in only ten bodies of water in Maine, are descendants of anadromous, or sea-run, arctic char (*Salvelinus alpinus*) that became isolated from the sea during the most recent glaciation.

Gardner Pond

From the campsite on the far-western tip of Deboullie Pond, an easy portage trail leads into Gardner Pond. In mid-June it was still pretty soggy. If Deboullie Pond is beautiful, Gardner is spectacular, wild, and dramatic, with tall, jagged, basalt cliffs and large patches of scree. When we paddled here ravens called from hidden nesting ledges on the cliffs below Gardner Mountain. A 42-acre patch of old-growth spruce-fir forest lies between the peak of Gardner Mountain and the pond. (In the Deboullie Management Unit there are five patches of old-growth spruce-fir forest totaling 153 acres.)

We watched an osprey dive for a fish and a bald eagle soar over Gardner Mountain. You can explore a few yards up the small inlet creek at the western end of Gardner Pond. Look here for the tiny sundew plant, whose sticky hairs trap small insects (see page 117 for more on Maine's carnivorous plants).

Togue Pond

Togue Pond, south of Gardner Pond and closer by road to Route 161, is less visually striking and somewhat less remote than Deboullie and Gardner ponds, but is nonetheless very nice. Unlike Deboullie and Gardner, Togue Pond is stocked with salmon to improve recreational fishing, and you are likely to see a number of motorboats here.

The shoreline of Togue Pond differs significantly from that of Deboullie and Gardner ponds. Northern white cedars, more prevalent here, extend right down to the water's edge, while on the more northern ponds alder dominates the shoreline.

Getting There

From the south, take Route 11 north to Fort Kent, then drive west on Route 161 along the St. John River for 22.0 miles. At the Cross Rock Restaurant, turn left on a gravel road, reaching the North Maine Woods St. Francis Checkpoint in 0.4 mile. Pass through the checkpoint (there is both a day-use fee and a camping fee) and follow the main gravel road for 7.0 miles. Then turn left onto a rougher road at the sign to Public Reserve Lands and Red River Camps. Stay on this road, following signs to Public Reserve Lands, reaching the boat access at Togue Pond in another 8.5 miles. The access onto Pushineer Pond is another 3.4 miles.

If you have a high-ground-clearance truck and the water level is not too high, you can ford the outlet stream from Pushineer Pond. Though rough, the ford is on solid rock, and many campers drive across in trucks. Or you can unload gear at the ford and park back up the hill out of the way of other vehicles. We made it in all right to Pushineer Pond in a low-ground-clearance VW Rabbit (driving very carefully), but would probably have floated away had we tried to ford the stream in mid-June. It appeared that the road would not have been easily passable a few weeks earlier because of mud. If you are unsure about road conditions, ask at the checkpoint or call in advance.

There are several campsites on Togue Pond along the road and at Pushineer Pond just across the ford. Several others are accessible only by boat. Some campsites are permitted for fires; with others you need a permit from the Maine Forest Service. There is a private sporting camp (Red River Camp) on Island Pond, just south of Pushineer Pond, which offers lodging and canoe rentals. There are also motel accommodations at the Cross Rock Inn near the St. Francis checkpoint and in the village of St. Francis.

About the Authors

A LEX WILSON is a writer in Dummerston, Vermont. He is an avid canoeist and naturalist and has written two other quiet water canoeing guides for the Appalachian Mountain Club: *AMC Quiet Water Canoe Guide: Massachusetts/Connecticut/Rhode Island* and *AMC Quiet Water Canoe Guide: New Hampshire/Vermont.* He is the editor and publisher of *Environmental Building News* and a widely published freelance writer on energy, building technology, and environmental issues for such magazines as *Architecture, Progressive Architecture, Journal of Light Construction, Fine Homebuilding, Popular Science, Home,* and *Consumers Digest.*

J OHN HAYES is a professor of biochemistry and environmental science at Marlboro College in Marlboro, Vermont. He has canoed and kayaked in Minnesota's Boundary Waters Canoe Area, in Georgia's Okefenokee Swamp, in Florida's Everglades, as well as throughout the Northeast. When not in the classroom, he often leads natural history field trips to Central America, the Southwest deserts, the Rockies, and the Everglades.

About the Appalachian Mountain Club

The Appalachian Mountain Club pursues an active conservation agenda while encouraging responsible recreation. Our philosophy is that succcessful, long-term conservation depends on firsthand experience of the natural environment. AMC's 64,000 members pursue interests in hiking, canoeing, skiing, walking, rock climbing, bicycling, camping, kayaking, and backpacking, and—at the same time—help safeguard the environment.

Founded in 1876, the club has been at the forefront of the environmental protection movement. As cofounder of several leading New England environmental organizations, and as an active member working in coalition with these and many other groups, the AMC has successfully influenced legislation and public opinion.

Conservation

The most recent efforts in the AMC conservation program include river protection, Northern Forest Lands policy, Sterling Forest (NY) preservation, and support for the Clean Air Act. The AMC depends upon its active members and grassroots supporters to promote this conservation agenda.

Education

The AMC's education department offers members and the general public a wide range of workshops, from introductory camping to intensive Mountain Leadership School taught on the trails of the White Mountains. In addition, volunteers in each chapter lead hundreds of outdoor activities and excursions and offer introductory instruction in backcountry sports.

Research

The AMC's research department focuses on the forces affecting the ecosystem, including ozone levels, acid rain and fog, climate change, rare flora and habitat protection, and air quality and visibility.

Trails Program

Another facet of the AMC is the trails program, which maintains more than 1,400 miles of trail (including 350 miles of the Appalachian Trail) and more than 50 shelters in the Northeast. Through a coordinated effort of volunteers, seasonal crews, and program staff, the AMC contributes more than 10,000 hours of public service work each summer in the area from Washington, D.C., to Maine.

In addition to supporting our work by becoming an AMC member, hikers can donate time as volunteers. The club offers four unique weekly volunteer base camps in New Hampshire, Maine, Massachusetts, and New York. We also sponsor ten-day service projects throughout the United States, Adopt-a-Trail programs, trails day events, trail skills workshops, and chapter and camp volunteer projects.

The AMC has a long-standing connection to Acadia National Park. Working in cooperation with the National Park Service and Friends of Acadia, the AMC Trails Program provides many opportunities to preserve the park's resources. These include half-day volunteer projects for guests at AMC's Echo Lake Camp, ten-day service projects, weeklong volunteer crews in the fall, and trails day events. For more information on these public-service volunteer opportunities, contact the AMC Trails Program, Pinkham Notch Visitor Center, P.O. Box 298, Gorham NH 03581; 603-466-2721.

Alpine Huts

The club operates eight alpine huts in the White Mountains that provide shelter, bunks and blankets, and hearty meals for hikers. Pinkham Notch Visitor Center, at the foot of Mt. Washington, is base camp to the adventurous and the ideal location for individuals and families new to outdoor recreation. Comfortable bunk rooms, mountain hospitality, and home-cooked, family style meals make Pinkham Notch Visitor Center a fun and affordable choice for lodging. For reservations, call 603-466-2727.

Publications

At the AMC main office in Boston and at Pinkham Notch Visitor Center in New Hampshire, the bookstore and information center stock the entire line of AMC publications, as well as other trail and river guides, maps, reference materials, and the latest articles on conservation issues. Guidebooks and other AMC gifts are available by mail order (1-800-262-4455) or by writing AMC, P.O. Box 298, Gorham NH 03581. Also available from the bookstore or by subscription is *Appalachia*, the country's oldest mountaineering and conservation journal.

Alphabetical Listing of Lakes and Ponds